W9-BXG-069

African American Eras

Segregation to Civil Rights Times

African American Eras

Segregation to Civil Rights Times

Volume 4:
Military
Popular Culture
Religion
Science and Technology

U·X·L
A part of Gale, Cengage Learning

GALE
CENGAGE Learning™

Detroit • New York • San Francisco • New Haven, Conn • Waterville, Maine • London

**African American Eras:
Segregation to Civil Rights Times**

Product Managers: Meggin Condino
and Julia Furtaw

Project Editor: Rebecca Parks

Rights Acquisition and Management:
Leitha Etheridge-Sims, Kelly Quin

Composition: Evi Abou-El-Seoud

Manufacturing: Rita Wimberley

Imaging: John Watkins

Product Design: Pamela Galbreath

For product information and technology assistance, contact us at
Gale Customer Support, 1-800-877-4253.
For permission to use material from this text or product,
submit all requests online at **cengage.com/permissions.**
Further permissions questions can be emailed to
permissionrequest@cengage.com.

Cover photographs reproduced by permission of Getty Images (photos of March on
Washington and Bessie Coleman) and AP Images (photo of Jackie Robinson).

While every effort has been made to ensure the reliability of the information presented
in this publication, Gale, a part of Cengage Learning, does not guarantee the accuracy of
the data contained herein. Gale accepts no payment for listing; and inclusion in the
publication of any organization, agency, institution, publication, service, or individual does
not imply endorsement of the editors or publisher. Errors brought to the attention of the
publisher and verified to the satisfaction of the publisher will be corrected in future
editions.

Library of Congress Cataloging-in-Publication Data

African American eras. Segregation to civil rights times.
    p. cm.
    Includes bibliographical references and index.
    ISBN 978-1-4144-3596-1 (set) -- ISBN 978-1-4144-3597-8 (v. 1) --
ISBN 978-1-4144-3598-5 (v. 2) -- ISBN 978-1-4144-3599-2 (v. 3) --
ISBN 978-1-4144-3600-5 (v. 4) 1. African Americans--History--1863-1877--
Juvenile literature. 2. African Americans--History--1877-1964--Juvenile literature.
3. African Americans--Segregation--History--Juvenile literature. 4. Segregation--
United States--History--Juvenile literature. 5. African Americans--Civil rights--
History--19th century--Juvenile literature. 6. African Americans--Civil rights--
History--19th century--Juvenile literature. 7. African Americans--Biography--
Juvenile literature. 8. United States--Race relations--Juvenile literature.
I. Title: Segregation to civil rights times.
    E185.6.A254 2010
    973'.0496073--dc22
                                                                    2010012405

Gale
27500 Drake
Farmington Hills, MI 48331-3535

ISBN-13: 978-1-4144-3596-1 (set)   ISBN-10: 1-4144-3596-7 (set)
ISBN-13: 978-1-4144-3597-8 (Vol. 1)   ISBN-10: 1-4144-3597-5 (Vol. 1)
ISBN-13: 978-1-4144-3598-5 (Vol. 2)   ISBN-10: 1-4144-3598-3 (Vol. 2)
ISBN-13: 978-1-4144-3599-2 (Vol. 3)   ISBN-10: 1-4144-3599-1 (Vol. 3)
ISBN-13: 978-1-4144-3600-5 (Vol. 4)   ISBN-10: 1-4144-3600-9 (Vol. 4)

This title is also available as an e-book.
ISBN-13: 978-1-4144-3705-7 ISBN-10: 1-4144-3705-6
Contact your Gale, a part of Cengage Learning sales representative for ordering
information.

Printed in Mexico
1 2 3 4 5 6 7 14 13 12 11 10

Table of Contents

VOLUME 2

VOLUME 3

chapter nine **Law and Justice** 551

chapter twelve **Religion** *757*

Reader's Guide

U•X•L *African American Eras: Segregation to Civil Rights Times* provides a broad overview of African American history and culture from the end of the Civil War in 1865 through the civil rights movement up to 1965. The four-volume set is broken into thirteen chapters. Each chapter covers a major subject area as it relates to the African American community. Readers have the opportunity to engage with history in multiple ways within the chapter, beginning with a chronology of major events related to that subject area and a chapter-specific overview of developments in African American history. They are next introduced to the men and women who shaped that history through biographies of prominent African Americans, as well as topical entries on major events related to the chapter's subject area. Primary sources provide a firsthand perspective of the people and events discussed in the chapter, and readers have the opportunity to engage with the content further in a research and activity ideas section.

The complete list of chapters is as follows:

- Activism and Reform
- The Arts
- Business and Industry
- Communications and Media
- Demographics
- Education

- Government and Politics
- Health and Medicine
- Law and Justice
- Military
- Popular Culture
- Religion
- Science and Technology

These chapters are then divided into seven sections:

Chronology: A timeline of significant events in the African American community within the scope of the chapter's subject matter.

Overview: A summary of major developments and trends in the African American community as they relate to the subject matter of the chapter.

★ **Headline Makers:** Biographies of key African Americans and their achievements within the scope of the chapter's subject matter.

❖ **Topics in the News:** A series of topical essays describing significant events and developments important to the African American community within the scope of the chapter's subject matter.

Primary Sources: Historical documents that provide a firsthand perspective on African American history as it relates to the content of the chapter.

Research and Activity Ideas: Brief suggestions for activities and research opportunities that will further engage the reader with the subject matter.

☞ **For More Information:** A section that lists books, periodicals, and Web sites directing the reader to further information about the events and people covered in the chapter.

OTHER FEATURES

The content of U•X•L *African American Eras: Segregation to Civil Rights Times* is illustrated with 240 black-and-white images that bring the events and people discussed to life. Sidebar boxes also expand on items of high interest to readers. Concluding each volume is a general bibliography of books and Web sites, and a thorough subject index that allows readers to easily locate the events, people, and places discussed throughout the set.

COMMENTS AND SUGGESTIONS

We welcome your comments on U•X•L *African American Eras: Segregation to Civil Rights Times* and suggestions for other history topics to consider. Please write: Editor, U•X•L *African American Eras: Segregation to Civil Rights Times*, 27500 Drake Rd., Farmington Hills, MI 48331-3535; call toll-free: 1-800-877-4253; or send e-mail via http://www.galegroup.com.

Chronology

1862   Congress passes the Homestead Act, which provides people with 160 acres of free land in the American West. The act, which applies to African Americans, sets the stage for the so-called "Colored Exodus" of the late 1870s and early 1880s.

1862   Freedmen's Hospital is founded in Washington, D.C., by the U.S. secretary of war. Its purpose is to meet the medical needs of African Americans, including newly freed slaves.

1865   **March 3**   Congress passes the Freedmen's Bureau Act, creating the Bureau of Refugees, Freedmen, and Abandoned Lands for the purposes of helping former slaves obtain property, employment, and an education.

1865   **December 2**   The Thirteenth Amendment to the United States Constitution, which formally outlaws slavery in the United States, is ratified.

1866   United States Congress commissions six all-black U.S. Army units. The units, which become known as the Buffalo Soldiers, serve the United States in the Indian wars and in the Spanish-American War, among others.

1868   Howard University College of Medicine is founded in Washington, D.C., as one of the few medical schools open to African Americans.

1868   **July 9**   The Fourteenth Amendment is added to the Constitution. Its most important provisions declare that African Americans who are born in the United States are citizens, that all persons are entitled to due process of law, and that no person shall be denied the equal protection of the laws.

1869   **May 1** Ebenezer Bassett becomes the first African American to serve the United States as a diplomat when President Ulysses S. Grant appoints him to be minister resident (the nineteenth-century equivalent of an ambassador) to Haiti.

1870   **February 3** The Fifteenth Amendment to the United States Constitution, which outlaws discrimination against voters based on race, is ratified.

1870   **February 23** Hiram Revels of Mississippi becomes the first African American to serve as a United States senator.

1875   **March 1** The Civil Rights Act of 1875, which forbids discrimination based on race for all public accommodations, is signed into law.

1877   **March** Under the Compromise of 1877, which enabled Republican candidate Rutherford B. Hayes to be elected president, the Republican Party agrees to withdraw the U.S. military from the South and end Reconstruction.

1883   **October 15** The Civil Rights Act of 1875 is declared unconstitutional by the Supreme Court, opening the way for Southern states to enact Jim Crow laws and institute policies of segregation.

1892   Journalist Ida B. Wells publishes *Southern Horrors: Lynch Law in All Its Phases,* the first comprehensive study of lynchings in the United States.

1895   **September 18** Booker T. Washington delivers a speech popularly known as the "Atlanta Compromise," in which he encourages African Americans to have patience and prove themselves worthy of equality to whites.

1896   **May 18** In the court case *Plessy v. Ferguson,* the United States Supreme Court rules that segregation is legal as long as blacks are provided "separate but equal" accommodations and facilities.

1899   **September 18** Scott Joplin publishes his first successful ragtime composition, "Maple Leaf Rag," which becomes the first instrumental sheet music to sell over one million copies.

1903   Author and activist W. E. B. Du Bois publishes *The Souls of Black Folk,* his landmark collection of essays about race relations in the United States.

1905   Madame C. J. Walker, a former employee of Annie Malone's Poro Systems, goes into business for herself, selling hair straighteners, creams, and other styling products designed specifically for African American women.

1906   **April**   William Joseph Seymour begins the Azusa Street Revival, which is often credited as a key development in the growth of the Pentecostal faith. The Azusa Street Revival becomes the longest-running continuous revival in United States history.

1908   **December 26**   Boxer Jack Johnson defeats Canadian heavyweight Tommy Burns in Australia to become the first African American world heavyweight champion.

1909   **February 12**   Civil rights activists gather to form the organization that becomes known as the National Association for the Advancement of Colored People.

1910   Sickle-cell anemia is scientifically described for the first time. James Herrick, a Chicago physician, publishes a report describing the disease in Walter Clement Noel, a young black student from Grenada in the West Indies.

1919   **March**   Oscar Micheaux's *The Homesteader,* the first feature-length film written and directed by an African American, premieres.

1920   Marcus Garvey, as part of his Back to Africa project, moves the headquarters of the Black Star shipping line to Liberia, a country in western Africa.

1925   Dancer and singer Josephine Baker arrives in Paris and quickly becomes the most popular American performer in Europe.

1927   **January 7**   The first officially recorded game featuring the Harlem Globetrotters is played in Illinois.

1931   **November 7**   The tragic death of Juliette Derricotte in a car accident in Dalton, Georgia, sparks a national outrage over segregated hospitals. Derricotte does not receive adequate medical care because the local hospital does not admit African Americans.

1936   **November 3**   Seventy-six percent of African Americans who vote in the presidential election cast their vote for Franklin D. Roosevelt, a Democrat. The election marks the beginning of a major shift of African American voters away from the Republican Party.

1937   **April 25**   The Brotherhood of Sleeping Car Porters becomes the first all-black union in American history to negotiate a labor agreement with a major corporation when it enters into a collective bargaining agreement with the Pullman Company.

1940   **February 29**   Actress Hattie McDaniel becomes the first African American to win an Academy Award for her portrayal of Mammy in the film *Gone with the Wind* (1939).

1941   **June 25**   President Franklin D. Roosevelt signs Executive Order 8802, making it illegal for government agencies and private companies that do business with the government to refuse to hire African Americans.

1945   **November**   John Harold Johnson launches the lifestyle magazine *Ebony,* which quickly becomes the most popular African American magazine in the nation.

1945   **November 1**   Brooklyn Dodgers owner Branch Rickey signs Negro League baseball player Jackie Robinson to play in the major leagues, the first African American in modern major league baseball.

1952   After completing a jail sentence for burglary, Malcolm Little adopts the new name Malcolm X and becomes the leading spokesperson for the Nation of Islam.

1954   **May 17**   The Supreme Court unanimously rules in *Brown v. Board of Education* that segregated schools are unconstitutional. The Court's ruling overturns its previous decision in *Plessy v. Ferguson* (1896) and marks the beginning of the end of legalized racial segregation.

1954   **October 30**   The last racially segregated unit in the United States military is disbanded, completing the military's transition from completely segregated to completely integrated in just over five years.

1955   **August 28**   Emmett Till, a fourteen-year-old African American boy from Chicago, Illinois, is taken from his uncle's house in Money, Mississippi, and murdered for allegedly whistling at a white woman.

1955   **December 1**   Rosa Parks is arrested after refusing to give up her seat to a white passenger on a Montgomery, Alabama, city bus; the arrest leads to a year-long bus boycott and the eventual desegregation of Montgomery city buses.

1957   Martin Luther King Jr. and Ralph Abernathy co-found the Southern Christian Leadership Conference (SCLC), a group that teaches the use of nonviolent direct action to protest injustice and promote civil rights for African Americans.

1957 **August 13** A postal worker alerts the suburb of Levittown, Pennsylvania, that a black family has moved into the neighborhood. This incident sparks a wave of violence and terrorism against the family as white residents attempt to force them to leave the neighborhood.

1957 **September 24** President Dwight D. Eisenhower deploys a U.S. Army division to Little Rock, Arkansas, and federalizes the Arkansas National Guard in order to protect nine African American students and enforce integration at Little Rock Central High School. The students become known as the "Little Rock Nine."

1958 Dancer Alvin Ailey forms the Alvin Ailey American Dance Theater in New York City, one of the most influential modern dance companies in the country.

1959 **March 11** The play *A Raisin in the Sun* by Lorraine Hansberry premieres, becoming the first Broadway play written by an African American woman.

1960 **February 1** Four college students stage a sit-in at a Woolworth's lunch counter in Greensboro, North Carolina, launching a massive campaign that results in the desegregation of lunch counters throughout the city.

1960 **April 14** Berry Gordy Jr. founds the recording label Motown Records in Detroit, Michigan.

1962 **October 1** James Meredith is admitted to the University of Mississippi as its first African American student; the event leads to riots among white supremacists.

1963 **January 14** Newly elected Alabama governor George C. Wallace famously declares in his inauguration day address that he will support "segregation now, segregation tomorrow, segregation forever."

1963 **August 28** At least two hundred thousand demonstrators participate in the March on Washington for Jobs and Freedom; millions of viewers around the world are moved by the event and by Martin Luther King's "I Have a Dream" speech.

1964 **March** Malcolm X leaves the Nation of Islam and founds his own religious organization, the Organization of Afro-American Unity, built on a belief in world brotherhood.

1964 **May 25** The Supreme Court rules in *Griffin v. County School Board of Prince Edward County* that state governments in the South cannot close their public schools as a strategy for avoiding the racial integration mandated by the Court's decision in *Brown v. Board of Education.*

1964   **July 2**   The Civil Rights Act of 1964, which outlaws segregation based on race in virtually all instances, becomes law.

1964   **December 10**   Martin Luther King Jr. is awarded the Nobel Peace Prize for his campaigns of nonviolent resistance.

1965   The federal programs Medicare and Medicaid are created, finally bringing an end to the long practice of segregated hospitals and medical discrimination.

1965   **February 21**   Malcolm X, while attending a meeting in Harlem, is shot dead by three members of the Nation of Islam.

1965   **August 6**   President Lyndon B. Johnson signs into law the Voting Rights Act of 1965, which prohibits all forms of racial discrimination in voting and the administration of elections. The Voting Rights Act and the Civil Rights Act of 1964 are widely regarded as the most important pieces of legislation enacted in the country in the twentieth century.

Era Overview

The American Civil War ended in 1865 with a victory for the North and freedom for African American slaves. The federal government quickly enacted several constitutional amendments aimed at establishing and protecting the rights of African Americans. The federal government was able to protect these rights during the period of time immediately following the Civil War known as Reconstruction. The presence of federal troops in the South during Reconstruction allowed African Americans to make impressive advances in a variety of fields. Numerous African Americans were elected to local and state offices as blacks exercised their right to vote. Schools were built throughout the South to help educate and train freed slaves for new careers in mainstream American society.

Federal troops remained in the South for more than a decade to enforce Reconstruction policies. Reconstruction ended in 1877 after the Northern Republicans agreed to withdraw federal troops from the South in exchange for Southern Democratic support of the Republican presidential candidate Rutherford B. Hayes (1822–93). The withdrawal of federal protection was devastating to the Southern black population. Many African Americans found themselves in circumstances as bad or worse than before the war. Southern blacks once again worked the plantation fields owned by whites—now as sharecroppers, trapped by debt just as they had once been bound by slavery.

To make matters worse, state governments throughout the South began to institute "black codes," which were laws aimed at restricting the rights of African Americans. These laws supported strict segregation throughout the

South. Separate public facilities—everything from schools to hospitals to water fountains—were created for blacks. These facilities were almost never equal in quality to those offered for white citizens. The constitutionality of this kind of segregation was tested in the United States Supreme Court case *Plessy v. Ferguson* in 1896. The Court ruled that "separate but equal" facilities for blacks did not violate the Fourteenth Amendment, which gave African Americans full citizenship. The "separate but equal" concept was used to justify segregation for many decades.

The South in particular saw increasing violence against blacks at the end of the nineteenth century, mainly in the form of lynching. Lynchings are executions held outside the bounds of the law, usually by large groups, and often without much proof that the victim had committed a crime. African American journalist and editor Ida B. Wells (1862–1931) exposed the racist motivations for lynchings in her pamphlets *Southern Horrors* (1892) and *A Red Record* (1895). She campaigned vigorously for stronger anti-lynching laws.

Even in the midst of segregation and lynchings, many African Americans in the South were furthering their educations thanks to schools such as the Tuskegee Institute in Alabama. Booker T. Washington (1856–1915), born into slavery, was the leader of the Tuskegee Institute and a persuasive voice in the struggle for African American acceptance by white society. Washington's philosophy was to provide African Americans with basic trade skills so they could prove their worth to whites as productive members of society. He felt that protests and demands for increased liberty would prove disastrous for blacks, and that the key component in defusing racial tension was time. Many African American intellectuals in the North, such as W. E. B. Du Bois (1868–1963), felt that blacks should not have to wait for whites to give them the rights they deserved. Du Bois was a driving force behind the creation of the National Association for the Advancement of Colored People (NAACP) in 1909. He utilized the organization's official publication, *The Crisis*, to rally African American readers in the struggle for civil rights.

In the first decades of the twentieth century, many African Americans began moving to growing cities in the North and Midwest in search of greater economic opportunities and freedoms. This became known as the Great Migration. By 1930, millions of African Americans had migrated to urban centers such as New York City, Detroit, and Chicago. One of the largest concentrations of African Americans in the North was found in Harlem, a neighborhood in New York City. The relative economic prosperity enjoyed by African Americans in the North, combined with the influx of cultural influences from the South, were key factors in the Harlem

Renaissance. The Harlem Renaissance was a flourishing of African American art and culture that began in the 1920s and continued into the 1930s.

Equally notable was the growing acceptance of African Americans by mainstream American society. While many white Americans reacted negatively to African American boxer Jack Johnson (1878–1946) when he won the heavyweight boxing title in 1908, Joe Louis (1914–81) was praised as an American hero when he secured the title in 1937. When Jackie Robinson (1919–72) debuted as the first African American baseball player in the major leagues in 1947, uncertainty among white fans quickly gave way to respect for his unquestionable talents.

African Americans made great strides in other fields as well. In 1939, Charles Drew (1904–50) invented a blood storage method that allowed for the creation of blood banks, thereby helping to save the lives of millions. Singer Marian Anderson (1897–1993) earned worldwide acclaim for her performances of both opera and traditional songs. And in 1940, Benjamin O. Davis Sr. (1877–1970) became the first African American to achieve the rank of general in the United States Army. In each case, however, these pioneers struggled against the widespread racism that still divided American culture. Drew resigned from the Red Cross in 1941 when the United States Army ordered that blood from black donors must be separated from blood donated by whites. In 1939, Anderson was barred from performing at Constitution Hall in Washington, D.C., because she was black. And while Davis served as a general in the U.S. Army during World War II (1939–45), the soldiers themselves were still divided on the battlefield according to their race.

One important factor in changing American perceptions about blacks was popular media. Even as the roles for African Americans in Hollywood films remained largely stereotypical, performers like Bill "Bojangles" Robinson (1878–1949) won over audiences with their talent and charm. Hattie McDaniel (1895–1952) became the first African American to win an Academy Award for her supporting performance as a servant in the 1939 film *Gone with the Wind*. Still, it would be fifteen years before another African American woman, Dorothy Dandridge (1922–65), would be nominated in the Best Actress category, and twenty-four years before Sidney Poitier (1927–) would become the first African American man to win an Oscar for Best Actor.

Even more significantly, the media played a key role in shaping American views on the growing struggle for civil rights for African Americans. The South was still as segregated in the 1950s as it had been in the 1800s, even as black Americans made important contributions to the worlds of art, science, and business. One of the most important challenges to segregation occurred in 1954. That year the United States Supreme Court ruled in the case *Brown v. Board of Education of Topeka* that separate schools for blacks and whites are, by definition, unequal, and therefore against federal law. Soon after, segregation was challenged on other fronts as well; for example, Alabama resident Rosa Parks (1913–2005) earned fame when she refused to give up her seat to a white bus passenger in 1955. Her arrest sparked the Montgomery bus boycott, one of the first major protest campaigns of the modern civil rights era. In 1957, nine African American students in Little Rock, Arkansas, defied the state's governor and National Guard troops to attend a high school that had previously admitted only white students.

The leading voice of the civil rights struggle in the South was Martin Luther King Jr. (1929–68), a clergyman and advocate of nonviolence in the struggle for civil rights. King's influence resulted in peaceful demonstrations such as sit-ins and boycotts of businesses that supported segregation, and earned him the Nobel Peace Prize in 1964. However, the peaceful efforts of King and other activists were often met with violence by whites. Activists such as Medgar Evers (1925–63) and James Chaney (1943–64) were brutally murdered because of their efforts to help African Americans secure their constitutional right to vote. Across the South, African American churches were bombed, and peaceful demonstrators were beaten—often by police and at the direction of state and local government officials.

In 1963, more than two hundred thousand demonstrators participated in the March on Washington for Jobs and Freedom, aimed at securing basic civil rights for African Americans nationwide. Massive media coverage of the event helped sway millions of white Americans to support civil rights reform. The following year, the Civil Rights Act of 1964 was passed by the United States Congress. This legislation formally ended segregation and guaranteed civil rights for all Americans regardless of race. More than a century after Abraham Lincoln issued the Emancipation Proclamation to free African American slaves, the federal government finally followed through on guaranteeing their basic rights as Americans.

chapter ten *Military*

1866 United States Congress commissions six all-black army units. The units, which are known as the Buffalo Soldiers, serve in the Indian wars and in the Spanish-American War.

1877 June 15 Henry Ossian Flipper becomes the first African American ever to graduate from the United States Military Academy at West Point and be commissioned as a military officer.

1882 June 30 Henry Ossian Flipper is dishonorably discharged from the U.S. Army after being convicted by a court martial of "conduct unbecoming an officer and a gentleman," despite a lack of any evidence to support the charge.

1889 August 31 Charles Young becomes the third African American cadet ever to graduate from the United States Military Academy at West Point.

1898 June 24 Buffalo Soldiers come to the aid of Theodore Roosevelt's Rough Riders at the Battle of Las Guasimas, a key moment leading up to the capture of the Spanish Navy in the Spanish-American War.

1898 July 1 Buffalo Soldiers fight alongside other American troops, including Theodore Roosevelt's Rough Riders, to win a U.S. victory at the Battle of San Juan Hill in the Spanish-American War.

1901 February Benjamin O. Davis Sr. is commissioned as a second lieutenant in the U.S. Army, raising the total number of African Americans serving as military officers to five.

1906 August 13 Three men are shot in the so-called "Brownsville Affair." The incident leads to a hasty, biased judgment that results in three companies of an African American military unit being dishonorably discharged without due process. The men are eventually pardoned by Congress in 1972.

1916 June 1 Charles Young becomes the highest-ranking African American officer in the U.S. Army when he is promoted to the rank of lieutenant colonel.

1917 Buffalo Soldiers ride with General John J. Pershing to defeat Mexican revolutionary leader Pancho Villa, who had attempted to invade the United States.

1917 August 23 The Houston Mutiny, an uprising of African American soldiers in Houston, Texas, leaves nineteen people dead. The uprising is the result of months of mistreatment of the black soldiers and slowly building racial tensions.

1917 August 27 Eugene Bullard, a member of the French Air Service during World War I, becomes the first African American ever to fly a combat mission in an aircraft.

1917 November 11 Under pressure from the American military, which believed that African Americans were incapable of serving as combat aviators, the French military transfers Eugene Bullard out of the air service and into infantry, ending his career as a pilot.

1918 May 15 Henry Johnson becomes the first American ever to be awarded the Croix de Guerre, France's highest military honor.

1919 The so-called Red Summer riots break out in cities across the United States, leaving hundreds dead and many more injured. The riots were fore-shadowed by the Houston Mutiny two years before.

1923 February 12 The Hospital for Sick and Injured Colored World War Veterans, which would later be renamed the Tuskegee Veterans Administration Hospital, is dedicated in Tuskegee, Alabama.

1923 July 3 The Ku Klux Klan protests the decision to staff the veterans hospital at Tuskegee with African American doctors and nurses by burning a forty-foot-tall cross and sending a seventy-car caravan to surround the hospital.

1936 June 12 Benjamin O. Davis Jr. graduates from the United States Military Academy at West Point, be-coming the first African American in the twentieth century to do so.

1940 October 25 Colonel Benjamin O. Davis Sr. is promoted to brigadier general, becoming the first African American ever to attain the U.S. Army's highest rank.

1941 June 25 President Franklin D. Roosevelt signs Executive Order 8802, prohibiting private companies that do business with the government from practicing racial discrimination in hiring. The order makes it possible for African Americans to obtain fair employment as part of the war effort.

1941 July 19 The U.S. Army Air Corps opens its first-ever flight school for the training of African American pilots at the Tuskegee Institute in Tuskegee, Alabama.

1941 December 7 Dorie Miller, a navy chef who had not received any formal combat training, shows great bravery and valor during the Battle of Pearl Harbor by rescuing the captain of the USS *West Virginia* and shooting down at least three Japanese planes.

1942 June 10 Dorie Miller is awarded the Navy Cross, the U.S. Navy's highest award for valor, and promoted to mess attendant first class in recogni-tion of the courage and devotion to duty he displayed during the Battle of Pearl Harbor.

1942 September Charity Adams Earley becomes the first African American woman to receive an officer's commission as a member of the Women's Army Auxiliary Corps.

1944 African Americans make up 8.3 percent of the industrial workforce dedicated to the U.S. war effort, up from just 2.5 percent at the beginning of 1942.

1946 March Charity Adams Earley retires from the Women's Army Auxiliary Corps (WAAC), having attained the rank of lieutenant colonel. At the time she retires, she is the highest-ranking African American officer in the WAAC.

1948 July 20 At the retirement ceremony of General Benjamin O. Davis Sr., President Harry S. Truman credits Davis with helping increase the number of African American officers in the military from only five to more than one thousand.

1948 July 26 President Harry S. Truman issues Executive Order 9981, which ends racial segregation in the military and requires all soldiers to be treated equally regardless of their race.

1954 October Benjamin O. Davis Jr. is promoted to the rank of brigadier general, and becomes the first African American general in U.S. Air Force history.

1954 October 30 The last racially segregated unit in the United States military is disbanded, completing the military's transition from completely segregated to completely integrated in just over five years.

1959 October 9 Eugene Bullard is made a chevalier in the French Legion of Honor, an order that recognizes France's most decorated and deserving citizens and veterans.

African Americans have served in every war in U.S. history, but their service was long undervalued and unrecognized. Congress commissioned several all-black military units in 1866. The soldiers in the all-black cavalry regiments came to be known as "Buffalo Soldiers." The Buffalo Soldiers are best known for their role in fighting the Plains Indians for control of the American West. They also guarded railroads and wagon trains, helped police and caught cattle thieves, and helped build infrastructure like buildings and telegraph lines. The Buffalo Soldiers also took part in important military engagements outside the American Indian Wars. They helped fight Mexican revolutionary leader Pancho Villa (1878–1923) on the U.S.-Mexico border. They also famously fought alongside Theodore Roosevelt's Rough Riders in the Battle of San Juan Hill in Cuba during the Spanish-American War.

In spite of their brave military service, black soldiers faced prejudice during the segregation era. This prejudice came from both within the military and outside the military. A famous example of this was the so-called "Brownsville Affair" in 1906. Three men were shot outside of Fort Brown in Brownsville, Texas. The U.S. Army's inspector was never able to determine exactly who was responsible for the attack. Motivated by racial bias and a rush to judgment, the inspector urged President Theodore Roosevelt (1858–1919) to discharge three companies of African American soldiers stationed at Fort Brown. The president did, and all of the men were dishonorably discharged without any kind of legal process or chance to demonstrate their innocence. Congress would eventually pardon them in 1972.

The Brownsville Affair set the stage for a bloody conflict between black soldiers and civilians several years later. The Houston Mutiny of 1917 involved black soldiers stationed at Fort Logan in Houston and white citizens of the city. The conflict began with the Houston police beating Corporal Charles Baltimore for supposedly interfering with their questioning of a black woman. More than 150 black soldiers took to the streets of Houston, leading white civilians to arm themselves in response. The conflict left nineteen men dead and led to the largest court-martial, or military trial, in United States history.

Almost 400,000 African Americans served in the military during World War I (1914–18), and 200,000 served in Europe. The vast majority of them were unable to receive quality medical care as veterans because of the policies of racial segregation. The opening of a veterans hospital in Tuskegee, Alabama, in 1923 was thus an important milestone in African

American military history. A veteran is a former military member. The hospital was controversial in the South when it opened because it employed African American doctors and nurses. The controversy eventually subsided, and the Tuskegee veterans hospital became a much-needed provider of medical care. The hospital was funded by the federal government with the full support of President Warren Harding (1865–1923)—a sign that the country was gradually coming to recognize the importance of African Americans' contributions to the military.

World War II (1939–45) gave African American service members a new opportunity to prove themselves in active duty to their country. The Tuskegee Airmen were the first group of African American pilots ever to serve in the United States military. Prior to World War II African Americans had been barred from serving as pilots because the U.S. Army believed they lacked the necessary skills and abilities. The Tuskegee Airmen were an experimental unit designed to test African Americans' flight worthiness. They passed with flying colors. All told, nearly 1,000 African American pilots served as Tuskegee Airmen during World War II. They compiled an exemplary record serving primarily as escorts during bombing runs. Their brave and capable service struck an important symbolic blow in favor of integration and racial equality. All-black "Buffalo Soldier" units also fought in World War II.

African Americans achieved another major victory in the military arena shortly after the end of World War II. The United States military had been racially segregated since the end of the Civil War (1861–65). This policy became subject to criticism during World War II. Many African Americans believed it was unfair for the United States to be fighting a war to protect freedom abroad when many African Americans lacked basic freedoms at home. Further, the valiant service of nearly one million African Americans during World War II was impossible to deny or ignore. President Harry S. Truman (1884–1972) decided to put an end to racial segregation in the military by issuing Executive Order 9981 on July 26, 1948. The military was completely integrated within five years. Truman's decision to end segregation in the military helped contribute to the end of segregation in civilian society just a few years later.

★ CHARITY ADAMS EARLEY
(1918–2002)

Charity Adams Earley was the first African American woman ever to be a commissioned officer in the U.S. Army. Adams Earley joined the Women's Army Auxiliary Corps (WAAC; later the Women's Army Corps) soon after the United States became involved in World War II. She quickly rose through the ranks and eventually had command of an entire battalion of female troops. She had attained the rank of lieutenant colonel by the time of her retirement from the military in March 1946, which made her the highest-ranking African American in the Women's Army Corps. Adams Earley was a pioneer who forged a path for women in general, and African Americans in particular, to obtain leadership positions at the highest levels of military service.

A Young Woman Answers the Call to Service

Charity Adams Earley was born under the name Charity Edna Adams on December 5, 1918, in Kittrell, North Carolina. She spent most of her childhood in Columbia, South Carolina. She was the oldest of four children born to the Reverend Eugene and Charity Adams. The Adams family placed a high value on education. Reverend Adams had worked to put himself through college and would purchase foreign newspapers to keep his language skills sharp. The elder Charity Adams was a schoolteacher who, even after her children were grown, would use a red pencil to mark any errors she found in the letters they sent her. Adams shared her parents' studiousness. She was the valedictorian of her high school class and earned a bachelor's degree from Wilberforce University in Ohio in 1938. She spent the next several years working as a schoolteacher in Columbia.

Charity Adams Earley.
© *Bettmann/Corbis*

The United States' entry into World War II at the end of 1941 created an opportunity for Adams to pursue a new career. The beginning of the war created a massive need for new combat soldiers. Many former civilians joined the military, and many existing military members who had formerly served in office positions moved over into combat units. This shift in personnel created a huge need for new military recruits who could fill the administrative void. The armed forces decided to target women for these positions. Mary McCleod Bethune (1875–1955), a prominent African American educator and political leader who was a close confidant of President Franklin D. Roosevelt, spearheaded a recruiting effort that specifically targeted African American women.

Bethune was particularly concerned with recruiting talented and educated African American women who were well groomed for leadership positions within the military. She sent letters to a number of all-black colleges and universities, asking them to recommend recent female graduates who would be good candidates for military service. Wilberforce University recommended Adams. Adams received a personal invitation in June 1942 requesting that she join the Women's Army Auxiliary Corps (WAAC). She decided to accept the invitation. She set out for a military base in Des Moines, Iowa, to begin her training.

Rises Through the Ranks of the WAAC

Adams's basic training introduced her to the fundamentals of military life. She and her fellow recruits learned precision marching, map-reading, and chain of command. Unfortunately, Adams and the other thirty-eight African American women in her basic training class also learned that racial segregation was a fundamental reality of military life. She and the other black recruits were forced to live in separate housing and take their meals at separate tables. Adams did not let this discourage her. She completed basic training on August 30, 1942. Within two weeks, she had received a commission in the WAAC, becoming the first African American woman to do so. A commission is a formal document issued by the U.S. government under the direct authority of the president. It certifies that the commission-holder is a military officer.

Adams was a natural leader and a quick study. For that reason, her first assignment as an officer in the WAAC was as the company commander of a new class of recruits undergoing basic training in Des Moines, Iowa. The number of trainees under Adams's command more than doubled as the WAAC's recruitment efforts intensified, but Adams was always able to keep her unit running smoothly. Her efficiency at her job earned her a promotion to the rank of captain, giving her new responsibilities overseeing the more advanced components of basic training. This position required her to travel between military bases and also to the military's headquarters at the Pentagon in Washington, D.C.

Adams used the prominence of her new position to combat the racial discrimination that African American members of the WAAC faced. Some military bases refused to employ African American members of the WAAC. Others would only employ them in the lowest-ranking, least prestigious positions. Adams attacked this problem in several ways. She helped persuade the U.S. Army to create an "opportunity school" to provide extra assistance to African American recruits whose educational background left them ill-prepared for military service. She also helped lead an effort to recruit more highly educated African American women to military service. Adams believed that each of these initiatives would help produce more qualified African American servicewomen, which in turn would increase their chances of being employed. These efforts helped Adams earn a promotion to the rank of major.

Overseas Duty Presents New Challenges

Adams received a new assignment in December 1944 that was as exciting as it was challenging. Adams was assigned to a U.S. military base in England to take command of the newly formed 6888th Central Postal Battalion. She became the first African American member of what was then known as the Women's Army Corps to be stationed overseas. The 6888th Battalion had been formed to handle and direct the incoming and outgoing mail to and from the more than seven million Americans in the military who were stationed in Europe at the time. It was a hugely important job because it was critical to the troops' morale that they regularly receive mail from home.

Adams's new job was as difficult and complicated as it was important. The troops were constantly on the move, so it was difficult to properly direct their mail. The volume of mail was massive. Adams also had to overcome a significant backlog in delivery. The 6888th Battalion was able to overcome these challenges thanks to Adams's leadership. Her hard work was rewarded with a promotion to lieutenant colonel in December 1945. By then, World War II was over and she was preparing to come home. Adams remained in England until March 1946. She left the military when she returned to the United States. She was the highest-ranking African American officer in the WAC when she retired.

Adams led a long and interesting life after her time in the military. She was married to Stanley Earley in 1949, earned a master's degree in vocational psychology, raised two children, and worked as a professor and educational administrator. Later in life, she donated her time as a volunteer member of various charitable organizations. She also received numerous honors and recognitions for her path-breaking career in the military. She wrote a book about her time in the military, titled *One Woman's Army: A Black Officer Remembers the WAC* in 1989. Adams had the honor of introducing the keynote speaker, President Bill Clinton

(1946–), at a dinner honoring African Americans' contributions to World War II on February 17, 1995. Adams died on January 13, 2002, at the age of eighty-three.

★ EUGENE BULLARD
(1894–1961)

Eugene Bullard was the first African American ever to fly a plane in combat. He did not fly that mission for the United States, where African Americans were not allowed to train as pilots. Bullard served as a fighter pilot during World War I (1914–18) for the French Foreign Legion, which is a special unit in the French Army that was created to allow foreign nationals to join the French military. Bullard served the Legion with great distinction. He made his way to France via a long, indirect route away from his American homeland, and he led an interesting, varied life in the years before and after his service as a combat aviator.

A Long, Winding Journey Begins

Eugene Jacques Bullard was born on October 9, 1894, in Columbus, Georgia. He was the seventh of ten children, although three of his siblings died while they were still infants. His father, Octave Bullard, had been born into slavery only three months before the end of the Civil War (1861–65). Octave Bullard was adopted and raised by the Bullards, the family that lived next door to the plantation where he was born. The Bullards had come to the United States from France. Octave Bullard himself believed the family line could be traced back to Martinique, an island in the Caribbean that at the time was ruled by France.

Octave Bullard's connections to France would have a powerful influence on the life of his son Eugene. The Bullard family suffered through terrible racial discrimination and violence as Eugene was growing up in the 1890s. One of Eugene's brothers was killed by a lynch mob (a mob without any legal authority that seizes and maims or executes a person). Octave Bullard was nearly murdered after a fight with a white man at his job. This racism in Georgia prompted Octave to tell stories about France and Martinique. Octave told his family, including Eugene, that blacks and whites were treated as equals in France and lived in harmony together. These stories captured Eugene's imagination when he was young. He became determined to make his way to France.

Eugene Bullard began his journey to France when he was just eight years old. In 1902, he sold his pet goat for $1.50. His plan was to take the money and walk to France. Of course, this proved to be impossible, so Eugene Bullard spent the next three years traveling the South. In 1905, he

arrived in Newport News, Virginia, where he stowed away (hid on board without paying) on a ship bound for Hamburg, Germany. Bullard was discovered and forced to get off the ship in Scotland.

Bullard spent the next eight years in the United Kingdom. He traveled to Ireland and northern England before eventually making his way to London. He worked a variety of odd jobs, taking whatever work he could find. He earned a living by dancing on street corners, keeping a lookout for illegal gambling halls, and handling freight as a stevedore (a person who loads and unloads ships at a port). Bullard found steady work as a boxer in 1911. It was through his career as a fighter that Bullard was finally able to make his way to France. Bullard met a vaudeville troupe (a group of performers that travels from city to city and puts on variety shows) at a fight club in London in 1913. The troupe invited Bullard to join them for a tour of Europe. Bullard accepted, and he took up residence in Paris, France, in the spring of 1914 after the tour was complete. His childhood dream of moving to France had finally come true.

Becomes a Combat Pilot

Bullard continued his career as a boxer in Paris until the beginning of World War I just a few months after he arrived. Bullard decided to join the French Foreign Legion, which is the only unit in the French Army that will enlist a person who was not born in France. Soldiers in the French Foreign Legion are famous for being tough and daring. Bullard fit right in. He fought in some of the most dangerous and violent battles of World War I. Bullard was twice injured in his leg at the Battle of Verdun in 1916, one of the longest and deadliest battles of the entire war. Both times he returned to the field of battle. After the battle, the French Army determined that Bullard's leg injuries were too serious for him to continue serving in the Army. He was discharged late in 1916.

It did not take long for Bullard to find his way back into action. Bullard had returned to Paris after his discharge. While in Paris he made a comment to an American friend that he was thinking about joining the French Air Service. His friend believed it would be impossible for an African American to serve as a combat pilot. Bullard bet his friend two thousand dollars—an enormous sum of money in those days—that he would succeed in becoming a combat pilot. Bullard used connections he had made during his time in the Legion to get himself accepted as a member of the Lafayette Flying Corps, which was the squadron of the French Air Service that accepted foreign nationals as pilots. Most of the Lafayette pilots were American. Bullard completed his pilot training on May 5, 1917, and he promptly collected his two thousand dollars from his friend.

Bullard served with distinction in the Air Service. He flew his first combat mission on August 27, 1917. He flew numerous combat missions from August to November, scoring one confirmed kill of a German airplane. Bullard was a colorful character as a pilot. He had a small pet monkey named Jimmy who accompanied him on all of his combat missions. He also painted the side of his airplane with the motto, "All Blood Runs Red." His flying style was aggressive and daring. He was the only African American in the French Air Corps. He thus earned the nickname "The Black Swallow of Death" and became a celebrity in France.

Racial Prejudice Ends Bullard's Tour as a Combat Pilot

The entry of the United States into World War I in 1917 caused Bullard's career as a combat pilot to be cut short. The United States invited all American pilots who were then serving for France to enlist in the U.S. military. Every pilot who applied for a transfer was accepted—except for Bullard, the only African American in the group. American stereotypes held that African Americans were not intelligent enough to serve as pilots. As a result, the U.S. military was determined to bring Bullard's flying days to an end. The French Air Service, in response to pressure from the United States, transferred Bullard out of the Air Service and back to an infantry unit on November 11, 1917. Bullard served out the rest of World War I in France on noncombat duty.

Bullard remained in France following the end of World War I in 1918. He picked up right where he had left off in civilian life. He undertook a wide variety of interesting pursuits in the years following World War I. He managed a gymnasium and trained boxers, toured France as a drummer for a jazz band, and managed a nightclub in Paris called Le Grand Duc. He was married to a woman named Marcelle Eugenie Henriette de Straumann in July 1923, and the couple had two daughters, one born in 1924 and the other in 1926. He separated from his wife in 1930 and, in an arrangement that was very unusual at the time, he took custody and sole responsibility for their two children. Bullard became the owner of a Paris nightclub called L'Escadrille in the late 1920s. He owned the club through the 1920s and 1930s, and it became very popular.

The outbreak of World War II (1939–45) finally prompted Bullard to make his way back to the United States. Germany invaded France in 1940. Bullard initially became a part of the French Resistance, but he soon decided to flee France for the United States. He escaped by riding a bicycle to Lisbon, Portugal, where he was evacuated by the Red Cross on a trans-Atlantic ship bound for New York. Bullard worked as a perfume salesman and an elevator operator in New York. He returned to France following the end of the war and tried to reopen his nightclub, but the club had been seized by the government. Bullard returned to New York, where he lived for the rest of his life.

Bullard finally received recognition for his historic accomplishments and interesting life during the 1950s. He was featured as a guest on the *Today Show* in 1954. That same year, he returned to Paris to be honored by the French government as a war hero. Bullard was one of three former soldiers chosen to participate in the ceremonial relighting of the Everlasting Flame over the Tomb of the Unknown Soldier in Paris. In 1959, Bullard was named a *chevalier* (knight) in the French Legion of Honor, which is the order that honors France's most decorated and deserving citizens and veterans. Bullard died in New York of stomach cancer on October 12, 1961, just three days after his sixty-seventh birthday. Bullard was a true trailblazer for African Americans in the fields of military service and aviation.

★ BENJAMIN O. DAVIS JR. (1912–2002)

Benjamin O. Davis Jr.
U.S. Air Force

Benjamin O. Davis Jr. enjoyed a long, successful career in the military. Davis was the first African American in the twentieth century to graduate from the United States Military Academy at West Point. During World War II, Davis commanded the legendary Tuskegee Airmen, an all-black squadron of fighter pilots. The Tuskegee Airmen flew combat missions bravely and skillfully under Davis's leadership. Later in his career, Davis became the first African American ever to attain the rank of general in the United States Air Force.

A Military Son Is Born to a Military Family

Benjamin Oliver Davis Jr. was born on December 18, 1912, in Washington, D.C. He was the second of three children born to Elnora Davis and Benjamin O. Davis Sr. (1877–1970), who was an officer in the U.S. Army. Davis was exposed to military life at a young age. He went for a ride in an open-cockpit airplane when he was fourteen, and became interested in becoming a pilot. After he graduated high school in 1929, Davis enrolled at Fisk University, an all-black university in Nashville, Tennessee. He still dreamed of becoming a pilot. However, in the early 1900s there were no African American pilots.

Davis concluded that joining the military would give him his best chance of becoming a pilot. He decided to pursue admission to the United States Military Academy in West Point. Admission to West Point requires nomination from a United States congressional representative. Davis's father used his military connections to convince Representative Oscar De Priest (1871–1951), the only African American in Congress at the time, to nominate Davis to West Point. Davis enrolled in 1932. He encountered open racism in the form of "silencing." None of the other cadets would room with him, eat with him, or even speak to him. Normally this treatment is reserved for cadets (West Point students) found guilty of violating the West Point honor code. Davis was targeted because of his race. This treatment lasted all four years Davis was a cadet.

Davis did not let the racist attitudes of his fellow cadets interfere with his studies or goals. He was an outstanding student at West Point. He graduated in 1936 ranked thirty-fifth in a class of 276. He was the first African American cadet to graduate from West Point since Charles Young (1864–1922) in 1889. The United States military rewards West Point graduates by allowing them to choose their assignments in order of class rank. Davis finished in the top 15 percent of his class, so he told the military he wanted to join the U.S. Army Air Corps (the military branch that later became the U.S. Air Force) so he could pursue his dream of becoming a pilot. The military turned him down, explaining that African Americans could only be assigned to all-black units, and there were none in the U.S. Army Air Corps.

Davis was disappointed but not defeated. He spent the next five years serving in the U.S. Army, including two years teaching military science at the Tuskegee Institute in Alabama. By 1940, political pressure was mounting on President Franklin D. Roosevelt (1882–1945) to make more and better opportunities available to African Americans in the military. One of Roosevelt's responses was to make Davis's father the first African American general. Roosevelt also ordered the U.S. Army Air Corps to begin training African American pilots for combat missions. Davis became a part of the first African American class selected for aviation training. He and four of his classmates completed training and received their pilot wings on March 7, 1942.

Dream of Being a Pilot Comes True

Davis's completion of the pilot training program put him on the path to a historic career. He was promoted to lieutenant colonel and selected to command the 99th Pursuit Squadron, a newly created all-black combat flying unit based at the Tuskegee Air Field. The 99th deployed to combat operations in North Africa in early 1943 and compiled a successful record. Davis was transferred in October 1943 to command of the 332nd Fighter Group, which was made up of four all-black fighter squadrons. The 332nd deployed to Europe in January 1944 and became heavily engaged in regular combat with German aircraft.

Davis and the men he commanded compiled an exemplary record of service. One of the 332nd Fighter Group's key responsibilities was to escort bombers on their bombing runs and prevent German fighters from shooting down the bombers. Not a single American bomber was shot down while being escorted by the 332nd. Davis himself flew more than sixty combat missions during World War II. He received the Distinguished Flying Cross, a medal awarded to pilots who display heroism or extraordinary skill during combat flight, and a Silver Star, the third-highest award for valor awarded by the U.S. military. Davis was the first African American ever to receive a Silver Star. Davis and his unit played a key role in proving false the stereotypes that African Americans were not smart enough, brave enough, or loyal enough to serve in the challenging position of combat pilot. Davis's service earned him a promotion to the rank of full colonel.

Davis returned to the United States after World War II. In the late 1940s and early 1950s, he helped the U.S. Air Force become the first branch of the military to fully comply with President Harry S. Truman's executive order that the military end its policy of racial segregation. Davis was promoted to the rank of brigadier general in October 1954. He followed in the trailblazing footsteps of his father, who was the first African American general in any branch of the armed forces. Davis Jr. became the first-ever African American general in the United States Air Force. By the time he retired from the military in 1970, he had risen to the level of a lietutenant—three-star—general.

Davis spent the years after his retirement from the military working in civil service posts, which means he was a civilian employee of the government. He wrote an autobiography titled *Benjamin O. Davis, Jr., American* in 1991. Davis died on July 4, 2002, at the age of eighty-nine.

★ BENJAMIN O. DAVIS SR.
(1877–1970)

Benjamin O. Davis Sr. was the first African American to become a general in the United States armed forces. Davis's promotion to the rank of brigadier general was the high point of a career in the military that lasted fifty years. Davis played a major role in convincing the U.S. Army to provide better treatment and opportunities to its African American soldiers. He also was instrumental in improving relations between black and white soldiers during World War II. Davis's work helped convince President Harry S. Truman (1884–1972) to end racial segregation in the military.

A Successful Military Career Is Launched

Benjamin Oliver Davis Sr. was born on July 1, 1877, in Washington, D.C. He was the youngest of three children born to Louis Patrick Henry Davis and Henrietta Stewart Davis. His mother was a nurse, and his father worked as a messenger for the federal government. His parents were both educated and literate and taught Davis to be the same. Davis was an excellent student, and he was interested in a career in the military. After he finished high school, he enrolled at Howard University in Washington, D.C. Davis joined the Washington, D.C., National Guard while at Howard. He joined the U.S. Army after the outbreak of the Spanish-American War in 1898.

Benjamin O. Davis Sr.
U.S. Army

Davis served as a volunteer soldier from 1898 to 1899. He held a temporary position as a lieutenant, a low-ranking officer. Davis joined the U.S. Army full-time after his term as a volunteer ended. He enlisted as a private on June 14, 1889. His education, literacy, and year of experience in the military enabled him to rise quickly through the ranks. He had attained the rank of sergeant major by 1901, which is the highest rank a noncommissioned officer can hold. Commissioned officers are persons who pass a test and hold the highest leadership positions in the military. Davis aspired to be a commissioned officer, so he took an officer examination. He passed, and in February 1901, Davis became a second lieutenant (the lowest commissioned officer's rank).

Davis held numerous different jobs all over the world. He served as a quartermaster (person responsible for purchasing food and clothing) in Wyoming, a military attaché (a high-ranking military officer who is assigned to guard and assist a group of diplomats that is stationed in another country) in the African nation of Liberia, a professor of military science in Ohio and later in Alabama, and a logistics officer in the Philippines. Davis steadily moved up the military ranks. He had become a major by 1917, he attained the rank of lieutenant colonel in the early 1920s, and he was promoted to full colonel in 1929.

For all his success, Davis's race remained a factor that limited his chance to advance. The military enforced a strict policy of racial segregation in the early 1900s. As an African American officer, Davis was prohibited from serving in a position that required him to command white soldiers. The military also barred African American soldiers from combat duty. This policy was based on the prejudicial view that African Americans lacked the intelligence, bravery, skills, and morale to serve in the line of fire. Most members of the military viewed combat duty as the most respected and prestigious kind of military service. The exclusion of African Americans from combat sent a message that they were not valued as highly as their white counterparts.

Uses His Position to Fight Racism

Davis was uniquely impacted by racism in the military in the 1930s after he became a colonel, the rank directly below general. General is the highest rank in the military. The military refused to promote Davis to general, despite his more than thirty years of loyal service. The military's refusal to promote any black officers to general became a political issue in early 1940 as President Franklin D. Roosevelt campaigned for a third term as president. African American voters, who had consistently supported Roosevelt and were essential to his reelection chances, expressed their outrage over racism at the highest levels of the military. Roosevelt responded by ordering that Davis be promoted to the rank of brigadier general. On October 25, 1940, Davis became the first African American ever to attain the rank of general.

As a general, Davis worked to fight racism and promote better race relations among soldiers during World War II. He was stationed in Europe from 1942 to 1945. Other military leaders consulted him on how to best use their African American troops. Davis also began taking proactive steps to improve the reputation of black soldiers and prevent interracial tensions. He produced several educational films documenting the success of all-black military units assigned to combat duty. Davis's work is believed to have had a major impact on the racial attitudes of top military leaders, including General Dwight D. Eisenhower (1890–1969) and General George S. Patton (1885–1945). By the time World War II ended, a much larger number of African American soldiers were participating in combat.

Davis retired from the military on July 20, 1948. He was honored with a ceremony at the White House hosted by President Harry S. Truman. President Truman credited Davis for helping increase the number of

African American officers in the military from the five there had been the year Davis was commissioned to more than one thousand. Just six days after Davis retired, President Truman signed Executive Order 9981. An executive order is a document signed by the president that gives legally binding instructions on how to comply with the law. Executive Order 9981 officially ended racial segregation in the military. It was a major civil rights victory, in which Davis played a significant part.

Davis remained active in public life after his retirement from the military. He traveled overseas on diplomatic missions and served as a member of the American Battle Monuments Commission. He also was able to witness his son, Benjamin O. Davis Jr. (1912–2002), become the first African American ever to attain the rank of general in the United States Air Force. Davis died November 26, 1970, at the age of ninety-three.

★ HENRY OSSIAN FLIPPER
(1856–1940)

Henry Ossian Flipper was the first African American to graduate from the United States Military Academy at West Point in New York. Flipper graduated from West Point in 1877. West Point is a very highly regarded institution. Flipper's graduation was viewed as a major milestone for the African American community. Unfortunately, Flipper was not able to serve a long career in the military. Racial prejudice led to his being dishonorably discharged from the U.S. Army just four years after his graduation from West Point. Flipper worked throughout the rest of his life to try to clear his name. It was not until forty years after his death that the Army acknowledged that Flipper had committed no crimes as a soldier and honored him for his service.

Henry Ossian Flipper.
National Archives and Records Administration

History Is Made at West Point

Henry Ossian Flipper was born on March 21, 1856, in Thomasville, Georgia, a small city in the southern part of that state. He was the oldest of five children, all sons, born to Festus and Isabella Flipper. Henry Flipper was born into slavery. After the Civil War brought an end to slavery, the Flippers moved to Atlanta,

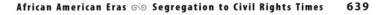

Georgia. Henry and his brothers attended schools there that were operated by the American Missionary Society, a religious group that was dedicated to the cause of equal rights for African Americans. Flipper attended high school at the preparatory department of Atlanta University, which had been established by the American Missionary Society in 1865. A preparatory department is a high school that is affiliated with a college. He began taking classes in the collegiate department in 1873.

Just as he was entering college at Atlanta University, Flipper decided he wanted to apply to West Point. Earning admission to West Point is very difficult. Students at West Point are called cadets. Each cadet must receive a nomination from his or her congressperson. Flipper wrote to his congressman, Representative James C. Freeman (1820–85), in 1872 and requested a nomination. Freeman agreed to provide the nomination after he received impressive letters of endorsement and recommendation from several of Flipper's teachers and professors. Flipper thus enrolled at West Point in the fall of 1873.

Flipper was not the first African American ever to attend West Point. That distinction belonged to James Webster Smith (1850–76), who was Flipper's roommate during his first year at West Point. (Smith was dismissed from West Point in 1874 after he failed a philosophy course.) Flipper's enrollment at West Point was nonetheless big news in the African American community. African American weekly newspapers such as the *Louisville Ledger* in Kentucky and the *New National Era and Citizen* in Washington, D.C., ran long stories providing details about Flipper's performance and experience at West Point.

Flipper did not disappoint. He achieved two notable firsts in 1877. He became the first African American ever to graduate from the United States Military Academy. West Point is a training ground for military officers. Its graduates receive commissions, which are documents certifying that the government has formally appointed them to be officers. Flipper's commission made him the first African American ever to serve as an officer in the United States military. Officers are the military's leaders. Leadership positions such as these had long been unavailable to African Americans. Flipper's graduation from West Point, therefore, was viewed as an important breakthrough for the African American community.

A Military Career Is Unfairly Cut Short

Flipper published a book the year after he graduated, providing an autobiographical account of his time at West Point. The book, entitled *The Colored Cadet at West Point,* describes all aspects of Flipper's life at the military academy. The book makes it clear that Flipper confronted significant racial prejudice and discrimination while he was at West Point.

The book describes how his white classmates refused to associate with him and the other African American cadets. They were required to allow Flipper to eat at the same table with them. Otherwise, they refused to interact with him socially. Some of the officers and instructors at West Point believed that African Americans did not deserve leadership positions in the military and treated him accordingly. Flipper nonetheless kept a positive attitude about his time at West Point.

Flipper received his first assignment as a military officer in January 1878. He was assigned to the Tenth Cavalry Regiment. A cavalry is a unit of soldiers that are mounted on horseback during combat. The Tenth Cavalry Regiment was one of the U.S. Army's first all-black regiments. It was one of two all-black regiments that came to be known as the "Buffalo Soldiers." The Buffalo Soldiers primarily fought against Native Americans and were respected for their bravery. During his time with the Tenth, Flipper was stationed in Texas and in Indian territory in what is now the western United States.

Initially Flipper's career in the U.S. Army went well. For example, he worked as the post engineer for a military post. Several pools of stagnant water had collected on the post. The pools were breeding grounds for mosquitoes that carried the deadly malaria parasite. Two previous engineers had been unable to drain the pools. Flipper succeeded in draining them. The project became known as "Flipper's Ditch."

Things took a turn for the worse in late 1880, when Flipper was assigned to a new post under the supervision of Colonel William R. Shafter (1835–1906). Shafter had a reputation as someone who treated the officers under him badly and unfairly. Flipper was serving as the post commissary, which means he supervised the grocery and general-supply store used by the soldiers. In 1881, Shafter had Flipper court-martialed (which means taken to a military criminal court) on charges that Flipper had stolen more than three thousand seven hundred dollars from the commissary. Flipper was also accused of "conduct unbecoming an officer and a gentleman," which is a special military crime that punishes officers for committing dishonest acts. The court-martial found Flipper not guilty of stealing the money, but somehow it found him guilty of "conduct unbecoming."

The verdict was illogical and unfair. Under the terms of military law, an officer can only be convicted of "conduct unbecoming" if he has committed a dishonest or indecent act. By acquitting Flipper of theft, the court-martial concluded that he had not committed a dishonest act. By nonetheless convicting him of "conduct unbecoming," the court-martial made it clear that it was convicting Flipper for something other than his conduct. Racial prejudice was almost certainly the basis for the conviction. The conviction caused Flipper to be dishonorably discharged from the military on June 30, 1882.

Fights to Clear His Name

Flipper took work as a mining engineer and land surveyor after his career in the U.S. Army was cut short. He worked in Mexico and the southwest portion of the United States. His work in the mining field eventually helped him become a recognized expert on Mexican land-use law. Flipper's expertise in the areas of engineering, mining, and mining law enabled him to have a long and distinguished career. He worked as an aide to a senator, as an assistant to the secretary of the interior, and as a consultant for a Venezuelan oil company. Flipper retired in 1930 and eventually died of a heart attack on May 3, 1940, at the age of 84.

The Army honored Henry Ossian Flipper with this bust at the Buffalo Soldier Monument at Fort Leavenworth in 2007.
AP Images

Throughout the later part of his life, Flipper fought to have his court-martial conviction overturned. He traveled to Washington, D.C., every single year to seek restoration of his status as an officer in good standing. But not even the personal pleas of the senator for whom Flipper worked, Albert B. Fall (1861–1944) of New Mexico, could convince Congress to set aside Flipper's conviction while he was still alive.

It was not until after Flipper died that his name was cleared. Flipper's niece took up his cause in 1975. With the help of an attorney, she was able to convince the U.S. Army to review Flipper's conviction. Flipper's conviction was reversed in 1976. Ninety-five years after his wrongful dishonorable discharge, Flipper finally received the honorable discharge he deserved. The next year, West Point honored the one-hundredth anniversary of the graduation of its first African American cadet by putting a bust (a sculpture of a person's head and shoulders) of Flipper on campus. And in 1999, President Bill Clinton (1946–) invited Flipper's descendents to the White House for a ceremony at which Flipper received a presidential pardon.

Henry Johnson after being awarded the Croix de Guerre for bravery during a battle with German soldiers in World War I.
© *Bettmann/Corbis*

★ HENRY JOHNSON
(1897–1929)

Henry Johnson was a soldier in World War I who earned the Croix de Guerre, France's highest military honor. Johnson earned the honor as a member of the French military. Johnson served in the French military because the U.S. military would not let African Americans serve in combat. Johnson was awarded the Croix de Guerre in recognition of exceptional bravery and valor during an attack by a German raiding party.

Military Service Offers Limited Options

Little is known about Johnson's early life. He was born in 1897. He was either born in Alexandria, Virginia, or Winston Salem, North Carolina. Johnson made his way to Albany, New York, at some point during his teenage years. He worked as a porter (a person who loads and unloads luggage) at a train station there.

The New York state legislature passed a law creating a special, all-black military unit in

1913. The unit was called the New York Fifteenth Infantry. An infantry unit is a group of soldiers specially trained for ground fighting on foot. Infantry warfare is the most dangerous and deadly kind of combat. World War I broke out in Europe in 1914. The United States stayed out of the war for several years, until Congress declared war on Germany on April 6, 1917. Johnson traveled south to Brooklyn, New York, two months later to enlist in the New York Fifteenth Infantry. After a few months of training, the New York Fifteenth deployed to Europe as part of the U.S. Army's 369th Infantry Regiment.

Racism limited the service of the men of the 369th. At the time, the U.S. military practiced a policy of racial segregation. African American soldiers could only serve in all-black units. Racial prejudice and stereotypes further limited their service in two important ways. First, military leaders wrongly believed that African Americans were not as intelligent as white Americans. African Americans were barred from serving as commanding officers and in other leadership positions. Second, the prevailing prejudices of the day held that African Americans lacked courage, bravery, and loyalty. As a result, African American soldiers were not allowed to serve in combat positions.

Wins Fame for His Bravery in Combat

The all-black 369th Infantry was one of the very first American units to arrive in Europe during World War I. At first, Johnson and his fellow members of the 369th were forced to work in grueling, low-status positions. They loaded and unloaded ships and dug latrines (outdoor ditches to be used as toilets). But soon after they arrived, the French military asked the United States for assistance. France had been involved in World War I for three years and had suffered heavy casualties. The French were facing a desperate shortage of able-bodied combat troops. They asked the American military to loan them some soldiers. Reluctantly, the United States assigned the 369th Infantry to the command of the French military.

The 369th thus became the first African American unit to see combat in the war. Johnson and his fellow soldiers were issued French uniforms, weapons, and rations. They received instruction in French language and combat tactics. They deployed to the Western front in early 1918.

On the night of May 14, 1918, Johnson and another African American soldier named Needham Roberts were on guard duty at a forward outpost. A forward outpost is a position close to enemy lines where soldiers scout the enemy and give advance warning of attacks. That night, a German patrol of between twenty-four and thirty soldiers attacked Johnson and Roberts's post. Roberts quickly suffered a serious injury and was not able to fight. Johnson single-handedly fought off the German patrol. At first he used grenades. When he ran out of grenades, he used his rifle. When he ran out of bullets, he used the butt of his rifle as a club. When his rifle splintered, he fought with his bolo knife (a large cutting tool similar to a machete).

Johnson's actions were heroic. He held off the group of Germans for more than an hour. During the battle, Johnson suffered twenty-one separate wounds on his arms, back, feet, and face, yet still he fought on. His bravery prevented him and Roberts from being captured or killed. French soldiers arrived the next morning to find four dead German soldiers and evidence that several other dead soldiers had been dragged away. The French soldiers were so impressed with Johnson's bravery that

New York governor George Pataki, right, along with Herman Johnson, left, and a member of the New York Army National Guard, prepare to place a wreath at the gravesite of Johnson's father, World War I hero Sergeant Henry Johnson at Arlington National Cemetery in Arlington, Virginia, January 10, 2002. *AP Images*

they nicknamed the men of the 369th Infantry "Hell-fighters." The 369th adopted the name and became known as the Harlem Hellfighters. Johnson's incredible bravery was proof that the stereotype of African American soldiers as lacking courage was utterly without foundation.

Johnson's conduct during the battle prompted France to award him the Croix de Guerre, that nation's highest military award. Johnson also received a golden palm on his Croix, which indicated he had displayed extraordinary valor. He became the first American ever to be so recognized. The 369th Infantry served out the remainder of World War I in combat duty under French command. Their service was so exceptional that the entire unit received a collective Croix de Guerre after the war ended.

The 369th Infantry was the toast of New York when they returned from Europe. The city hosted a huge parade to welcome them home. Johnson was a star. The hero's treatment was short-lived. When Johnson was discharged, the U.S. Army refused to acknowledge that he had been injured in battle and was entitled to disability pay. Johnson returned home to Albany after his discharge. He enjoyed a moment of celebrity, but his war wounds made it impossible for him to return to his old job as a porter. Unable to work and wrongfully denied disability pay from the military, Johnson fell into alcoholism and poverty. Little is known of the last years of his life. He died on July 2, 1929, and was buried in the Arlington National Cemetery in Arlington, Virginia, the largest and most famous military cemetery in the nation.

★ DORIS "DORIE" MILLER (1919–1943)

Dorie Miller was a chef and kitchen worker in the U.S. Navy during World War II. Miller gained renown (fame, recognition, and respect) for his courageous actions on board the battleship USS *West Virginia* during the Japanese attack on Pearl Harbor on December 7, 1941. Miller's bravery saved the life of his ship's captain. Miller also was able to shoot down at least three attacking Japanese planes. He received an award from the U.S. Navy, but he did not receive a Congressional Medal of Honor, the highest possible honor a military service member can earn. Many historians believe that Congress's failure to award Miller a Medal of Honor was caused by racial prejudice.

Doris Miller was born on October 12, 1919, on a farm near Waco, Texas. He was the third of four sons born to Henrietta and Connery Miller. Miller's parents were sharecroppers. Sharecroppers are people who farm land that they do not own. The owner of the land allows them to

OPPOSITE PAGE
Dorie Miller.
National Archives and Records Administration (NARA)

farm there in exchange for a share of the farm's profits. The sharecropping system is economically disadvantageous to the sharecropper and advantageous to the landowner. Miller's family was very poor. As a child, Miller frequently was required to help his parents farm their fields. As a teenager, Miller was a strong, solidly built young man who played fullback on the football team and earned the nickname "Raging Bull." Miller's childhood on a farm also helped him become an accomplished hunter and an excellent marksman.

Miller did not aspire to a life of farming. After he graduated high school at the age of nineteen, he wanted to broaden his horizons and see the world. He traveled to Dallas, Texas, to meet with a U.S. Navy recruiter. Miller enlisted for a six-year term in the U.S. Navy on September 17, 1939. Racial segregation and discrimination were still rampant in the U.S. Navy at this time. African Americans were not allowed to serve as sailors or in combat positions. The only position open to Miller was in the messman branch. "Mess" is a military slang term for meals; a "messman" is a military cook. Miller's duties as a messman in the U.S. Navy were thus limited to cooking, serving food, clearing tables, and waiting on the officers.

Displays Valor and Courage at Pearl Harbor

Miller never received weapons training or learned any combat skills. His only role in combat would be to handle ammunition and help gunners reload their weapons. This lack of training did not prevent Miller from answering the call of duty on December 7, 1941. That day, Miller was working aboard the USS *West Virginia*, a battleship that was anchored in Pearl Harbor, Hawaii. Early in the morning of December 7, several hundred Japanese fighter planes, bombers, and torpedo planes attacked the U.S. Navy base at Pearl Harbor. The *West Virginia* was anchored next to the USS *Arizona*,

a battleship that was one of Japan's primary targets. As the *Arizona* took heavy fire, the *West Virginia* came under attack as well.

Miller was working below deck in the kitchen when the battle alarm sounded. He ran up to the deck and saw that Mervyn Bennion, the ship's captain (its highest-ranking commanding officer) had been severely injured by a bomb. Miller rescued Bennion, picking him up and dragging him to a place where he was out of harm's way.

Japanese planes were flying overhead and spraying the *West Virginia* with machine-gun fire. Many of Miller's shipmates, desperate to avoid the gunfire, were abandoning ship and jumping overboard. But Miller did not join them. He took control of one of the ship's anti-aircraft machine guns even though he had never received training on the gun. His marksmanship and childhood experience as a hunter served him well. He is confirmed to have shot down at least three Japanese planes and may have downed as many as six. Eventually, the gun Miller was firing ran out of ammunition, and the *West Virginia* sustained heavy damage from the Japanese attack. Miller was ordered to save himself and exit the ship.

A Career in the Navy Is Cut Short

Miller's actions during the Battle of Pearl Harbor were heroic and remarkable. They also challenged racial stereotypes and prejudices that were deeply entrenched in U.S. Navy policy. African Americans were barred from serving in any role other than a messman because the U.S. Navy believed they lacked composure and initiative to serve in combat. Miller's heroism at Pearl Harbor debunked the U.S. Navy's racist policies. President Franklin D. Roosevelt joined newspapers and civil rights groups across the country in calling for the U.S. Navy to recognize Dorie Miller's service at Pearl Harbor.

Miller received the honor he deserved on June 10, 1942. That day Admiral Chester W. Nimitz (1885–1966), the commander in chief of the U.S. Navy's Pacific fleet, presented Miller with the Navy Cross. The Navy Cross was the U.S. Navy's highest award for valor and bravery in combat. Miller was the first African American ever to receive a Navy Cross. Miller was also promoted in rank and became a mess attendant first class. Miller received other honors and recognition for his courage at Pearl Harbor. For example, in 1983 the U.S. Navy named a frigate (a small warship) in his honor. But Miller never received the U.S. government's highest military decoration for bravery in combat, the Congressional Medal of Honor. Many historians believe that Miller would have received a Medal of Honor but for the racial prejudice of certain members of Congress in the 1940s.

Miller's career in the U.S. Navy came to an untimely end just two years later. Miller received a promotion from messman to the position of ship's cook by November 1943, and he was assigned to an aircraft carrier, the USS *Liscome Bay*. The ship deployed to the South Pacific to participate in combat operations against the Japanese. The *Liscome Bay* was sunk by a Japanese torpedo on November 20, 1943. Only 272 of the ship's 635 crew members were rescued. Miller did not survive the attack. But his bravery at Pearl Harbor struck an important blow in favor of equal treatment for African Americans in the U.S. Navy.

★ CHARLES YOUNG
(1864–1922)

Charles Young was an accomplished military officer who had a distinguished career in the late 1800s and early 1900s. Young became the highest-ranking African American officer in the U.S. Army when he rose to the rank of lieutenant colonel in 1916. Young earned respect and recognition as a college professor and as an author early in his career. Later in his military service, Young did important work as a cartographer (a person who surveys land and draws maps of it). Young also served

Charles Young. © *Corbis*

as the superintendent of Sequoia National Park in California. His work there was crucial to the preservation of one of the country's most treasured natural resources.

Charles Young was born on March 12, 1864, in Mayslick, Kentucky. Mayslick is a small town in the north-central part of Kentucky, about seventy miles from Cincinnati, Ohio. Both of his parents were slaves at the time of his birth. When Young was nine, his family moved across the Ohio River to Ripley, Ohio, which is just southeast of Cincinnati. Young attended an all-black high school in Ripley. He was a talented student with a particular aptitude for mathematics and foreign languages. Young graduated from high school in 1880 and accepted a job as a high school teacher.

Young had a chance to earn admission to the United States Military Academy at West Point in 1883. Earning admission to West Point is very difficult. Students at West Point are called cadets. Each state in the United States is allowed to send a certain number of cadets to West Point. Young and other students in Ohio took a competitive examination to determine which of them would become a cadet. Young received the second highest score. The person who earned the highest score dropped out of the competition, so Young was admitted to West Point. He did not have an easy time there. The white cadets subjected him to racial discrimination, ostracism, harassment, and hazing. Young persevered, and on August 31, 1889, he became the third African American cadet ever to graduate from West Point.

A Promising Military Career Is Launched

Young was commissioned as a second lieutenant after graduation, which means he received a formal document from the U.S. government certifying he was a military officer. Second lieutenant is the lowest rank of officer in the U.S. Army. Young was initially assigned to the Tenth Cavalry. He later joined the Ninth Cavalry. A cavalry is a unit of soldiers who are mounted on horseback during combat. The Ninth and Tenth Cavalry Regiments were the U.S. Army's first two all-black regiments. Together, their members were known as the "Buffalo Soldiers." The Buffalo Soldiers primarily fought against Native Americans and were renowned (famous and respected) for their bravery. Young served as a Buffalo soldier from 1889 to 1894.

Young became a college professor once his time as a Buffalo soldier ended. He taught in the military department at Wilberforce University in Ohio. Wilberforce is the oldest privately run African American university in the United States. Young was a professor there from 1894 to 1898. He taught classes on military strategy, military theory, mathematics, and French. He also was promoted to first lieutenant.

Young asked the U.S. Army to transfer him away from Wilberforce and back to combat duty in 1898 in response to the outbreak of the Spanish-American War. Young was put in charge of an all-black volunteer infantry unit and received a wartime (temporary) promotion to the rank of major. He eventually left the volunteer unit and rejoined his old unit, the Ninth Cavalry. While serving with the Ninth Cavalry, he received a permanent promotion to captain on February 2, 1901. Young saw combat duty in the Philippines during this time. His bravery and leadership in combat earned him the nickname, "Follow Me."

Young returned to the United States in October 1902 and was stationed in California. He was acting superintendent of the Sequoia and General Grant National Parks, serving from October 1902 to late 1903. These parks are home to groves of massive and ancient sequoia trees. These groves are one of the country's most treasured natural resources.

Young is credited with increasing the public's appreciation for the beauty of these trees during his time as the superintendent of the parks. He oversaw the construction of roads that greatly increased public access to the parks.

Young also took important conservationist steps that preserved and protected the health of the sequoias. He recognized that the trees were being damaged by the countless tourists who were trampling their roots. Young and his troops were the first to put up fences around the trees to protect them from abuse. The National Park Service unveiled a mural in August 2003 honoring Young and the Ninth Cavalry for their contributions to protecting the sequoias.

Becomes a Colonel

Young's military service once again took him overseas in 1904. This time he was assigned to be an assistant to the U.S. military attaché in Port-au-Prince, Haiti. A military attaché is a high-ranking military officer who is assigned to guard and assist a group of diplomats that is stationed in another country. Young began practicing cartography (the science of making maps) during his time in Haiti. He rode the island on horseback, revising old maps and creating new maps of territory that was previously uncharted. Young remained in Haiti until 1907, when he again returned to the United States. He alternated duty between the United States and the Philippines from 1907 to 1912.

In 1912, Young accepted an assignment as a military attaché to Liberia, a small nation on the western coast of Africa. In Liberia, Young again began practicing cartography. He traveled the country and mapped previously uncharted territory. Young was promoted to major on August 28, 1912. Just one month later, Young was shot in the right arm while he was engaged in a rescue mission. Despite the injury, Young served out his tour in Liberia. He finally returned to the United States in 1915, where he was put in charge of the Tenth Calvary. Young led the Tenth in battle during the Mexican-American War. Young was promoted to the rank of lieutenant colonel in recognition of his outstanding leadership on June 1, 1916. The promotion made him the highest-ranking African American officer in the U.S. Army.

Young's career was on the rise. A promotion to full colonel—and eventually a chance to become the first African American general in American history—seemed within reach. Young expected to get a chance to earn those promotions with continued combat service when the United States entered World War I in April 1917. However, the military declared that the arm injury he had suffered five years earlier in Liberia was a physical disability that made him unfit for combat. It made no difference that Young had served in combat in the Mexican-American War after he suffered the injury. The declaration of physical disability was almost certainly the result of racial prejudice on the part of white military officers who did not want to see Young rise any higher in the ranks. Young decided to prove his physical fitness by riding his horse from Ohio to Washington, D.C., to protest the military's decision. Young was reinstated to military duty once World War I was over. But his chance to rise even higher had already come and gone.

Young's last assignment was a second tour as a military attaché in Liberia. He arrived in 1919. In early 1922, Young fell ill while on a diplomatic mission to Nigeria. He died of a kidney infection on January 8, 1922, at the age of fifty-seven. He was first buried in Nigeria. After a year, his wife successfully petitioned to have his body returned to the United States. On June 21, 1923, Young was buried in the Arlington National Cemetery in Arlington, Virginia, the largest and most famous military cemetery in the nation.

❖ BUFFALO SOLDIERS EARN RESPECT IN U.S. WARS

About one hundred eighty thousand African Americans fought in the U.S. Army during the Civil War (1861–65). They fought in segregated regiments, or military units. The United States needed fewer troops once the Civil War ended, so military units were consolidated, or reduced. The black regiments that fought during the Civil War were consolidated into four units. These units were known as the Buffalo Soldiers and included two cavalry units (soldiers on horses) and two infantry units. They are best known for fighting in the Indian Wars on the American Western frontier. They also fought in the Spanish-American War and helped defeat Mexican revolutionary commander Pancho Villa (1878–1923).

Admission to the Buffalo Soldier units was very competitive. Four or five times as many African American men wanted to serve in the U.S. Army

Group shot of Buffalo Soldiers during World War I. *National Archives and Records Administration (NARA)*

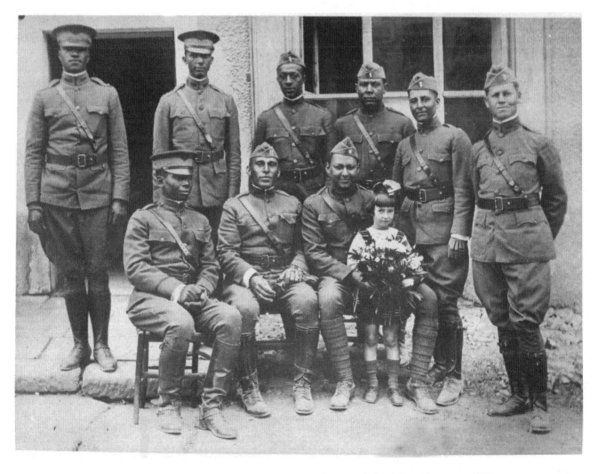

Cathay Williams: A Female Buffalo Soldier

Cathay Williams is the only woman known to have served as a Buffalo soldier. Williams was born a slave in 1842. She was freed soon after the beginning of the Civil War. She went to work for the Union Army as a servant to Colonel Thomas Hart Benton and to General Phillip Sheridan. She experienced military life firsthand while working for these men.

Williams wanted to continue her military service after the war. Women were not allowed to serve in the military at that time, so in 1866, the year Congress first authorized creation of the units that became the Buffalo Soldiers, Williams enlisted—as a man. She called herself William Cathay. She served with the Thirty-Eighth Infantry division for a few years before it was discovered that she was a woman. She received an honorable discharge from the U.S. Army.

as there were spots available. There were few economic opportunities for African Americans in the late 1800s; thus, many saw the military as a desirable career option. The Army also gave African American soldiers a chance at education they would not have otherwise had. Many learned to read in after-hours courses available to the troops.

Buffalo Soldiers Fight in the American West

The Buffalo Soldiers are best known for fighting in the Western frontier during the second half of the nineteenth century, especially for fighting in wars against the Native Americans. This is where the Buffalo Soldiers got their name, from the Plains Indians. Some accounts say the Indians called the African American soldiers Buffalo Soldiers because they thought their curly, coarse hair resembled that of a buffalo. Other accounts say they were called Buffalo Soldiers because their fighting spirit was strong like a buffalo's. Either way, it is agreed that the designation, or name, was embraced by the Buffalo Soldiers. They saw it as a name of honor.

The great majority of Buffalo Soldiers were stationed at forts throughout the American Western frontier in the late nineteenth century. Many of their duties did not involve fighting, but instead involved helping with the westward expansion of the country. The Buffalo Soldiers built and repaired buildings. They installed telegraph lines to allow communication with Western settlements. They guarded railroads and protected railroad property against thieves and striking workers. They provided police-type protection, too, by protecting wagon trains and chasing down cattle thieves.

Buffalo Soldiers also had many battles with Native Americans. The Native Americans proved a problem for the country's goal of expanding its border to the Pacific Ocean and settling the West. The Indians had occupied the lands the United States wanted to annex for thousands of years. The United States sought to contain or in many cases simply eliminate tribes in the Great Plains and Southwest as it expanded. The Buffalo Soldiers were a central part of this effort. They fought the Apaches of the Southwest and the Cheyenne and Comanche of the Great Plains. Buffalo Soldiers won nineteen Medals of Honor during the Indian Wars. The Medal of Honor is the highest military honor in the United States.

Fighting in Cuba During the Spanish-American War

The United States went to war with Spain in 1898 over the issue of Cuban independence. People in Cuba had been pressing for independence from Spain, and the United States supported their cause. They supported the Cubans in part because of sympathy with their efforts to throw off colonial rule (as the United States had done during the American Revolution). The United States government was also interested in taking over Spanish colonies (including the Philippines, Puerto Rico, and Guam) for its own use. Buffalo Soldiers were dispatched to fight in Cuba after war was declared.

The Buffalo Soldiers fought bravely in the Spanish-American War. Their most important victory came in the Battle of San Juan Hill, which was a key turning point in the war and its most famous land battle. It was part of the United States military's effort to take over the Spanish-occupied city of Santiago de Cuba. This was important because Spanish naval forces were stationed in the harbor on the other side of Santiago de Cuba.

The Battle at San Juan Hill is most popularly remembered for the involvement of Theodore Roosevelt (1858–1919), who would go on to become president of the United States. Roosevelt led the First Cavalry Unit, a diverse, all-volunteer unit known as the "Rough Riders." The Tenth Cavalry and the Fourth Cavalry of the Buffalo Soldiers first fought alongside the Rough Riders at the Battle of Las Guasimas. Las Guasimas was an important position in the U.S. efforts to take Santiago de Cuba. The Rough Riders stormed the village of Las Guasimas on June 24, 1898. They fought valiantly but found themselves trapped by Spanish gunfire. The Tenth Cavalry Unit came to the rescue. They fought their way through

dense jungle to come to the aid of the Rough Riders. Eventually, they joined forces and chased off the Spanish troops, taking the village.

Once Las Guasimas was secured for U.S. forces, the Tenth Cavalry joined the Rough Riders in the siege on San Juan Hill. They were joined by two other Buffalo Soldier units, the Twenty-Fourth and Twenty-Fifth Infantry Units. The Buffalo Soldiers fought courageously as they charged up the hill under heavy enemy fire. The Tenth Cavalry lost 20 percent of its men. The Twenty-Fourth Infantry and Twenty-Fifth Infantry charged past white units that were too scared to advance. Their heroic fighting prompted a fellow soldier, Frank Knox, who would go on to become secretary of the navy, to comment, "I must say that I never saw braver men anywhere" than the Buffalo Soldiers. They secured the hill and proceeded to lay siege to Santiago de Cuba. The city surrendered two weeks later. It was the last major military engagement of the war. The United States had won, thanks in large part to the efforts of the Buffalo Soldiers.

Fighting in the Philippines and Mexico

Buffalo Soldiers also went to the Philippines to aid in U.S efforts to free the region from Spanish control. The United States promptly took possession of the Philippines, prompting the angry Philippine freedom fighters to launch the Philippine-American War, in which the Buffalo Soldiers also fought. (The United States won and retained control of the Philippines until 1946.)

The Buffalo Soldiers also took part in a famous mission in Mexico known as the Mexican Expedition. The Mexican Revolution had started

Celebrating the Buffalo Soldiers

The Buffalo Soldiers continued to be honored in different ways even decades after disbanding. The following are some notable celebrations of the Buffalo Soldier legacy.

- 1983: Reggae singer Bob Marley's song "Buffalo Soldiers" is released.
- 1992: Monument to Buffalo Soldiers is opened at Fort Leavenworth, the original home of the Tenth Cavalry. African American general Colin Powell dedicates the memorial to the brave service of the Buffalo Soldiers.
- 1994: United States Postal Service honors Buffalo Soldiers with the release of a commemorative stamp.
- 2000: Buffalo Soldier Museum is opened in Houston, Texas.

in 1910 as a struggle against the tyrannical rule of Porfirio Diaz (1830–1915). It soon became a complex, multisided struggle that involved many paramilitary groups (fighting groups that do not belong to a national military branch). The wily guerrilla fighter Pancho Villa led such a group. After he led his men in an attack in U.S. territory, the U.S. military retaliated in 1916 by sending troops to Mexico. The aim was to capture Villa. Though Villa escaped them, the Buffalo Soldiers fought bravely.

The End of the Buffalo Soldier Era

The Buffalo Soldier units fought in U.S. wars through World War II (1939–45). Black soldiers played an integral part of the effort in World War II. The bravery and successes of the Buffalo Soldier units inspired military leaders to recognize the successes and importance of black soldiers. This recognition is at least partly responsible for President Harry Truman's decision to sign Executive Order 9981 on July 28, 1948. The order permanently ended racial segregation in the United States military. Like civilian desegregation, desegregation of the military did not happen overnight. The process took some years to complete. By the time the Korean War broke out in 1950, there was only one remaining unit of Buffalo Soldiers, the Twenty-Fourth Infantry Unit. The Twenty-Fourth Unit was officially deactivated on October 1, 1951, signaling full desegregation of the United States military.

❖ BROWNSVILLE AFFAIR DISCRIMINATES AGAINST BLACK SOLDIERS

Black soldiers routinely had to deal with discrimination based on race during the segregation era. Such racism often came from the military establishment. The Brownsville Affair is a good example of this discrimination. The Brownsville Affair resulted in the dishonorable discharge of three companies of black soldiers without any opportunity for a legal defense after three men were shot outside of Fort Brown, Texas.

The Incident and Initial Response

Brownsville, Texas, is a town on the U.S.–Mexico border. It is just across the border from the Mexican town of Matamoros. It was also the home to Fort Brown, a United States military base during the late 1800s and early 1900s. A number of African American soldiers were stationed at Fort Brown in 1906. The soldiers were members of the all-black military unit, the 25th Infantry Regiment. The First Battalion of the 25th Infantry had three companies of soldiers stationed at Fort Brown.

A button protests the discrimination experienced by the black soldiers unfairly discharged in the Brownsville Affair.
© *David J. & Janice L. Frent Collection/Corbis*

There had been tensions between the African American soldiers and the white population of Brownsville. Brownsville, like many other towns in the American South, was strictly segregated. This segregation was enforced by the townspeople and also by Jim Crow laws, which were state and local laws that required racial segregation in public places. The white townspeople spread rumors and false charges about the black soldiers stationed at Fort Brown. They accused members of the 25th Infantry of trying to force white women to have sex with them and of public drunkenness. They also physically assaulted some of the African American soldiers.

Tensions in Brownsville reached a boiling point on the night of August 13, 1906. Soon after midnight on August 14, gunfire rang out from the area between Fort Brown and the town limits. Soldiers on duty that night came to attention, assuming the fort was under attack. In actuality, the people who had been killed were a white barkeeper, a Mexican American police officer, and another Mexican American man. Some white townspeople immediately concluded that the African American soldiers must have been responsible for the attack. Their suspicions were confirmed by the reports of the two Mexican American victims.

A U.S. Army inspector first began to investigate the incident. He concluded quickly that the black soldiers at Fort Brown must have been responsible for the attack. The morning after the attack, cartridges from Army-issued guns were found in the streets in Brownsville. The inspector thought this pointed to the soldiers as culprits.

The U.S. Army inspector reported his findings and suspicions to President Theodore Roosevelt. He was not able to pinpoint any specific people responsible for the attack, so he recommended that Roosevelt simply discharge all of the black soldiers at Fort Brown. The president responded swiftly. He dishonorably discharged all of the soldiers in companies B, C, and D of the 25th Infantry. The soldiers did not receive any kind of due process, or formal legal proceedings, either criminal civilian proceedings or military proceedings known as a court martial. This means that the soldiers had no chance to defend themselves, and the government never had to prove that any of the soldiers had actually been responsible.

The Investigation

The fact that the government never actually proved who was responsible for the shootings led to criticism and suspicion. This was even true among some white observers. A civil rights organization, the Constitution League, first took up the soldiers' cause. They found a defender in Senator Joseph E. Foraker (1846–1917). Senator Foraker, a Republican from Ohio, was not motivated entirely by concern for the soldiers. He was a rival of President Roosevelt, and he wanted to highlight Roosevelt's questionable judgment.

Senator Foraker went to the Senate Committee on Military Affairs. He wanted the committee to investigate the incident in Brownsville and force the president to answer for his actions in connection with it.

Senator Foraker and another Republican senator, Morgan G. Bulkeley (from Connecticut), delved deeply into investigating the Brownsville Affair. The Senate's investigation lasted more than a year, from February 1907 to March 1908. They gathered a wealth of evidence that created doubt as to whether the soldiers at Fort Brown had been responsible for the attack. First, they argued, the eyewitnesses who had pointed to the soldiers were not reliable. Second, there was evidence that the U.S. Army's investigators were racially prejudiced. Third, it was well known that the people of Brownsville, who had been harassing the soldiers for some time, were prejudiced against African Americans. Fourth, all of the men in the battalion had an alibi. They could account for their whereabouts in the moments after the incident, along with the whereabouts of their guns and ammunition. Fifth, the bullets found in the street did not all match the cartridges that had been used during the shooting. Foraker and Bulkeley concluded that it was likely that someone else was responsible for the shooting, but had tried to make it seem as though the soldiers at Fort Brown were responsible.

The Legacy of the Brownsville Affair

President Roosevelt and his administration did not take the Foraker and Bulkeley report seriously, nor did the Senate Committee on Military Affairs. The committee voted to uphold the president's decision. Their vote was nine votes to uphold to four votes against upholding the decision. Still, the War Department of the federal government did allow some of the dishonorably discharged soldiers to reenlist in the military. Fourteen soldiers were allowed to reenlist in 1910.

The Brownsville Affair continued to be controversial for years. Some critics, motivated by racial bias, had long argued that African Americans should not be permitted to serve in the United States military. These racist critics argued that the Brownsville incident proved that African Americans should not be allowed to be armed or serve as combat troops. For others, the Brownsville Affair was a clear demonstration of racial injustice in the United States. As the fight for civil rights in the United States was in its early years, the Brownsville Affair served as a powerful reminder of the many ways in which African Americans were denied equal protection of the law in the United States.

In 1972, Congress revisited the Brownsville incident decades after it occurred. Congress concluded that it was likely that the Army inspector who initially pointed the finger at the African American soldiers was biased and had probably prejudged the incident before conducting his investigation.

Congress granted the men who had been banished honorable discharges. The one surviving member of the battalion was then able to collect his military pension.

❖ HOUSTON MUTINY OF 1917 RESULTS IN NINETEEN EXECUTIONS

The Houston Mutiny was a violent confrontation between African American soldiers and white townspeople in Houston, Texas. The incident, which took place on August 23, 1917, was the result of months of racial tensions between townspeople and the African American soldiers stationed at Camp Logan. The U.S. military executed nineteen of the black soldiers found to be involved, and sentenced sixty more to life in prison. The speed with which the military carried out its sentences alarmed many in the black community. The incident was a forerunner to violent race riots that occurred in several U.S. cities just two years later.

The Lead-Up to the Mutiny

Various men from the Third Battalion of the all-black Twenty-Fourth Infantry Unit were stationed at Camp Logan in 1917. Camp Logan was in Houston, Texas. The United States was embroiled in World War I (1914–18) at the time. Camp Logan was used as a training camp for the United States military during the war. The infantrymen of the Third Battalion had been sent to Camp Logan to protect military building projects.

Relations were tense between the black soldiers at Camp Logan and the white citizens of Houston, Texas. Houston, like many other cities in the

The court martial of African American soldiers on trial for the Houston Mutiny. © *Corbis*

American South at the time, was strictly segregated under a system of Jim Crow laws. Jim Crow laws were laws that required segregation of white people and African American people in public places and in public accommodations like restaurants, buses and trains, and housing.

Many white people harbored racist prejudices about African Americans in the military. Many did not believe that African Americans should be permitted to own firearms or serve in combat. Tensions between townspeople and the black soldiers increased in the months leading up to the mutiny at Camp Logan. The African American infantrymen were harassed by Houston police officers. The soldiers quickly grew tired of the harassment. Many African American soldiers had grown used to the relative equality they experienced in the military. White civilians, on the other hand, feared that African American civilians would come to expect more equal treatment if they saw that African American servicemen stood on closer to equal footing.

A Riot Breaks Out

This tense environment proved explosive when the Houston riot broke out in 1917. The riot was spurred by rumors that an African American serviceman had been killed by the Houston police. It was rumored that Corporal Charles Baltimore had been murdered by Houston police for interfering with the interrogation, or police questioning, of a black woman by the Houston police. In actuality, Baltimore had not been murdered. He had, however, been severely beaten by the Houston police. The rumors about the incidents surrounding Charles Baltimore's treatment by the police contributed to the violent uprising that broke out. Another factor was the climate of frustration over mistreatment by Houston authorities and citizens.

As news of Charles Baltimore's mistreatment by the police spread, black soldiers took to the streets of Houston. About one hundred fifty soldiers marched through the city streets in protest, armed with their weapons. In response, local white people took up their own firearms. The result was a violent confrontation that left nineteen people dead. Four black soldiers were killed, along with fifteen local residents. Around a dozen others were injured in the confrontation. To make matters worse, the leader of the troops took his own life. He killed himself after his troops killed a national guardsman whom the troops accidentally believed was a Houston police officer.

The Largest Court Martial in U.S. History

The soldiers who participated in the Houston Mutiny had to face a court martial, or military trial. It was, at the time, the largest court martial in United States history. The court martial took place at Fort Sam Houston

Houston Mutiny Foreshadows Red Summer Riots of 1919

In many ways, the Houston Mutiny foreshadowed the "Red Summer" Riots of 1919, which happened about two years after the riot in Houston. Red Summer Riots is the term commonly used to refer to the multiple race riots that broke out in major American cities in the summer and fall of 1919. Like the Houston Mutiny, the Red Summer Riots were the result of simmering racial tensions in American cities.

One of the most violent Red Summer Riots took place on July 27, 1919, in Chicago, Illinois. Like the Houston Mutiny, the riots in Chicago were spurred by the African American community's perception of police mistreatment. After a black youth was drowned in a stone-throwing contest in a public swimming area that had been claimed by whites, Chicago police refused to arrest the white men involved. They arrested a black man instead. Fights broke out across the city between groups of white and black citizens. The riots continued for thirteen days, leaving 37 people dead and 537 injured. The homes of one thousand black families were destroyed in the riots.

in San Antonio, Texas. Numerous soldiers from the Third Battalion were tried at the court martial. Thirteen of the black soldiers were sentenced to death. Forty-one received sentences of life imprisonment. Four received several years in prison. Five were acquitted, or found not guilty.

The men who were sentenced to death at the first court martial were swiftly executed. Many African Americans were outraged and shocked at the way the men's sentences were carried out. They were secretly hanged, and their hangings did not follow official procedure. Generally, the public was able to learn of a court martial sentence before it was carried out. The president and the secretary of war were also typically allowed to review and approve a death sentence before it was carried out. By contrast, many white members of the Houston community were happy with the swift executions.

The military conducted two more courts martial in 1918. In those courts martial, sixteen more men were sentenced to death. By this time, word had spread of the military's handling of the first executions. Black leaders were outraged and put pressure on President Woodrow Wilson (1856–1924). President Wilson, responding to this pressure, commuted the death sentences of ten of the men. Commuting a death sentence means changing it to a sentence of life in prison. By the end of the military trials, sixty soldiers received life in prison for participating in the Houston Mutiny.

❖ THE TUSKEGEE VETERANS HOSPITAL CARES FOR BLACK VETERANS

The opening of a hospital for African American veterans (former members of the military) in Tuskegee, Alabama, was an important development in African American military and medical history. Hundreds of thousands of African Americans had served in World War I. Many of these veterans needed medical care that they could not get at segregated hospitals in the South in the 1920s. The Tuskegee Veterans Hospital was opened to fill this need. The hospital's decision to employ only African American doctors and nurses was very controversial. But the facility thrived and continued in operation into the twenty-first century.

A Need Arises for a Black Veterans Hospital

World War I provided the impetus (incentive or driving force that causes something to occur) for the opening of the Tuskegee Veterans Hospital. The United States drafted an army of more than four million men during World War I, including three hundred eighty thousand African American soldiers. Approximately two hundred thousand African Americans were deployed to Europe, roughly forty-two thousand of whom engaged in combat. Many American soldiers suffered serious but non-fatal injuries during World War I. Many of these injured soldiers needed continuing medical care after the war ended in 1918. African American veterans were no exception.

The policies of racial segregation that were in place throughout the South at the time made it impossible for most African American veterans to receive medical care in the same hospitals as white veterans. Many African American veterans were denied government-provided medical care entirely. Others were forced to receive their care in inferior, underfunded facilities. The lack of medical care for black veterans in the South was especially problematic. This was because a very large percentage of the nation's African American residents lived in the South in the early 1900s. More than three hundred thousand of the three hundred eighty thousand African Americans who were veterans of World War I lived in the South in the early 1920s.

An all-black veterans hospital was needed. The National Association for the Advancement of Colored People (NAACP) began lobbying President Warren G. Harding to provide federal funding for an all-black veterans hospital in the early 1920s. The Tuskegee Institute in Tuskegee, Alabama, emerged as the logical place to locate an African American veterans hospital. The Tuskegee Institute is an all-black university that was founded by Booker T. Washington (1856–1915) in 1881. It was one of the most highly regarded African American institutions of higher learning in the nation in the early 1900s. In addition, the Tuskegee Institute Hospital and Nurse Training School had been in operation there since 1892. The Tuskegee Institute Hospital provided medical care to the black students and faculty of the Tuskegee Institute and to the African American community in the surrounding area.

A New Veterans Hospital Faces Controversy

The Tuskegee Institute and the NAACP partnered with the National Medical Association (NMA), a black physicians' group dedicated to promoting the medical well-being of African Americans. The Tuskegee Institute agreed to donate three hundred acres of land adjacent to its campus where the new veterans hospital could be located. The NMA and the NAACP lobbied Congress to provide funding. Their lobbying efforts paid off in 1923. Congress authorized the United States Treasury to build a hospital exclusively dedicated to providing medical care to African American veterans. The hospital was built on the land donated by the Tuskegee Institute at a cost of $2.5 million. It comprised (was made up of) twenty-seven buildings and had six hundred beds.

Robert Moton made sure that the new Tuskegee veterans hospital was staffed with black doctors and nurses. *Fisk University Library. Reproduced by permission*

The dedication ceremony for the new veterans hospital took place on February 12, 1923. Vice President Calvin Coolidge (1872–1933) officiated the ceremony. The hospital began operation as the Hospital for Sick and Injured Colored World War Veterans. The name was later changed to the Tuskegee Veterans Administration Hospital, or V.A. Hospital for short.

One of the most controversial aspects of the new veterans hospital was the racial composition of its staff. Robert R. Moton (1867–1940), the president of the Tuskegee Institute, joined with the NAACP and local African American residents in calling for the hospital to employ black doctors and nurses and be run by a black administrative staff. White residents of Tuskegee and throughout the South, on the other hand, believed the hospital should only employ whites. When the hospital was first dedicated, a "whites only" hiring policy was in place. Moton and the NAACP fought back. They lobbied President

Harding and members of his administration to change the policy. Their lobbying worked. Less than two weeks later, on February 23, 1923, President Harding ordered that, to the greatest extent possible, the hospital should be staffed by African American doctors and nurses.

The Tuskegee V.A. Hospital Leaves a Lasting Legacy

Harding's decision sparked outrage in the South. White politicians in Alabama argued it was dangerous to allow African Americans to run a major institution such as a hospital because it made them less subject to white control. Moton received letters threatening to burn down the hospital and the rest of the Tuskegee Institute, too. The local chapter of the Ku Klux Klan (KKK) marched on Tuskegee on July 3, 1923. The KKK burned a forty-foot-tall cross, and a caravan of seventy cars surrounded the hospital.

Ultimately, the KKK's efforts at intimidation failed. Moton refused to compromise his commitment to having an all-black staff at the hospital. Six African American doctors began treating African American veterans at Tuskegee in August 1923. By July 1924, the hospital employed twenty-one African American physicians and dentists. The Tuskegee V.A. Hospital thus became the first and only hospital in the South staffed exclusively by African American medical professionals. The opportunity to work in an all-black facility attracted the best young African American medical professionals to Tuskegee for many years. The facility thrived and provided first-class medical care to African American veterans.

The Tuskegee V.A. Hospital remained in operation as of 2010. Segregation in hospitals became illegal in 1965, after which Tuskegee V. A. Hospital provided care to veterans of all races, and employed doctors and nurses of all races as well. The hospital celebrated its eighty-fifth anniversary in February 2008. It became part of the Central Alabama Veterans Health Care System in 1997. As of 2010, it was one of four sites in that system that serviced 143,000 veterans in more than 40 counties in Alabama and Georgia.

❖ THE TUSKEGEE AIRMEN BATTLE NAZIS AND STEREOTYPES

The Tuskegee Airmen were the first group of African Americans ever to serve as pilots for the United States military. For years, the military had refused to let African Americans serve as pilots because of racial stereotypes. Political pressure caused the Tuskegee Airmen to be organized as a unit immediately before the United States entered World War II. The Tuskegee Airmen were pioneers who participated in a novel form of combat. They frequently endured unfair criticism and racial prejudice. But they proved their mettle (courage and ability) in combat. They compiled an exemplary record of service during World War II. The Tuskegee Airmen are remembered as heroes who struck an important symbolic blow in favor of integration and racial equality.

Resistance to Black Pilots Is Overcome

There were no African American pilots in the U.S. Army Air Corps (which would later become the U.S. Air Force) in the years before World War II. All branches of the military practiced a strict policy of racial segregation during those days. The roles of African Americans were limited by institutional racism. Being a pilot was considered a prestigious and advanced form of military service. The prevailing racial stereotypes of the day held that African Americans were not capable of being pilots. The U.S. Army even had conducted a study in 1925 that claimed to have "scientifically" proven that African Americans were not brave enough to serve in combat and also lacked the intelligence and skills to perform technically complex jobs such as pilot and aircraft mechanic.

African Americans who were working as civilian pilots began to challenge the U.S. Army's policy in the late 1930s. The National Airmen's Association (NAA), a group of black pilots, arranged a meeting in May 1939 with Missouri senator (and future president) Harry S. Truman (1884–1972). The NAA wanted Truman to help them force the military to start training black pilots. Truman told them he did not think that goal was

These men were among the first group of Tuskegee Airmen to be sent into combat. © *Bettmann/Corbis*

feasible. However, he agreed to sponsor a bill in Congress that would allow African Americans to be admitted to the federal government's Civilian Pilot Training Program. Congress passed the bill. The new black pilots would be trained at the Tuskegee Institute in Tuskegee, Alabama, a well-respected college for African American students.

The program soon expanded from the civilian field to the military. The first group of African American pilots had completed their civilian pilot training at Tuskegee by December 1940. At the same time, the U.S. Army Air Corps and President Franklin D. Roosevelt (1882–1945) were under political pressure to increase the opportunities available to African Americans in the military. Roosevelt's wife, Eleanor Roosevelt (1884–1962), proposed to the U.S. Army that they expand the ongoing civilian training program at Tuskegee into a military facility for the training of African American combat pilots. Roosevelt's proposal specifically stated that the admissions criteria and qualifications for this experimental program should be identical to the criteria used to train white pilots. A longtime supporter of civil rights, Eleanor Roosevelt believed that the program offered the opportunity to disprove powerful negative stereotypes about African Americans.

The Tuskegee Airmen Are Born

The 66th Air Force Contract Flying School was established at the Tuskegee Army Field in July 1941. The graduates of the training program would make up a black flying unit, the 99th Pursuit Squadron. ("Pursuit squadron" was the World War II–era name for a fighter squadron.) Thirteen African American pilots formed the first class. The airmen completed their classroom work at the Tuskegee Institute and then received flight training at the nearby airfield. The first five Tuskegee Airmen earned their flight wings, which means they were certified as combat-ready pilots, in March 1942. As the first batch of airmen began their service overseas, more and more African American pilots began training at Tuskegee. Nearly one thousand would complete the training and earn their wings before the war ended.

The first Tuskegee Airmen entered combat service in North Africa in May 1943. They then were stationed in the European theater, first in Italy and eventually in Germany. The Tuskegee Airmen were fighter pilots. As the war went on, their primary responsibility became flying escort missions with bombers. Bombers are large planes that fly at high altitudes to drop bombs on the ground below. They are large, slow, and vulnerable to attack from enemy fighters because fighter planes are smaller and quicker. The job of a fighter flying an escort mission is to patrol the skies around the bomber it is escorting and protect it from enemy fighters. The Tuskegee Airmen flew escort missions above Germany throughout 1944 and 1945.

The Tuskegee Airmen compiled an incredible combat record during World War II. They flew more than 15,000 sorties (a mission flown by a single plane), shot down 111 enemy aircraft, destroyed 200 grounded aircraft, and demolished nearly 1,000 automobiles and railroad cars. The achievement of which the unit was the most proud was the fact that they flew more than two thousand bomber escort missions without allowing a single American bomber to be destroyed by enemy fire. Individually, the airmen earned a large number of decorations and honors. These included 150 Distinguished Flying Crosses, which are awarded for heroism or extraordinary achievement during combat aerial flight, and 744 Air Medals, which are awarded for meritorious achievement during aerial flight. The Tuskegee Airmen made up one of the most decorated units in World War II.

The legacy of the Tuskegee Airmen extends beyond their service in World War II. Their bravery, expertise, and loyalty changed the culture of the military forever. No longer would African American soldiers be excluded from serving as pilots or in other desirable positions because of stereotypes about their intelligence. Many historians believe that the record of service compiled by the airmen helped convince Truman to end racial segregation in the military in 1948. Their influence did not end there. The Tuskegee Airmen continued to captivate and inspire the American public for decades to come. In recognition of their unique place in United States history, Barack Obama, the first African American ever to be elected president, invited all of the surviving Tuskegee Airmen to attend his presidential inauguration ceremony in early 2009.

❖ TRUMAN DESEGREGATES THE MILITARY

July 26, 1948, was a historic day for African Americans in the military. That day, President Harry S. Truman issued Executive Order 9981. An executive order is a document signed by the president that gives legally binding instructions on how to comply with the law. Executive Order 9981 required the military to provide equal opportunity and treatment to all soldiers, without regard to their race. This ended the military's policy of racial segregation. Truman's decision came only after the United States was subject to fierce criticism at home and abroad because of its racially segregated military. The integration of the military was a major civil rights victory.

Racial Segregation in the Military Draws Criticism

The United States military had a long history of racial segregation. In 1866, following the conclusion of the Civil War, Congress ordered all African American soldiers to be reorganized into single-race regiments.

African American soldiers were largely commanded by white officers, and they could not serve alongside white soldiers. As states throughout the South passed laws requiring racial segregation in the late 1800s, the military followed suit. Military bases, including mess halls, social venues, and barracks, became segregated. Black soldiers served loyally and courageously in the military throughout the early twentieth century, but they faced significant racial discrimination.

The United States became subject to criticism because of racial segregation in its military during World War II. Some of this criticism came from other countries around the world. The enemies of the United States in World War II were Germany, Italy, and Japan, known as the Axis powers. These countries promoted openly racist, anti-Jewish policies. The United States and its allies argued they were fighting the war to promote the triumph of democracy and freedom over racial and religious intolerance. The Axis powers rightly pointed out that the United States had a segregated military, which was evidence that it was being hypocritical in its defense of freedom and equality. Even some U.S. allies questioned whether racial segregation in the armed forces was consistent with democratic government.

The most heated criticism came on the home front. Many African Americans were angry that the nation was willing to fight a war overseas in

Picketers protest racial segregation in the military outside of the Democratic National Convention in 1948. © *Bettmann/Corbis*

the name of protecting freedom but was unwilling to protect the freedom of African Americans at home by ending racial segregation. African Americans knew that the nation needed them to support the war effort. Black leaders and newspapers wanted to couple their support of the war effort with demands for racial integration and equal treatment. To that end, they came up with the "Double V" slogan. The two Vs stood for two victories, one over enemies abroad and the other over racism at home. The Double V campaign built important momentum for the civil rights movement that began in the 1950s.

World War II Sparks Integration

Support for racial segregation in the military began to break down during World War II. Some people had argued that segregation was necessary for white soldiers' morale, but the necessities of combat caused black and white soldiers to fight side-by-side and live in close quarters during the war, and still the U.S. armed forces won victory after victory. Others contended that African American soldiers did not deserve equal treatment because they were not as smart or as brave as white soldiers. However, numerous black soldiers won awards for their bravery and valor in combat. In addition, African American officers became able commanders, and the success of the legendary Tuskegee Airmen proved that no military task was beyond the ability of African American soldiers. By the end of World War II, it was apparent that racial segregation in the military was based on nothing more than stereotypes and prejudice.

The movement to desegregate the military gained momentum after World War II ended. More than one million African Americans had served their country during the war. Yet when they returned home, many were greeted with violence and scorn at the hands of white Americans, especially in the South. In 1946, the number of lynchings of African Americans (lawless, racially motivated murders by mobs) in the South was the highest it had been in decades. These problems prompted President Harry Truman to ask Congress to create a commission to determine how best to protect African Americans' civil rights. The President's Commission on Human Rights issued a report in 1947 that called for a variety of legal reforms. Senators from the South refused to allow Congress to pass legislation enacting any of the proposed reforms.

Truman decided to take matters into his own hands. The U.S. Constitution makes the president the commander in chief of all branches of the armed forces. As a result, the president has the authority to determine a wide range of military policies. Truman decided to use his authority as commander in chief to end segregation in the military. Truman believed desegregating the military would serve two main benefits. First, it would help the military attract more African American recruits. Second, it would be a victory for civil rights and would help promote equality in society at large. Truman issued Executive Order 9981 on July 26, 1948. The order required all soldiers to be treated equally, regardless of race. It also ordered the military to set up a new committee to determine how best to integrate existing military forces. The committee was called the Committee on Equality of Treatment and Opportunity in the Armed Services.

Truman's Order Brings Lasting Changes

Many officers in the military were opposed to Executive Order 9981 at the time it was issued. Despite the experience of World War II, they continued to argue that integrating the troops would undermine morale and cause white soldiers to begin disobeying orders. The military was slow to submit plans for integration. The U.S. Air Force was the first branch to do so. It submitted an integration plan in 1949. The U.S. Navy and U.S. Army followed suit in 1950, as did the U.S. Marine Corps in 1951. As integration proceeded, the fears of unrest proved to be unfounded. Soldiers are accustomed to following orders and obeying the chain of command. When orders came down that they were to serve in racially integrated units, they simply obeyed the orders. As a result, racial integration in the military proceeded smoothly and quickly. By 1953, 95 percent of all African Americans in the military were serving in integrated units. The last racially segregated unit in the American military was disbanded on October 30, 1954. The military had achieved total integration in barely five years.

Truman's decision to integrate the military had several important benefits. Sociologists (academics who study the way society works) have long known that the best way to combat racism and prejudice is to have people of different races live and work together. A racially integrated military brought together African Americans and white Americans from all over the country and all walks of life. This did much to break down racial stereotypes among white soldiers. Those soldiers, in turn, helped break down prejudice and stereotypes among their family and friends outside the military.

The successful integration of the military also helped bring about the end of racial segregation in the South. Just five years after the U.S. Air Force became the first integrated branch of the military, the Supreme Court ruled in *Brown v. Board of Education* that segregated schools were unconstitutional. By integrating the military, President Truman sent a strong signal that the Jim Crow laws of the South were no longer acceptable.

AFRICAN AMERICAN PRESS COVERAGE OF FLIPPER'S TIME AT WEST POINT (1878)

Henry Flipper (1856–1940) was the first African American cadet ever to graduate from the United States Military Academy at West Point. He graduated in 1877. West Point is the training ground for military officers. A military officer serves in a leadership position. Important leadership positions had long been unavailable to African Americans. Flipper's graduation from West Point, therefore, was viewed as an important breakthrough for African Americans everywhere.

Flipper's experience at West Point was covered in both the mainstream and African American press. The following excerpts are from two articles in African American newspapers—the first from a newspaper in Thomasville, Georgia, and the second from the *Louisville Ledger*. They provide an especially insightful view of the discrimination Flipper faced and discuss the coverage of Flipper's experience in the mainstream press.

• •

[From the Thomasville newspaper]

It is not generally known that Atlanta has a negro cadet at the United States National Military Academy at West Point. This cadet is a **mulatto** boy named Flipper. He is about twenty years old, a **stoutish** fellow, weighing perhaps one hundred and fifty pounds, and a smart, bright, intelligent boy. His father is a shoemaker, and gave him the **euphonious** name of Henry Ossian Flipper.

Flipper has been at the great soldier factory of the nation for a year. He was recommended there by our late Congressman from the Fifth District, the Hon. J. C. Freeman. Flipper has made a **right booming** student. In a class of ninety-nine he stood about the middle, and triumphantly passed his examination, and has risen from the fourth to the third class without difficulty.

The only two colored boys at the Academy were **the famous Smith** and the Atlanta Flipper. It is thought that Smith at the last examination failed. If so, Atlanta will have the distinguished honor of having the sole African representative at West Point.

Flipper has had the privilege of eating at the same table with the poor white trash; but Smith and Flipper bunked together in the same room alone, without white companions.

It is an astonishing fact that, socially, the boys from the Northern and Western States will have nothing to do with these colored brothers. Flipper and Smith were socially **ostracized.** Not even the Massachusetts boys will associate with them. Smith has been a little rebellious, and attempted to thrust himself on the white boys; but the

Mulatto
A person of mixed black and white ancestry

Stoutish
Physically strong or bulky

Euphonious
Pleasing to the ear

Right booming
A nineteenth-century slang term for "very good"

The famous Smith
A shorthand reference to James Webster Smith, the first African American ever to be admitted to West Point

Ostracized
Excluded from receiving the privileges and acceptance of a group

Radical extraction
Being a supporter of the then-ongoing project of Radical Reconstruction

Deportment
Manner of conducting oneself around others

Venerable
Deserving of praise and respect

Antecedents
Origins or roots

Third Class
The West Point term for a sophomore

Intimate
To communicate delicately and indirectly

sensible Flipper accepted the situation, and proudly refused to intrude himself on the white boys.

The feeling of ostracism is so strong that a white boy who dared to recognize a colored cadet would be himself ostracized by the other white cubs, even of **radical extraction.**

We copy the above from the **Atlanta Herald** of last week, for the purpose of remarking that among colored men we know of none more honorable or more deserving than Flipper, the father of the colored West Point student of that name. Flipper lived for many years in Thomasville as the servant of Mr. E. G. Ponder—was the best bootmaker we ever knew, and his character and **deportment** were ever those of a sensible, unassuming, gentlemanly white man. Flipper possessed the confidence and respect of his master and all who knew him. His wife, the mother of young Flipper, was Isabella, a servant in the family of Rev. R. H. Lucky, of Thomasville, and bore a character equal to that of her husband. Young Flipper was baptized in his infancy by the **venerable** Bishop Early. From these **antecedents** we should as soon expect young Flipper to make his mark as any other colored youth in the country.

. . . .

[From the **Louisville Ledger.**]

It is just possible that some of our readers may not know who Flipper is. For their benefit we make haste to explain that Flipper is the solitary colored cadet now at West Point. He is in the **third class,** and stands forty-six in the class, which numbers eighty-five members. This is a very fair standing, and Flipper's friends declare that he is getting along finely in his studies, and that he is quite up to the standard of the average West Point student. Nevertheless they **intimate** that he will never graduate. Flipper, they say, may get as far as the first class, but there he will be "slaughtered."

A correspondent of the **New York Times** takes issue with this opinion. He says there are many "old heads" who believe Flipper will graduate with honor, and he thinks so too. The grounds for his belief, as he gives them, are that the officers are gentlemen, and so are the professors; that they believe merit should be rewarded wherever found; and that they all speak well of Flipper, who is a hard student, as his position in his class proves. From this correspondent we learn that Flipper is from Georgia; that he has a light, coffee-colored complexion, and that he "minds his business and does not intrude his company upon the other cadets," though why this should be put down in the list of his merits it is not easy to understand, since, if he graduates, as this writer believes he will, he will have the right to associate on terms of perfect equality with the other cadets, and may in time come to command some of them. We are afraid there is some little muddle of inconsistency in the brain of the **Times**' correspondent.

The Chicago Tribune seems to find it difficult to come to any conclusion concerning Flipper's chances for graduating. It says: "It is freely asserted that Flipper will never be allowed to graduate; that the prejudice of the regular army instructors against the colored race is insurmountable, and that they will drive away from the Academy by persecution of some **petty** sort any colored boy who may obtain admittance there. The story does not seem to have any substantial basis; still, it possesses considerable vitality."

We don't **profess** to understand exactly what sort of a story that is which has "considerable vitality" without any substantial basis, and can only conclude that the darkness of the subject has **engendered** a little confusion in the mind of the **Tribune** as well as in that of the writer of the **Times.** But the **Tribune** acquires more confidence as it warms in the discussion, and it assures us finally that "there is, of course, no doubt that some colored boys are capable of receiving a military education; and eventually the presence of colored officers in the regular army must be an accepted fact." Well, we don't know about that "accepted fact." The white man is mighty uncertain, and **the nigger won't do to trust to,** in view of which truths it would be unwise to bet too high on the "colored officers," for some years to come at least.

But let not Flipper wring his **flippers** in despair, notwithstanding. Let him think of Smith, and take heart of hope. Smith was another colored cadet who was sent to West Point from South Carolina. Smith mastered readin', 'ritin', and 'rithmetic, but chemistry mastered Smith.* They gave him three trials, but it was to no purpose; so they had to change his base and send him back to South Carolina. But what of that? They've just made him inspector of militia in South Carolina, with the rank of brigadier-general. How long might he have remained in the army before he would have become "General Smith?" Why, even Fred Grant's only a lieutenant-colonel. Smith evidently has reason to congratulate himself upon being "plucked;" and so the young gentleman from Georgia, with the "light, coffee-colored complexion," if he meets with a similar misfortune, may console himself with the hope that to him also in his extremity will be extended from some source a helping flipper.

*Cadet Smith failed in Natural and Experimental Philosophy. In Chemistry he was up to the average. He was never appointed Inspector-General of South Carolina. He was Commandant of Cadets in the South Carolina Agricultural Institute at Orangeburg, S. C., Which position he held till his death November 29th, 1876.

Petty
Having little or no importance or significance

Profess
To claim or declare

Engender
To cause, create, or bring about

The nigger won't do to trust to
An expression, suggesting that white Americans do not and should not trust African Americans, used here by an African American writer to both describe and criticize this attitude that he attributes to white Americans

Flippers
A slang term for "hands," used here as a play on words involving Flipper's last name

◈ TRUMAN ORDERS INTEGRATION OF THE MILITARY (1948)

President Harry S. Truman (1884–1972) struck an important blow for racial equality on July 26, 1948, when he issued Executive Order 9981. The order ended racial segregation in the United States military. An executive order is a document signed by the president that gives legally binding instructions on how to comply with the law. Many African Americans had served bravely and honorably in World War II. Truman's decision to desegregate the military recognized this service. It also helped strengthen public opposition to racial segregation in the South. The text of Executive

Order 9981 is reproduced below. The executive order explains the importance of equal treatment, mandates racial integration, and sets up a committee to enforce the order.

· ·

Whereas

In view of the fact that

Whereas it is essential that there be maintained in the armed services of the United States the highest standards of democracy, with equality of treatment and opportunity for all those who served in our country's defense:

Hereby

By these words, means, or actions

Now, therefore, by virtue of the authority invested in me as President of the United States, and as Commander in Chief of the armed services, it is **hereby** ordered as follows:

1. It is hereby declared to be the policy of the President that there shall be equality of treatment and opportunity for all persons in the armed services without regard to race, color, religion or national origin. This policy shall be put into effect as

Effectuate

To cause to occur or bring about

rapidly as possible, having due regard to the time required to **effectuate** any necessary changes without impairing efficiency or morale.

2. There shall be created in the National Military Establishment an advisory committee to be known as the President's Committee on Equality of Treatment and Opportunity in the Armed Services, which shall be composed of seven members to be designated by the President.

3. The Committee is authorized on behalf of the President to examine into the rules, procedures and practices of the armed services in order to determine in what respect such rules, procedures and practices may be altered or improved with a view to carrying out the policy of this order. The Committee shall confer and advise with the Secretary of Defense, the Secretary of the Army, the Secretary of the Navy, and Secretary of the Air Force, and shall make such recommendations to the President and to said Secretaries as in the judgment of the Committee will effectuate the policy hereof.

4. All executive departments and agencies of the Federal Government are authorized and directed to cooperate with the Committee in its work, and to furnish the Committee such information or the services of such persons as the Committee may require in the performance of its duties.

5. When requested by the Committee to do so, persons in the armed services or in any of the executive departments and agencies of the Federal Government shall testify before the Committee and shall make available for use of the Committee such documents and other information as the Committee may require.

6. The Committee shall continue to exist until such time as the President shall terminate its existence by Executive Order.

Harry Truman
The White House
July 26, 1948

Research and Activity Ideas

1. African American soldiers joining the military during the segregation era found that, in some ways, they were treated more equally in the military than in civilian life. Why do you think this might be? Make a list of characteristics of the military and military service that might have caused this phenomenon. Write an essay discussing each of these aspects of military life. Be sure to explain in detail why you think each might contribute to African Americans being treated more equally within the military than in other walks of life. Then, add some examples for contrast. Find examples from this chapter of African Americans being treated worse than their white counterparts in the military.

2. The Brownsville Affair and the Houston Mutiny were two violent uprisings that occurred in the early 1900s involving black soldiers and white townspeople. Read the entries for each from this chapter. How were the Brownsville Affair and the Houston Mutiny similar? How were the incidents different from each other? Can you think of any reasons for these similarities and differences? Write an essay comparing and contrasting the two incidents.

3. The Tuskegee Airmen are some of the most memorable figures from the World War II era. They were the first group of African Americans ever to serve as military pilots in the United States. Their time as combat pilots and bomber escorts captivated the public imagination. Their service also broke down barriers for African Americans in the military. Working with several of your classmates, have a group discussion about the impact and influence of the Tuskegee Airmen. Why do you think they have been so influential on the public? What are some ways that their service helped break down stereotypes about African American soldiers and African Americans in general?

4. Many African American soldiers, pilots, officers, and generals rose to positions of prominence and great accomplishment between 1865 and 1965. This chapter profiles notable military service members who made important contributions to the armed forces and attained notable firsts within that field. Prepare a speech in which you explain which of the African American military service members whom you read about in this chapter you admire the most. Why are you especially impressed or inspired by this person's accomplishments? What kind of obstacles did this person have to overcome? How did their work benefit others?

5. President Harry S. Truman struck a major blow for civil rights and racial equality when he integrated the military in 1948. At the time,

some military leaders believed that racial integration would be bad for military morale. They argued that it was risky to have soldiers of different races living and working in close quarters. Imagine that you are an African American soldier in 1947. Write a letter addressed to these leaders in which you argue in favor of integration. Give at least three specific reasons why their concerns about the effect of racial integration on troop morale are unfounded.

For More Information

BOOKS

Barbeau, Arthur E., and Florette Henri. *The Unknown Soldiers: African-American Troops in World War I*. Philadelphia, PA: Da Capo Press, 1996.

Davis, Benjamin O., Jr. *Benjamin O. Davis, Jr., American: An Autobiography*. Washington, D.C.: Smithsonian Institution Scholarly Press, 2000.

Field, Ron, and Alexander Bielakowski. *Buffalo Soldiers: African American Troops in the US Forces, 1866–1945*. Oxford, United Kingdom: Osprey Publishing, 2008.

Fletcher, Marvin. *America's First Black General: Benjamin O. Davis, Sr., 1880–1970*. Lawrence: University Press of Kansas, 1989.

Flipper, Henry Ossian. *The Colored Cadet at West Point*. Lincoln, NE: Bison Books, 1998.

Homan, Lynn M., and Thomas Reilly. *Black Knights: The Story of the Tuskegee Airmen*. Gretna, LA: Pelican Publishing Company, 2001.

Hughes, Langston. *Famous Negro Heroes of America*. New York: Dodd, Mead & Co., 1958.

Lloyd, Craig. *Eugene Bullard, Black Expatriate in Jazz-Age Paris*. Athens: The University of Georgia Press, 2002.

MacGregor, Morris J. *Integration of the Armed Forces, 1940–1965*. Washington, D.C.: Center of Military History, 1981.

McGuire, Phillip. *Taps for a Jim Crow Army: Letters from Black Soldiers in World War II*. Santa Barbara, CA: ABC-Clio, 1983.

WEB SITES

Davis, Sanford L. *Buffalo Soldiers & Indian Wars*. http://www.buffalosoldier.net/ (accessed on December 15, 2009).

Jones, Philip H. *African-American "Firsts" Key to Army History*. http://www.army.mil/-news/2009/02/05/16455-african-american-firsts-key-to-army-history/ (accessed on December 15, 2009).

McRae, Bennie J., Jr. *African American Military History: From the Revolutionary War to the Persian Gulf*. http://www.lwfaam.net/ (accessed on December 15, 2009).

Tuskegee Airmen, Inc. *Tuskegee Airmen History*. http://www.tuskegeeairmen.org/Tuskegee_Airmen_History.html (accessed on December 15, 2009).

chapter eleven *Popular Culture*

1875 May 17 African American jockey Oliver Lewis wins the first-ever Kentucky Derby.

1878 African American baseball player Bud Fowler becomes the first black man to play professional baseball, before major-league teams make an unspoken agreement to prevent African Americans from joining the league.

1891 Isaac Murphy wins his second consecutive Kentucky Derby, becoming the first jockey to win the race back-to-back.

1908 Runner John Baxter Taylor becomes the first African American to win an Olympic gold medal at the 1908 Olympics in London.

1908 December 26 Boxer Jack Johnson defeats Canadian heavyweight Tommy Burns in Australia to become the first African American world heavyweight champion.

1910 African American inventor Garrett Morgan develops a chemical hair relaxer that straightens textured hair, allowing African Americans to adopt styles popular in mainstream white culture.

1910 July 4 Boxer Jack Johnson successfully defends his heavyweight champion title against the undefeated champion James Jeffries, the "Great White Hope," who came out of

retirement in an attempt to show that whites are superior to blacks.

1915 April 5 Boxer Jack Johnson loses his heavyweight champion title to Jess Willard, a white boxer from Kansas, after a twenty-six-round match in Havana, Cuba.

1921 Henry King becomes the last African American jockey to race in the Kentucky Derby for seventy-nine years.

1923 October 29 The Charleston, a wildly popular dance based on early African American dances, first appears in the Broadway show *Runnin' Wild*.

1927 January 7 The first officially recorded game featuring the Harlem Globetrotters is played in Illinois.

1935 May 25 During a college meet in Michigan, track and field athlete Jesse Owens breaks three world records and matches a fourth in the span of less than an hour.

1936 June 19 Heavyweight boxer Joe Louis is handed his first loss as a professional boxer by German fighter Max Schmeling.

1936 August Jesse Owens wins four gold medals at the 1936 Olympic Games in Berlin, Germany, in front of Adolf Hitler and other Nazi officials.

1937 June 22 Heavyweight fighter Joe Louis defeats Jim Braddock to become the second African American world heavyweight champion, twenty-two years after Jack Johnson lost the title.

1938 June 22 Heavyweight champion Joe Louis defeats Max Schmeling in the first round in a rematch painted by the press as a battle between democracy (Louis) and Nazism (Schmeling).

1943 June 3 The zoot suit, a garment made popular by African Americans in New York and later adopted by Mexican Americans in California, becomes a source of tension between civilians and soldiers in Los Angeles, erupting in a series of attacks in which mobs of military personnel strip down and beat anyone they see wearing a zoot suit.

1945 November 1 Brooklyn Dodgers owner Branch Rickey signs Negro League baseball player Jackie Robinson to play in the major leagues as the first African American in modern major league baseball.

1946 August Kenny Washington becomes the first African American to play in the National Football League (NFL) since blacks had been excluded from the league in 1934.

1947 April 15 Baseball player Jackie Robinson debuts as a member of the major league Brooklyn Dodgers; his outstanding performance earns him the first Rookie of the Year Award.

1948 High jumper Alice Coachman becomes the first African American woman to win an Olympic gold medal.

1948 July 9 Legendary Negro League pitcher Satchel Paige debuts in the major leagues as a Cleveland Indian at the age of forty-two, becoming the oldest rookie ever to play major league baseball.

1949 Café Nicholson opens in New York, featuring Edna Lewis—future legend of country cooking—as its chef.

1949 March 1 Joe Louis officially retires from boxing, ending his reign as heavyweight champ; he held the title for almost twelve years and defended it through twenty-five matches.

1950 Actor and activist Paul Robeson has his American passport revoked by the State Department, which claims he poses a threat to the nation's safety for his outspoken views; it takes eight years and a Supreme Court decision before his passport is returned.

1950 August 28 Althea Gibson becomes the first African American to participate in the U.S. Open tennis championship.

1953 Designer Ann Lowe creates Jacqueline Bouvier's dress for her wedding to Senator John F. Kennedy.

1957 Althea Gibson wins the Wimbledon women's singles championship, becoming the first African American to win a singles title at Wimbledon.

1960 Golfer Charles Sifford becomes the first African American to receive a player card from the Professional Golf Association (PGA).

1962 August 1 Cook and businesswoman Sylvia Woods opens her first restaurant in Harlem, offering a variety of soul food that helps launch a trend in American cuisine.

1963 Tennis star Althea Gibson becomes the first African American woman to play in the Ladies Professional Golf Association (LPGA).

1967 Charlie Sifford becomes the first African American golfer to win a PGA tournament, the Greater Hartford Open Invitational.

The history of African Americans in popular culture parallels closely the history of racial relations in the United States. African Americans enjoyed a brief period of direct influence on mainstream American culture in the years following the Civil War (1861–65). The end of Reconstruction in 1877, however, ushered in an era of harsh segregation and lynchings, resulting in a decline of African American cultural influence. Finally, as white Americans began to accept ideas of integration, many aspects of African American culture found their way into America's popular identity.

The most important area of popular culture that shows this progression is sports. Most of the successful jockeys involved in organized horse racing were African Americans in the 1870s. Oliver Lewis (1856–1924) was the first winner of the Kentucky Derby in 1875; that inaugural starting lineup included fourteen African American jockeys, and only one white jockey. The most successful jockey of the era was Isaac Burns Murphy (1861–96), who won three Kentucky Derbys, four Clark Handicaps, four American Derbys, and five Latonia Derbys, as well as many others. His winning percentage dwarfs that of other successful jockeys, and will likely never be surpassed.

African Americans also enjoyed success in other sports in the late nineteenth century. Bud Fowler (1858–1913) played professional baseball across the United States and Canada as early as 1878, earning praise from sportswriters wherever he went. Resentment from white fans and players provided an indication of things to come for African American athletes. Fowler was forced to change teams often, and by the end of the nineteenth century, was no longer allowed on the field with white players. Similarly, horse racing—previously dominated by African American riders—instituted new rules that all but eliminated black jockeys from the major competitions.

African American athletes who dared challenge the superiority of whites were often ridiculed and viewed as troublemakers. The boxer Jack Johnson (1878–1946) is a prime example. Johnson's skill in the ring clearly earned him a rightful shot at the heavyweight championship title, yet undefeated title-holder James Jeffries (1875–1953) refused to give any nonwhites a chance to fight against him. White Canadian boxer Tommy Burns (1881–1955) took the title years later and agreed to fight Johnson. Johnson's victory in the fight caused many Americans to respond not with happiness that an American had won the title back, but with outrage that a black fighter had defeated a white champion. The outrage grew more intense when Johnson defeated Jeffries, who had come out of retirement to prove once and for all the superiority of whites. Criticism of Johnson was heavy from both fans and the media, and the federal government even went out of its way to prosecute Johnson on questionable charges and sentenced him to jail time during his heavyweight championship reign. It is not surprising that no other African American boxer would get a chance at the title for more than twenty years after Johnson lost it.

During this time, African American athletes found themselves increasingly excluded from the world of sports. It is perhaps no coincidence that around this time, professional sports were finally being viewed as legitimate businesses rather than wasteful pastimes. Professional football moved to exclude African Americans in the 1930s, and the first professional basketball organizations also kept blacks from playing. Still, African American athletes found ways to continue doing what they loved. The Negro leagues allowed black baseball players to make relatively substantial incomes, and black basketball players formed their own leagues. The Harlem Globetrotters, successful as competitive players and as entertainers, even opted not to join the ranks of professional basketball when offered the chance. Even with success, though, African American athletes lived in a culture separate from mainstream America.

Things began to change with the rise of Nazism in Germany. Adolf Hitler (1889–1945) had seized control of the country by promoting the idea that people of German descent, members of what he called the Aryan race, were superior to all others. He encouraged the persecution of Jews and other minorities; white Americans—though they engaged in similar behavior toward African Americans—recognized him as a dangerous fanatic. Hitler planned to show the world the superiority of the Aryan race through athletic victory at the 1936 Summer Olympic Games in Berlin, Germany. He was foiled in his plan by Jesse Owens (1913–80), an African American track star who won four gold medals and defeated a German favorite, Lutz Long (1913–43), in the long jump. For the first time, a large number of white Americans embraced an African American athlete as a hero.

Soon after, heavyweight title holder Joe Louis (1914–81) became a champion of American values and ideals when he fought German former heavyweight champ Max Schmeling (1905–2005). Their 1938 fight was characterized as a battle between democracy and Nazism; when Louis defeated Schmeling in the first round, he was hailed as a hero, not just by the black community, but by all Americans.

Doors once closed to African American athletes began to reopen after the end of World War II (1939–45). The National Football League (NFL) fielded its first African American player in 1946, and Jackie Robinson debuted as the first modern major league baseball player in 1947. African

Americans were allowed into the newly formed National Basketball Association (NBA) in 1950.

African American women, too, benefited from an increased push for integration. Alice Coachman (1923–) became the first African American woman to win a gold medal at the 1948 Olympic Games in London. Tennis player Althea Gibson (1927–2003) became the first African American— man or woman—allowed to participate on the world tennis tour in 1950. Gibson also went on to become the first African American in the Ladies Professional Golf Association (LPGA) in 1963, just three years after Charlie Sifford (1922–) broke through the "whites only" exclusion written into the PGA constitution. Sifford paved the way for future champion African American golfers like Calvin Peete (1943–) and Tiger Woods (1975–).

★ Headline Makers

★ ALICE COACHMAN
(1923–)

Alice Coachman overcame enormous obstacles to earn a place in history as the first black woman to win a gold medal in the modern Olympic Games. Her parents had actively discouraged her athletic talents and, living in the segregated South, she was denied access to facilities and equipment used by white athletes. Despite these obstacles, she went on to become a ten-time national high jump champion, and the only member of the 1948 United States women's Olympic track and field team to earn a gold medal.

Modest Roots, Major Talent

Coachman was born in Albany, Georgia, to Fred and Evelyn Coachman, the fifth of what would be a family of ten children. Her father was a laborer and the family was poor, which meant that the children often had to help out by picking cotton and performing other jobs to make ends meet. Coachman revealed herself to be athletically gifted at a young age, but her father—who thought girls should act dainty and delicate—punished her when she participated in physical sports and games.

Alice Coachman stands atop the winner's platform at the 1948 Olympics after winning the women's high jump. *AP Images*

Coachman had the support of her aunt Carrie, and when she reached fifth grade at Monroe Street Elementary, she found a new ally in her teacher, Cora Bailey. Both women encouraged her interest in sports and convinced her parents to let her develop her talents. She participated in track and field sports, though she had to train on her own makeshift equipment since she was not allowed to use the public equipment available to white students in town. She entered Madison High School and began training under coach Harry Lash, at which time her special abilities were quickly noticed.

Scouts from the Tuskegee Institute in Alabama, one of the premier African American colleges in the country, offered an athletic scholarship to Coachman for their high school program. Tuskegee was aggressively developing its track team to be the best in the country, and even before Coachman began her school year there, she was already competing in—and winning—Amateur Athletic Union (AAU) championships for the school. She dominated the high jump event, winning the AAU national championships for an astounding ten years in a row. She also won national championships in the 50-meter dash, 100-meter dash, and 400-meter relay. She was chosen for four consecutive All-American track and field teams, and in every case was the only African American on the team. In addition to her success as a track and field star, Coachman was part of the Southern Intercollegiate Athletic Conference championship basketball team for three years in a row.

Coachman's successful college athletic career made her an obvious choice to participate in the Olympic Games. She was not able to do so for several years, however, since her high school and most of her college career overlapped with World War II (1939–45). The Olympics were not held in 1940 or 1944 because of the world conflict. Coachman finished her college education with a degree in dressmaking in 1946, making her the first member of her family to obtain a college degree.

Success as an Olympian

Coachman finally got her opportunity to display her talents in a global arena in the 1948 Olympics. She not only qualified but also set an American record for women's high jump with a height of five feet four inches during her tryouts for the U.S. team. The Olympic Games for that year were held in London, England, and Coachman's main competition was Dorothy Tyler, a woman representing England on her home turf. Tyler had also participated in the 1936 Olympic Games, earning a silver medal.

The high jump competition took place in Wembley Stadium on the final day of the Games, as the final track and field event. Despite a lingering back injury, Coachman cleared five feet six and one-eighth inches. Tyler matched the jump, but because she had required more attempts, Coachman was awarded the gold medal. She became the first black woman of any nationality to win a gold medal in the modern Olympic Games, and was the only member of the 1948 United States women's track and field team to win a gold medal.

Coachman was welcomed as a hero when she returned to the United States. A procession led her from Atlanta, Georgia, to her hometown of Albany, and the parade at the end of the procession was attended by thousands. The honor did not exempt her from segregation practices in the South. Even as she sat onstage for a celebration thrown in her honor, she was segregated from the mayor and other white citizens on the stage, separated by a piano placed between them.

Coachman retired from track and field after her Olympic win. She became the first black woman with an endorsement deal for an American product—Wrigley's Gum—though these endorsements were only seen overseas. The Coca-Cola Company offered her an endorsement deal in 1952, and she became the first African American woman featured in an ad campaign within the United States.

Coachman continued her college education, earning a second degree from Albany State College in 1949. She then became a coach and a teacher for several schools across the South, including elementary schools, high schools, and South Carolina State College. She was inducted into the United States National Track and Field Hall of Fame in 1975, and in 1994, she formed the Alice Coachman Track and Field Foundation, a nonprofit organization that provided assistance to aspiring young athletes.

★ ALTHEA GIBSON
(1927–2003)

Althea Gibson was a trailblazer in the sport of tennis. She was the first black person allowed to participate in any of the so-called Grand Slam events of tennis, such as Wimbledon and the U.S. Open. She was also the first black person of any nationality or either gender to win all of the four major championships in the sport.

From Table Tennis to American Tennis Association Champion

Gibson was born in Silver, South Carolina, to Daniel and Annie Gibson, poor sharecroppers who lived with their extended family in a tiny shack. Sharecroppers were farmers who worked land owned by others, and in exchange for growing and harvesting the crops, they were allowed to keep a small portion for themselves. The family had difficulties making ends meet with so many mouths to feed, and when the Great Depression began in 1929, economic conditions got even worse. The Gibson family earned only seventy-five dollars from working the land in 1930. Like many other African Americans in the South at the time, the Gibsons believed that life would be better if they moved north to a large city like New York. Althea went north to live in Harlem with an aunt, and soon after the rest of the family followed.

Gibson was considered a troublemaker as a child. She ran away from home on more than one occasion, and was subjected to physical abuse from her father. One of her favorite places to spend time was the Police Athletic League (PAL), where she was able to participate in games and

Althea Gibson holds the winner's plate after winning the women's singles competition at Wimbledon in 1958. *Keystone/Hulton Archive/ Getty Images*

sports instead of roaming the street. She became an expert at one sport in particular: table tennis. She became the New York City Police Athletic League's table tennis champion when she was ten, and held the title for five years. She was also the pitcher for a champion softball team, and was the only girl on the team.

One of the youth leaders at the PAL, Buddy Walker, saw promise in Gibson's masterful table tennis skills. He bought two used tennis rackets and taught Gibson the basics of the sport when she was twelve. She proved to be a fast learner, almost immediately applying her table tennis talents on a larger scale at Harlem River Tennis Courts. Within an hour she had acquired an audience, and one of them told Fred Johnson, the pro for the Cosmopolitan Tennis Club, about her. He and other spectators were impressed enough to buy Gibson a new racket and a membership to the club.

Gibson won her first New York State Open Championship in 1942, and she repeated the feat in 1944 and 1945. The following year, she received an offer from Walter Johnson, a key figure in the advancement of African American tennis players. Johnson founded the American Tennis Association Junior Development Program, which helped young African Americans get involved in the sport. Most African Americans had no contact at all with tennis, since it was usually played at a country club, and only a few country clubs even allowed black members. Black players were not allowed to compete in the United States Lawn Tennis Association (USLTA), so they formed the American Tennis Association (ATA). Gibson made it to the finals of the 1946 ATA women's championships, but lost.

Johnson was instrumental in helping Gibson hone her skills as a player. He and Hubert Eaton brought Gibson to North Carolina, where she lived with the Eatons and focused on both tennis and her education. She had dropped out of high school while in New York; Eaton required her to complete her schooling. Beginning in 1947, Gibson dominated the ATA women's championships for a full ten years in a row. She also won the mixed doubles championships for seven of those years, partnered with Johnson's son.

Breaking the Color Barrier

Gibson graduated from high school near the top of her class in 1949, at the age of twenty-one. She enrolled in Florida Agricultural and Mechanical College, where she was offered a scholarship. The school did not technically offer a tennis scholarship, so Gibson was brought on as a basketball player. She also got a job as an assistant in the women's physical education department at the school. She divided her time between studies and tennis practice, a stark contrast to the mischievous child she had once been in Harlem.

Her winning streak at the ATA championships had not gone unnoticed by the USLTA, though its officials were hesitant to allow an African American to participate in their league. It took an impassioned editorial from white tennis legend Alice Marble (1913–90) to convince the USLTA to allow Gibson a chance to play in the U.S. Open, the most prestigious American tennis tournament. She became the first African

American to play in the U.S. Open in 1950. Even though she lost in the second round, she had opened up an entirely new world to African American athletes.

Gibson made her first appearance at Wimbledon in England the following year. Wimbledon is the most renowned tennis competition in the world. She did not win, but she became a ranked player on the tennis circuit. She continued to develop her talents and work on her education, completing her degree in 1953. She then spent several years as a physical education teacher and as a tennis ambassador, touring the world and participating in exhibition matches.

She returned to competitive tennis in 1956, becoming the first black player to win the French Open both in singles and doubles matches. She followed this victory with a women's doubles win at Wimbledon the same year, accompanied by her usual partner Angela Buxton, who would remain her lifelong friend. Gibson virtually destroyed the competition the following year, winning singles championships at Wimbledon and the U.S. Open, and doubles championships at Wimbledon, the U.S. Open, and the Australian Open. At the U.S. Open, she won against the woman who had beaten her in her very first U.S. Open competition seven years before.

Gibson finished the year as the number one ranked female tennis player in the world, and appeared on the cover of *Time* magazine in August. She was also selected as the Associated Press Female Athlete of the Year. Gibson continued her winning streak in 1958 with singles and doubles championships at Wimbledon, and another singles championship at the U.S. Open. For the second year in a row, she was ranked number one in the world.

Unlike modern tennis, there were few financial opportunities for tennis champions in the 1950s. Gibson retired from the circuit in an effort to use her fame to generate income. She secured some minor endorsement deals, wrote an autobiography, released an album as a singer, and toured with the Harlem Globetrotters, playing exhibition matches. However, she was unable to earn the same kind of money that white tennis champions were able to earn—primarily because she was still not allowed to play exhibitions at many segregated country clubs.

In 1964, Gibson struck another blow against segregation in sports when she became the first African American to play in the Ladies Professional Golf Association. She had only recently practiced the sport, so becoming a professional was a noteworthy accomplishment. She failed to earn much as a golfer, and later became an athletic commissioner for the state of New Jersey. She ran for the United States Senate in 1977, but could not secure the Democratic nomination. After being debilitated by several strokes, Gibson retired in 1992. She died in 2003 at the age of seventy-six.

★ JACK JOHNSON
(1878–1946)

Jack Johnson was the first African American heavyweight boxing champion of the world, and one of the most controversial African Americans of the twentieth century. His success in the ring was paired with a brazen attitude that did not fit well with how whites believed African Americans should act. He had relationships with many white women, even marrying some of them. The practice of interracial marriage was considered so taboo in many parts of the South that it was actually illegal in several states. At the same time, his accomplishments were celebrated by many African Americans, who suffered daily under the accepted notion that blacks could not perform as equals to whites in any arena.

From Timid Boy to King of the Battle Royal

Jack Johnson.
The Library of Congress

Johnson was born John Arthur Johnson in Galveston, Texas, to two former slaves. His father, Henry Johnson, was a janitor, while his mother, Tiny, took care of the home and washed laundry to bring in some extra money. Johnson was not expected to attend high school or college, though he did learn to read and write—something neither of his parents could do. He was the third child of the family and had two older sisters who sometimes had to protect him from bigger boys. His mother found out he was being terrorized by bullies, and told him she would whip him herself if he did not fight back. After that, Johnson never backed away from a fight, and rarely lost one. According to Johnson's own accounts, he never fought boys who were smaller or weaker than he was.

Many details of Johnson's early life remain in doubt. He is known to have introduced some fictional elements into his own accounts of his life, and official records occasionally contradict his statements. One of his claims is that, at the age of twelve, he ran away from home and traveled to New York City to meet his idol, Steve Brodie. Brodie was a charismatic man whose only achievement was that he claimed to have jumped off the Brooklyn Bridge and survived. Johnson's colorful account of this trip across the country is viewed with doubt by at least some, if not most, modern historians.

The facts surrounding his entry into boxing are more widely accepted. Johnson completed five years of schooling, and began work as the apprentice to a Galveston carriage painter who also happened to box for recreation. Johnson began practicing, using the painter's gloves and equipment, and before long had learned the basics of the sport. He got a job at a gymnasium and purchased his own gloves. For young African Americans, however, boxing opportunities in Galveston were largely limited to "battle royals," in which eight to ten men were put in a boxing ring together—sometimes blindfolded—and made to fight each other until only one remained standing. The winner would be the only fighter who earned money, which amounted to whatever coins the white spectators threw into the ring after the fight. Johnson became a frequent winner, and also made money performing various odd jobs such as janitor and dockworker.

A Devastating Storm and an Unlikely Mentor

Boxing was mostly a segregated sport in the late nineteenth century, with African American fighters only participating in matches against other African Americans. This followed not only the tradition of the South, in which most other public areas were segregated, but also the convention set by white boxing legend John L. Sullivan (1858–1918). Sullivan is credited as the fighter who helped turn boxing into a legitimate sport. During his reign as the first heavyweight champion, Sullivan refused to fight any man who was not white.

Johnson fought his first known match against a white opponent, Jim Scanlon, in May 1900. After knocking him out, Johnson began to fight other white opponents with regularity, usually winning. Some white promoters felt that Johnson was trying to challenge the superiority of white fighters, and sent their best men to match up against him. His rise to fame was derailed for a time when Galveston was struck by the worst natural disaster ever seen in the United States: the hurricane of 1900. The city of Galveston is located on an island that runs parallel to the Texas coast, and most of the buildings on the island sat very close to sea level. When the hurricane struck in September 1900, over three-fourths of all the buildings in Galveston were destroyed, and at least six thousand people were killed. Johnson's parents' home, where he still lived with them, was one of the buildings destroyed. Johnson was among the many survivors who immediately set to work helping to clear debris and assist the injured.

Galveston was an important port for shipping, and was quickly rebuilt despite the extensive damage. Johnson's family found a new house, and he resumed his boxing career. In 1901, he fought a well-known Jewish boxer named Joe Choynski in an "exhibition match" arranged by some boxing promoters. At the time, boxing for a cash prize was very popular and, in many states like Texas, illegal. Though most prizefights were overlooked or ignored, those involving prominent fighters were sometimes cancelled or interrupted. Choynski was a well-known boxer who had fought and nearly beat several heavyweight champions and contenders. Even though Choynski was ten years older than Johnson, he managed to score a knockout against Johnson in the third round, after which the two boxers were immediately arrested for participating in a prizefight.

The two men spent twenty-four days in jail together, where they shared cell space and were often allowed to spar for the benefit of small groups of spectators. It was a chance for Johnson to learn technique from one of the most accomplished boxers of the era. He took Choynski's lessons to heart, and when the two were released from prison, Johnson left Texas and immediately resumed fighting. He continued challenging both black and white opponents, but even when he won, he often had to endure racial insults being yelled at him from white spectators.

Johnson and the "Fight of the Century"

The current heavyweight champion at the time was James Jeffries (1875–1953), who, like Sullivan before him, had stated many times that he would not fight a black man in the ring. Johnson arranged instead to fight the champion's younger brother, Jack Jeffries, while the champ himself watched. The fight took place in the Jeffries' hometown of Los Angeles in May 1902, and Johnson faced a hostile crowd. However, he showed only complete confidence as he stepped into the ring. He even reportedly passed a note to the event promoter predicting exactly when he would score a knockout against Jeffries. Johnson lived up to his prediction, knocking Jack Jeffries out less than a minute into the fifth round.

James Jeffries still refused to fight Johnson, but his defeated brother Jack trained another white boxer named Fred Russell for the challenge. During the fight, Russell kneed Johnson several times and punched him below the belt, resulting in a win for Johnson. Just a few months later, Johnson defeated Denver Ed Martin to become the World Colored Heavyweight Champion. What he wanted most, though, was a chance to fight James Jeffries for the world heavyweight title. Jeffries retired in 1905 without being defeated, and a Canadian boxer named Tommy Burns won the title the following year.

At first, Burns—like Jeffries—refused to offer Johnson a chance at the title. However, an Australian boxing promoter raised enough money to convince Burns to fight. The match occurred on December 26, 1908, in Sydney, Australia, in front of an audience of twenty thousand. The fight lasted until the fourteenth round, when police had to stop the match for Burns's own safety. Johnson was declared the winner.

The general reaction from white Americans was not pride that an American had won back the title, but anger that an African American had somehow beaten a white man. Throughout 1909, Johnson successfully defended his title against several contenders who stepped up to the challenge put forth by many sports journalists: regain the championship title for the whites. Johnson had always endured racial slurs from spectators, but now—as the recognized champion of the world—he faced boos and hate-filled threats. He never backed down in the face of such hate, and even spurred it on with an attitude many would describe as arrogant. He also made a habit of dating white women, three of whom he married at a time when many states had laws forbidding marriage between people of different races.

The biggest fight of Johnson's career came not when he won the heavyweight championship, but when James Jeffries finally agreed to square off against him in the ring. Jeffries was thirty-five years old—just three years older than Johnson—and had been retired for five years, but wanted to prove the superiority of the white race. The fight took place on July 4, 1910, in Reno, Nevada. The fight lasted fifteen rounds, with Johnson knocking Jeffries to the mat. It was the first time Jeffries had been knocked down in his boxing career. Jeffries's corner stopped the fight so that Johnson would not have an opportunity to knock out the previously undefeated boxer.

A Champion and a Fugitive

Johnson held the heavyweight championship title for over six years— a reign longer than James Jeffries's and nearly equal to John L. Sullivan's. During that time he was subjected to discrimination and even criminal prosecution on charges that he transported women across state lines for immoral purposes. Johnson's womanizing habits had left a trail of scorned ex-lovers, and in 1912, the government found one who agreed to testify against him on such charges. Johnson was found guilty by a jury of white men, and sentenced to one year and one day in jail. He fled the country before he could be taken into custody.

Johnson traveled the world from 1913 through 1920, defending his title until a 1915 bout against Jess Willard (1881–1968) in Havana, Cuba. It was the only fight he lost between 1905 and 1926. Johnson finally returned to the United States in 1920 and surrendered to authorities. He

A headline in the *San Francisco Chronicle* promotes the fight between James Jeffries (left) and Jack Johnson in 1910. © *Corbis*

completed his year-long sentence in Leavenworth Prison, located in Kansas. While there, he won four more matches against inexperienced fighters and invented an improved wrench that he later patented. He also co-patented an early theft-prevention device for automobiles.

Johnson had hoped to return to championship boxing after serving his sentence. Willard had since lost the heavyweight title to Jack Dempsey (1895–1983), and Johnson—already in his forties—wanted a chance to win it back. However, like Sullivan and Jeffries before him, Dempsey refused to fight against a black man. It was not until 1937 that another African American, Joe Louis (1914–81), would earn the title of heavyweight champion. Johnson fought lesser-known boxers to earn money, and also appeared in stage shows. Though he was considered a legend among African Americans, the white public still viewed him as a villain for his proud and unapologetic attitude.

Johnson continued to fight well into his fifties, and lost his final match when he was sixty years old. He died in 1946 in a car crash near

Raleigh, North Carolina, on his way to see Joe Louis fight against Billy Conn. He was sixty-eight.

★ EDNA LEWIS
(1916–2006)

Edna Lewis was one of the first African American chefs to achieve fame for promoting a cooking style that is characterized as Southern. Decades before Southern cooking was widely recognized by food experts and critics as a uniquely American cuisine, Lewis wowed diners with her simple and perfectly executed meals.

Lewis was born in Freetown, Virginia, and was one of eight children. Freetown was founded in part by one of her ancestors who was a former slave, and was built by freed slaves. Lewis grew up celebrating holidays like Emancipation Day. Every holiday revolved around a huge home-cooked meal. Freetown was a rural community, so these meals focused on freshly grown, seasonal ingredients. Lewis's early connection to the land and its bounties inspired her to become not a chef, but a botanist. She set this dream aside after her father died. Lewis became less concerned with schooling and more concerned with helping to provide for the family.

Edna Lewis in 1989.
© James Marshall/Corbis

Lewis left Virginia to live with relatives in Washington, D.C., and from there moved to New York City. She was only sixteen and without a high school education, so she found herself working odd jobs. One of these was as a seamstress, and she proved skillful enough that she thought she would pursue it as a career.

She became friends with John Nicholson while working in the design industry. Like Lewis, Nicholson had hoped to become a fashion designer or an antiques dealer, but was having little success. He decided instead to open a restaurant in 1949 called Café Nicholson, and Lewis—whose culinary skills from her youth had continued to develop—became both cofounder and head cook. The restaurant was popular among people in the fashion world, and its decorative interiors were often used for photo shoots. Its main claim to fame, however, was Lewis. Her Southern-influenced cuisine brought celebrities like

William Faulkner (1897–1962) and Tennessee Williams (1911–83) to the restaurant time and again.

She worked at the Café Nicholson until 1954. She moved on to other restaurants in New York and in the South, always bringing her distinctive Southern style and love of fresh, seasonal ingredients with her. She briefly owned her own restaurant in Harlem, and ran an organic farm with her husband Steve Kingston. Her greatest fame came after she broke her leg during the 1960s, and could not work as a chef for an extended period. She kept herself busy during her rehabilitation by writing down her many Southern recipes. They were collected in the *Edna Lewis Cookbook*, published in 1972. Her follow-up book, *The Taste of Country Cooking* (1976), is recognized as one of the first and best books on the subject of Southern cuisine.

Lewis continued to work as a professional chef until 1992. She also cofounded the Society for the Revival and Preservation of Southern Food, and was selected as the first recipient of the James Beard Living Legend Award in 1995. Lewis's final cookbook, *The Gift of Southern Cooking,* was published in 2003. She passed away in 2006, at the age of eighty-nine.

★ JOE LOUIS
(1914–1981)

Joe Louis, also known as the "Brown Bomber," was heavyweight boxing champion of the world from 1938 until 1949. He was not the first African American heavyweight champion, but he was one of the first African American athletes to be widely accepted and praised by white sports fans. His championship came at a time when much of the world was on the brink of war, and his promoters and members of the press were quick to emphasize his patriotism and high moral fiber rather than his race.

Cultivating a Career and an Image

Joseph Louis Barrow was the seventh of eight children born to sharecroppers Munroe and Lillie Barrow near La Fayette, Alabama. His father was committed to a mental institution when Joseph was still an infant, and the family was informed that he died there a few years later. In truth, he lived for over twenty years in confinement at the institution. Lillie Barrow remarried in 1920, and several years later, the family moved north to Detroit, Michigan. They were part of the Great Migration, in which millions of African Americans left the South for greater safety and economic opportunities in the North.

Joe Louis.
Hulton Archive/Getty Images

Joseph's mother tried to keep him out of trouble in Detroit by giving him money for violin lessons. He used the money to join a gym instead, where he first learned to box. It was around this time that he became known as Joe Louis, dropping his last name, quite possibly to keep his mother from finding out that he had taken up boxing. He also got a job to help support the family, since the country was in the midst of the Great Depression. The Great Depression was a time of economic hardship and high unemployment that began with the stock market crash of 1929. Louis became serious about his boxing training at the age of nineteen and began fighting in amateur matches at least once a week. He won nearly all of them, usually by knocking out his opponent. He became the Golden Gloves champion of Detroit, and the following year, he won both the Golden Gloves Chicago Tournament of Champions and the Amateur Athletic Union championship.

Many white boxing promoters were interested in managing Louis's professional career, but he chose a local African American named John Roxborough as his manager. Roxborough worked with a promoter named Julian Black to build Louis's reputation. They knew it was a difficult time for an African American heavyweight fighter to prosper. Ever since Jack Johnson (1878–1946) held the championship title from 1908 until 1915, no African American boxer had been allowed a chance at the title. This was partly because Johnson was seen as disrespectful and arrogant, and was unpopular among the majority of white fans. In addition, nearly all white heavyweight champions before and after Johnson carried out a tradition of fighting only whites, believing the sport should be segregated. Roxborough told Louis that in order to succeed as a heavyweight champion, he would have to act with humility, politeness, and restraint. His manager also wanted Louis to avoid even the appearance of having relationships with white women, which had been a frequent criticism of Johnson. Louis put much of that fear to rest when he married an African American secretary named Marva Trotter in 1935. Still, one of Louis's seven "commandments" of behavior was never to have his picture taken alone with a white woman.

The Brown Bomber Goes Pro

Louis began his professional career in July 1934 and finished the year with twelve straight wins, most of them by knockout. He continued his winning streak with eleven more matches in 1935, the most important against former heavyweight champion Primo Carnera (1906–67). A native Italian, Carnera had lost his championship title just one year before fighting Louis. When it came to public sentiment, Carnera was a victim of his native country's politics. The dictator Benito Mussolini (1883–1945) had taken control of Italy, and was preparing to invade the virtually defenseless north African country of Ethiopia to expand Italy's empire. Many spectators drew parallels between the boxing match and the invasion, since Louis was of African descent and Carnera was Italian. Carnera outweighed Louis by more than sixty pounds and stood several inches taller, yet Louis dropped him to the canvas three times in six rounds before the fight was stopped and Louis was declared the winner. For the first time, Louis had achieved something that Jack Johnson was never able to achieve: he was embraced by white spectators for his defeat of a white opponent. He was seen as a symbolic warrior against dictatorships and tyranny.

Louis went on to defeat Max Baer (1909–1959), another former heavyweight champion who had just lost his title only months before Louis knocked him out in four rounds. Louis's final fight of 1935 was his first at Madison Square Garden. This was a victory in itself since Madison Square Garden was one of the most popular boxing venues in the country and was tightly controlled by promoter James J. Johnston. Louis proved himself a box-office draw, finally achieving the kind of fame that would earn him a chance to fight for the championship title.

Louis first had to face another former heavyweight champ, a German fighter named Max Schmeling (1905–2005). Schmeling was unpopular with Americans for two reasons: He had won his heavyweight championship title because the other fighter was disqualified rather than through his own skills; and he was German at a time when Adolf Hitler (1889–1945) rose to power in Germany through his tyrannical Nazi Party. The crowd supported Louis, but he lost to Schmeling after twelve rounds in 1936. This was his first professional loss, and would remain his only loss until 1950.

Louis regrouped after his loss to Schmeling and continued his winning streak through the rest of 1936 and into 1937. Louis became the first African American since Jack Johnson to fight for the heavyweight championship in June 1937. He fought James Braddock (1905–74), who was able to knock Louis down once in the first round, but ultimately lost his title to Louis by a knockout in the eighth round.

Holding the Title and Seeking a Rematch

After he became champion, Louis had only one goal: a rematch against Schmeling. The match occurred on June 22, 1938, in Yankee Stadium with over seventy thousand spectators and tens of millions listening to the match by radio. Schmeling, regardless of his own beliefs, had become a poster boy for the Nazi German government, and Louis represented American freedom and democracy. It was one of the most publicized matches in boxing history, and it was over within a single round. After just two minutes and four seconds of Louis's intense blows, Schmeling's trainer stopped the fight. It was the first time a heavyweight championship had lasted less than one round.

Louis defended his title twenty-one times over the next four years, but his career came to a halt in 1942. World War II was already raging across Europe, and the Japanese attack on Pearl Harbor at the end of 1941 ensured that the United States would enter the war. Louis enlisted in

January 1942. He went through basic training, but was not placed in combat because he was considered too valuable as a morale booster for troops. Instead, he spent three and a half years fighting nearly one hundred exhibition matches to entertain over two million American soldiers. By the time he left in October 1945, he had attained the rank of sergeant.

Louis continued to defend his championship title after the war. He won another four matches before officially retiring in March 1949. He had defended his title more times than any other modern boxer, before or since, and held his title for longer than any other heavyweight champion. Another African American boxer, Ezzard Charles (1921–75), assumed his title as heavyweight champion. Massive financial difficulties prompted Louis's decision to return to the ring in 1950. His first fight was against Charles, in the hopes of reclaiming the heavyweight title. Louis lost the fifteen-round fight in a unanimous decision by the match judges. Still in need of money, Louis won eight more matches over the course of a year before being knocked out by up-and-comer Rocky Marciano (1923–69) in 1951. That was his last professional match.

Even as his boxing career ended, Louis played an important role in the integration of professional golf. At the time, no African Americans—or other minorities—were allowed to play in events run by the Professional Golfers' Association (PGA) of America. Louis was an excellent amateur player, winning the United Golf Association's (UGA) amateur title in the same year he lost in the ring to Marciano. He and another African American player were invited to play in the San Diego Open golf tournament in 1952, but the PGA later revoked their invitations, pointing to its "Caucasians only" rule. Louis's fame and enduring stature as an American hero led the press to criticize the PGA, even comparing the organization's leader to Hitler. The PGA eventually allowed Louis to play, and allowed other African American players to participate in PGA events on a case-by-case basis. These exceptions were rare, and the PGA continued to officially discriminate for years, but Louis had helped to pry open the doors of exclusion for future African American players.

His money problems continued, and he tried various careers, including celebrity spokesperson and professional wrestler. Louis eventually got a job as a celebrity greeter at a Las Vegas casino. He died of a heart attack in 1981 at the age of sixty-six, and his family received special permission from President Ronald Reagan (1911–2004) for Louis to be buried in Arlington National Cemetery. Max Schmeling, his former rival and later friend, helped pay for the funeral and served as one of the pall bearers.

Joe Louis played an important role in the integration of golf as his boxing career was coming to a close. *Joseph Scherschel/Time & Life Pictures/Getty Images*

★ ANN LOWE
(1898–1981)

Ann Lowe was a high-fashion dress designer with improbable roots in the deep South. At a time when African American fashion designers were virtually unheard of, Lowe made dresses by request of some of the country's wealthiest and most powerful families, including the Rockefellers, the Roosevelts, and the DuPonts. Her most famous creation is the wedding dress she made for the marriage of Jacqueline Bouvier (1929–94) and John F. Kennedy (1917–63) in 1953.

Jackie Kennedy's wedding dress, shown on display at the Kennedy Library, was one of Ann Lowe's most famous creations.
© *Brooks Kraft/Sygma/Corbis*

Lowe was born in Clayton, Alabama, the granddaughter of a slave. Both her grandmother and her mother were dressmakers and specialized in creating evening gowns for wealthy white women in the area. Lowe learned their craft and developed one enduring element of her style: As a child, she took the scrap material left over from the dresses her mother made and used them to create fabric flowers.

Lowe got married at the age of fourteen and had a son named Arthur soon after. Her mother passed away when Lowe was sixteen and working as her mother's assistant. Her mother's death left unfinished four dresses intended for the First Lady of Alabama. Lowe finished the dresses and began her own career as a dressmaker. She moved to Tampa, Florida, at age seventeen to create dresses for a wealthy family there. She then moved to New York City to attend fashion school, and returned to Tampa to run a dress shop three years later.

Lowe saved her money, and in 1927 moved back to New York and opened her own business. She designed and made dresses for high-fashion stores and salons, but did not have a store of her own. For this reason, she did not receive credit for much of her work—such as the dress actress Olivia de Havilland (1916–) wore to the 1947 Academy Awards, where she won Best Actress for the film *To Each His Own* (1946).

Still, Lowe's name became known among the wealthy elite, and she often worked at the request of specific families. She was hired to create the wedding dress worn by Jacqueline Bouvier for her marriage to John F. Kennedy, a senator who later became president of the United States. This was one of her highest-profile jobs, and it nearly ended in disaster. After she had spent eight weeks creating the dresses for the wedding party, most of them were ruined when her workplace was flooded just a week before the wedding. Lowe re-created the dresses in five days, and she ended up losing three times as much money as she was paid to do the work. However, the Kennedy wedding dress became an icon of American culture and is among the most famous wedding dresses ever created.

Lowe frequently experienced financial difficulties despite her creative successes. Her son Arthur took care of her accounting needs until his death in 1958, but her confusing mix of different types of business arrangements led to a severe underpayment of federal taxes. She also failed to set appropriate prices for her dresses, and often spent more on the fine materials than the dress's selling price. Friends in the fashion industry—and anonymous benefactors from among the wealthy families for whom she had created dresses—helped her straighten out her financial problems.

In 1961, Lowe lost sight in one eye to glaucoma, a disease that slowly reduces a person's field of vision. She hired an illustrator to put her designs to paper, and she opened a new shop under her own name on Madison Avenue in the mid-1960s. Failing vision ultimately ended her career, and she passed away in 1981 at the age of eighty-two. Her dresses have been included in collections at the Smithsonian Museum, the Metropolitan Museum of Art in New York, and the Black Fashion Museum in Harlem.

★ JESSE OWENS
(1913–1980)

Jesse Owens stands atop the victor's platform at the 1936 Olympics in Berlin. *AP Images*

Jesse Owens was one of the greatest track and field athletes of the twentieth century. He broke several world records while still in college, but is most famous for the four gold medals he won during the 1936 Olympic Games in Berlin. German leader Adolf Hitler wanted to show the world the superiority of the Aryan race, or non–Jewish white people, at the Games that year. Owens's substantial victory as an African American, therefore, showed Hitler's ideas to be false.

James Cleveland Owens—known to family and friends as "J. C."—was the tenth of eleven children born to Henry Cleveland Owens and Emma Fitzgerald Owens, sharecroppers in Oakville, Alabama. Sharecroppers farm land they do not own in exchange for a portion of the crops they grow, and generally live in poverty. The Owens family was no exception. Most of the children helped out with the farming, but J. C. was one of the youngest and was prone to illness, so he was not usually up to the task of physical labor. J. C.'s father decided to move the family north to Ohio in 1921. They became part of the Great Migration, the mass movement of millions of African Americans from the South to urban centers in the North. Economic opportunities were better there, and segregation was often not as strictly enforced. The Owens family settled in Cleveland, Ohio, when J. C. was just nine years old.

J. C. attended an integrated public school for the first time in Cleveland. He also received a new name when one teacher mistakenly thought he had said "Jesse" instead of "J. C." when he asked him his name. Rather than call attention to the mistake, Owens simply accepted it. From then on, J. C. was known to almost everyone as Jesse.

Owens met a physical education teacher and track coach named Charles Riley at his new school. Riley was concerned about Owens's frail build and apparently fragile health. He convinced the boy that running would be good for him since it would make him stronger. Owens eventually joined the track team. He worked several part-time jobs after school to help support the family, so Riley agreed to let Owens practice in the morning before school.

Owens stuck with track all through junior high and high school. He attended the National Interscholastic Championship in Chicago, Illinois, during his senior year. There, he tied the existing world record time for the 100-yard dash: 9.4 seconds, which was also a new high school world record. Owens's strong athletic performance earned him a scholarship to Ohio State University. He told school officials that he would only attend if they found a job for his unemployed father. They agreed.

Owens continued his record-setting performance on the track in college. He won four National Collegiate Athletic Association (NCAA) championships in 1935 and again in 1936. At one Detroit meet in 1935, Owens broke three world records and tied a fourth in the span of less than an hour. He set new world records in the 220-yard sprint (20.7 seconds), the 220-yard hurdles (22.6 seconds), and the broad jump (26 feet 8 1/4 inches—almost six inches farther than the previous world record). Another major milestone in Owens's life occurred in 1935 as well: He married longtime girlfriend Minnie Ruth Solomon, whom he had known since junior high school.

Owens easily qualified for the United States track and field team for the 1936 Olympic Games in Berlin, Germany. The Olympics were a source of great controversy around the world because Germany was ruled at the time by Nazi leader Adolf Hitler. Hitler sought to use the event as a grand display of the superiority of his country's "Aryan race." Owens put these ideas to rest by winning four gold medals, for the 100-meter sprint, the 200-meter sprint, the long jump, and as part of the 400-meter relay team.

Owens returned from the Olympics a hero, but financial opportunities for African American athletes were few. He resorted to stunt races against racehorses and cars, and at one point managed a dry-cleaning business. He moved his family to Chicago in 1946 and opened a public relations agency. In the 1950s, he was appointed to the Illinois State Athletic Commission and the Illinois Youth Commission. He became very involved with helping children who were underprivileged, as he once was.

Owens was inducted into the United States Track and Field Hall of Fame in 1974. He was presented with the Presidential Medal of Freedom for his accomplishments two years later. After spending several decades as a habitual smoker, Owens passed away from lung cancer in 1980 at the age of sixty-six.

★ SATCHEL PAIGE
(1906–1982)

Satchel Paige was one of the most popular baseball players of the Negro Leagues. The first official Negro League began in 1920 to organize teams of black players. Black players had been segregated from white

Satchel Paige. *AP Images*

players in the major leagues by an 1890 "gentleman's agreement" amongst white owners that they would not hire black players. Paige was undoubtedly one of the best pitchers to ever play the game, though his carefree spirit and tendency to follow the largest paycheck often got him into trouble with league officials. He became the seventh African American signed to a major league contract in 1948, at the age of forty-two, after the integration of major league baseball.

Rocks and Reform School

Leroy Robert Page was born in Mobile, Alabama, into a family that would eventually include eleven children. His father, John, was a landscaper, and his mother washed laundry. The family later changed the spelling of their last name by adding an "i" to it. Paige claimed that he threw rocks for fun as a boy because the family could not afford any toys. The family fished for their food during times when they were too poor to buy food from the store.

Paige occasionally attended school, but the family's need for money took priority over his education. He began to work at the train depot at the age of seven, hauling luggage for passengers. He only earned a dime for each bag he hauled, so he built a device using a rope and pole that allowed him to carry several bags at once. The other boys working at the depot told him that he looked like a "walking satchel tree," and from then on Paige was known by the nickname "Satchel." One of his childhood friends disputes this tale, however, and insists that Paige earned the nickname when he was caught trying to steal a passenger's satchel.

Paige also got a job sweeping at a local baseball park. He began practicing his own pitching after watching the semiprofessional pitchers there, using rocks instead of baseballs. He was chosen to play for the W. H. Council School baseball team at age ten. He was not originally selected as a pitcher, but the first time he was brought in to relieve the regular pitchers, he retired sixteen batters in a row.

Paige was caught stealing from a local store just after he turned twelve, and was sent away to the Industrial School for Negro Children, a reform school in Mount Meigs, Alabama. He spent five and a half years there, attending school and staying out of trouble. He also used that time to develop his skills as a pitcher. He was released from the reform school at the age of eighteen. He tried out for a local semiprofessional ball team called the Mobile Tigers just a month after his release. He and his brother Wilson both played for the team, but their earnings were meager. Paige was able to rack up two years of consistent wins before signing a contract with a professional Negro Southern League team, the Chattanooga Black Lookouts, in 1926. He earned fifty dollars per month.

A Varied Career in the Minors and Majors

Paige's career was one of frequent team changes, unofficial exhibition matches, and "for-hire" pitching engagements intended to increase attendance for flagging teams. He also played "barnstorming" matches against white professional ball players, striking them out as easily as any batters he faced in the Negro Leagues. Paige left Chattanooga after one season in order to play for the Birmingham Black Barons. He led his league in strikeouts during the three seasons he played with the Barons. He also played a series of games in Cuba for the Santa Clara Leopards.

Paige's roaming continued until 1935, when he was banned from the Negro National League for failing to honor a contract with the Pittsburgh Crawfords. He was allowed to rejoin the team, only to leave shortly thereafter to play for a team in the Dominican Republic. The team was overseen by Rafael Trujillo (1891–1961), the dictator who ran the country. Paige next went to the Mexican League, after first returning to the United States for a series of exhibition matches across the Midwest. He bounced back and forth between foreign leagues, all-star touring exhibitions, and regular season play for the Kansas City Monarchs. He took the Monarchs to the Negro World Series twice, in 1942 and 1946.

The decline of the Negro Leagues began with the integration of major league baseball by Jackie Robinson (1919–72) in 1947. Paige was already forty years old by the time of this historic achievement, but felt that his popularity made him the natural choice to be the first instead of Robinson. Paige's age did not stop him from following in Robinson's trailblazing path to become the seventh African American signed to a major league team. He signed with the Cleveland Indians in 1948. He became the oldest rookie ever to play in the major leagues at age forty-two, and was part of a World Series–winning team.

Sports team owner Bill Veeck (1914–86) was instrumental in continuing Paige's professional career. Veeck sold the Cleveland Indians, and purchased a controlling interest in the St. Louis Browns. The Indians new management team ended Paige's contract so Veeck persuaded Paige to play for the Browns. Paige became the first African American pitcher chosen for an American League All Star team during his time with the Browns. He continued playing on various minor league teams across the country after leaving the Browns, still maintaining an impressive record. Amazingly, Paige returned to the major leagues in 1965, at the age of fifty-nine, for one final game. He had discovered that he needed to pitch three more innings in order to be eligible for a major league baseball player's pension. The owner of the Kansas City Athletics signed Paige to a single-game contract and let him pitch his last three innings. He did not allow a single run.

Paige did not give up the sport completely. He played several more minor league and exhibition games for the money. He finally retired as a player in 1967. He is estimated to have pitched more than two thousand five hundred games during his career, with over two thousand wins. He signed on as a pitching coach for the Atlanta Braves in 1969. In 1971, Paige was inducted into the Baseball Hall of Fame. He passed away in 1982, at the age of seventy-five.

★ JACKIE ROBINSON
(1919–1972)

Jackie Robinson earned a place in history as the first African American to play modern major league baseball. He integrated the major leagues in 1947 after signing a contract with the Brooklyn Dodgers. He endured

Jackie Robinson. *AP Images*

significant abuse from sports fans who did not want to see a black baseball player on the same field as white players. He withstood the racial insults and threats to his life to not only succeed in baseball, but also to win over fans of all colors with his personality and charm. His success in the major leagues opened up opportunities for many other African American baseball players who had spent their careers as victims of segregation.

An All Star Athlete

Jack Roosevelt—nicknamed "Jackie"—Robinson was the youngest of five children born to Jerry and Mallie Robinson, sharecroppers who lived near Cairo, Georgia. Sharecropping was a hard life, in which the family lived and worked on land they did not own. In exchange for growing crops there, they were allowed to keep a portion of what they grew as payment. His father left the family while Jackie was still an infant, forcing the family to leave the plantation where they had been staying. Mallie decided to take her children to Pasadena, California, where her brother lived, because it seemed to offer opportunities that did not exist in the South.

Mallie worked as a laundress, and the family managed to scrape by with nothing to spare. Jackie was often left in the care of his older siblings, usually his sister Willa Mae. The year before Jackie was old enough to attend school, Willa Mae received special permission to bring him to her school and let him play in the sandbox all day while she went to class. Jackie got into some minor troubles as a member of a gang when he got older, but quickly turned to school and athletics as positive outlets for his energies. He became a lettered athlete in baseball, basketball, football, and track at John Muir Technical High.

Jackie received great encouragement from his brothers, who were also athletic. His brother Matthew "Mack" Robinson won a silver medal in the 1936 Olympic Games in Berlin, finishing second in the 200-meter sprint right behind Jesse Owens. Jackie attended Pasadena College after high school, where his continuing athletic accomplishments earned him the attention of larger universities. He chose to attend the University of California in Los Angeles (UCLA) because it was the closest to where his family lived. He became the first UCLA student to letter in four different sports. Also during his time at UCLA, he met his future wife, Rachel Isum.

Robinson left UCLA after two years in order to secure a job so he could help support his mother and siblings. He became an assistant athletic director at a youth camp for a short time, and then in 1941 traveled to Hawaii to play for the Honolulu Bears, a semiprofessional football team that featured both African American and white players. Professional football at the time was still segregated. Robinson left Hawaii after finishing the season to return to California on December 5, 1941. Two days later, Japanese forces attacked Pearl Harbor, the site of an American naval station just miles away from Honolulu. More than two thousand soldiers and civilians were killed, and the attack assured America's entry into World War II.

An Officer and a Trailblazer

Robinson was drafted into the U.S. Army in May 1942. He applied for Officers' Candidate School, but was kept waiting along with several other African American applicants. It was only after heavyweight champion boxer Joe Louis arrived on base and assisted the candidates that their applications were finally approved. He became a second lieutenant and morale officer, ultimately stationed with a tank battalion at Fort Hood, Texas. He was brought up for a court martial after refusing to change seats on a military transport bus. The bus driver had spotted Robinson talking to a white woman—the wife of another lieutenant—and ordered him to move to the back. Robinson refused to move, knowing that the U.S. Army had recently passed regulations against segregation while traveling on army bases. He was ultimately acquitted of all charges, and received an honorable discharge in November 1944.

Robinson was not sure what to do after leaving the service until he met another serviceman who had played baseball in the Negro Leagues for the Kansas City Monarchs. Robinson was accepted by the team, earning four hundred dollars per month. He found that life on the road with a Negro League team was hard to endure. Aside from the nonstop travel from city to city, team members were often excluded from hotels and restaurants because of their race.

Robinson came to the attention of Branch Rickey (1881–1965), the manager of the major league team the Brooklyn Dodgers. It was 1945, and conditions had only recently allowed for the possibility that an African American baseball player might be brought into the major leagues. Rickey was determined to be the first to sign an African American for a major league team. Robinson's excellent college athletic and military record made him an ideal choice. Rickey offered Robinson a contract in

November 1945. According to the contract, Robinson first had to play a season for the Dodgers' minor league farm team, the Montreal Royals.

Robinson proved to be an enormous asset to the team, earning the title of Most Valuable Player in the league and boosting attendance at Royals games. He also faced frequent occurrences of racism, including insults, threats, and refusal of service from various businesses. At Rickey's urging, Robinson did not fight back against these injustices. He knew the importance of what he was doing, and did not want to give racist critics any ammunition against him or other future African American players.

Major League Success

Robinson joined the Dodgers in April 1947 and became the first African American baseball player in the modern major leagues. Some players in the league—including some on his own team—threatened not to participate if Robinson was allowed to play. They were quickly shut down by the baseball commissioner and the league president, who laid out stiff penalties for any player protesting Robinson's presence. Still, he endured many verbal attacks by opposing teams and their fans. Despite this hostile environment, Robinson's outstanding performance earned him the very first major league Rookie of the Year award.

Robinson's success spurred other major league teams to sign African American players the following year. The Dodgers also signed three more African American players. However, few players in professional baseball— black or white—could equal Robinson's amazing success. He was a solid hitter and a reliable fielder, earning him the National League's Most Valuable Player award for the 1949 season. His inspiring story was even adapted to film in 1950 with great success; the baseball player portrayed himself in *The Jackie Robinson Story,* while his wife was played by actress Ruby Dee (1924–).

Robinson continued his successful career as a Dodger through much of the 1950s, and in 1955 he helped the Dodgers lead the league and win the World Series. He soon began to display physical problems associated with diabetes, and at the same time the manager of the Dodgers made an agreement to trade Robinson to the New York Giants. He decided to retire after the 1956 season.

Robinson took a position as vice president of a popular lunch counter chain, and also used his fame to fight for civil rights causes. He was the chairman of the National Association for the Advancement of Colored People's (NAACP) Freedom Fund Drive, and later created a construction company to build affordable housing for the poor. Robinson became the first African American inducted into the Baseball Hall of Fame in 1962. In

1972, the Dodgers (now a Los Angeles team) announced that his team jersey number—42—would be retired forever, meaning no other player for the team could ever be given that number. It was the 25th anniversary of Robinson's major-league debut. Robinson did not live long after the honor, passing away from complications related to diabetes just four months later, at the age of fifty-three. In 2004, major league baseball designated April 15 of each year as Jackie Robinson Day, in honor of the date he first played in the major leagues.

★ CHARLIE SIFFORD
(1922–)

Charlie Sifford was the first African American golfer to be recognized as a member of the Professional Golfers' Association (PGA). His membership marked the official end of segregation in professional golf. Prior to becoming a member of the PGA, he was one of the most successful golfers in the United Golf Association (UGA), created specifically for African American players.

Sifford was born in Charlotte, North Carolina, at a time when segregation was a normal way of life in the South. He lived in an area that offered relatively more tolerance and opportunities for African Americans than other places in the South. At the age of ten, he got a job as a caddie at the Carolina Country Club, a local whites-only golf course. He carried bags for club members and learned much about the sport. The caddies were allowed to play the course on Mondays, when the course was closed to the public. Sifford practiced diligently, even arriving early to practice on other days before the course opened.

Sifford developed a reputation as an outstanding golfer while he was still a teenager. The owner of the course told Sifford that he should quit as a caddie because the white club members were reacting badly to his success. Sifford decided to move to Philadelphia, which, unlike Charlotte, offered public golf courses open to African Americans. He continued to work on his game, dreaming of becoming a professional.

Charlie Sifford. *AP Images*

Golf was a segregated sport at the time. Many other sports, like baseball and tennis, relied on tradition and social pressure to keep African Americans out of the most prestigious leagues. The exclusion of African Americans and other minorities from professional golf was actually written into the bylaws of the PGA of America. In fact, the written exclusion—requiring members to be "of the Caucasian race"—was not added to the organization's constitution until 1943, just four years before professional baseball officially became integrated.

The only opportunity available for African American golfers was as part of the UGA, which offered smaller prizes and less prestige. Sifford was one of the top performers in the UGA. He won his first Negro National Open tournament in 1948, and won five more times by 1960. Several African American golfers challenged the PGA bylaws as discriminatory and illegal during the 1940s and 1950s. Bowing to public pressure, the PGA began to allow African American players to participate in some tournaments, but only as specially invited guests and never as members of the PGA. Sifford won the Long Beach Open tournament in 1957, and he sued the PGA to allow him to join. Finally, the PGA issued Sifford a player card in 1960—though they did not remove the "Caucasians only" rule from their bylaws until 1961. He was the first African American to be recognized as a member of the premier golf organization in the country.

Sifford placed second in his first tournament as an official PGA player, enduring death threats and racial insults over the course of the event. Though he was not allowed to enter the PGA until his late thirties, he continued playing on the regular tour well into his fifties, winning the 1967 Greater Hartford Open and the 1969 Los Angeles Open. Despite his consistent success, he was never allowed to play in the PGA Masters Tournament, an invitational event whose participants are determined by the Augusta National Golf Club in Georgia. (Lee Elder was the first African American to play in the Masters Tournament in 1975. The club remained closed to African American members until 1990, and, as of 2009, it had yet to admit a female member.) Even many years after he received his PGA player card, Sifford was frequently denied admission to whites-only golf courses and refused service at club restaurants.

Sifford began to play in the PGA Seniors' Tournament in the 1970s. The tournament was created for eligible golfers at least fifty years of age. He won the Seniors' Tournament in 1975, and continued to play on the Senior PGA Tour (now called the Champions Tour) throughout the 1980s and 1990s. He won his last tournament, the Liberty Mutual Legends of

Golf, in 2000. In 2004, Sifford was selected as the first African American to enter the World Golf Hall of Fame.

★ SYLVIA WOODS
(1926–)

Sylvia Woods helped establish the popularity of soul food in modern cuisine as a cook and restaurateur. Her restaurant in the New York neighborhood of Harlem earned her the title "Queen of Soul Food." Her business enterprise included a successful line of canned and bottled products.

Woods was born Sylvia Pressley in Hemingway, South Carolina, the only child born to Van and Julia Pressley. Her father died while she was an infant, and her mother went to New York to earn money as a laundry worker when Sylvia was just three. She was raised primarily by her grandmother, a midwife. Her mother returned to Hemingway when Sylvia was eight, and had saved enough money to buy forty acres and build a house next to her own mother.

Hemingway was a rural farm community, and everyone—including the children—was expected to help with the crops during harvest time. Sylvia picked cotton, tobacco, and green beans every day after school. She encountered a boy named Herbert at age eleven who would eventually become her husband. Their courting was interrupted in 1941, when Sylvia's mother sent her to New York City so that she could attend a cosmetology school. She returned to Hemingway and ran a beauty salon out of her mother's farmhouse. Sylvia and Herbert married in 1944.

By 1950, the couple relocated to Harlem, where he drove a cab and she worked as a hairdresser at home. Woods eventually took a job as a waitress at Johnson's Luncheonette, a position that was given to her after her cousin decided to quit and return to school. She worked there as a waitress for eight years. In 1962, the owner of the restaurant needed to sell, and asked if she wanted to buy it. She was interested, but did not have the twenty thousand dollars she would need. Her mother, still in South Carolina on her large farm, took

Sylvia Woods stands outside her famous restaurant with her husband, Herbert, c. 1988. © *Jacques M. Chenet/Corbis* out a mortgage to help Woods buy the restaurant. She took ownership on August 1, 1962.

Woods at first relied upon the traditional menu of hamburgers and other basic luncheonette offerings. She eventually renamed the restaurant Sylvia's and began to include the food of her childhood, such as pig's feet, black-eyed peas, and collard greens. The authentic Southern food was an immediate hit in the neighborhood. It was especially popular with the many African Americans who had moved north years before and still longed for the food they had eaten in their youth.

Harlem was the scene of massive riots following the murder of Martin Luther King Jr. (1929–68) in April 1968. Sylvia's was one of the few businesses that rioters did not damage. The restaurant moved to a new, larger location soon after, a former hardware store that allowed Woods to expand her customer capacity and her Southern menu. The restaurant's reputation continued to grow, spurred on by a glowing review in *New York* magazine written by respected food critic Gail Green. Woods expanded the restaurant's dining area in 1982, again in 1986, and yet again in 1989.

As the restaurant boomed, Woods recognized another opportunity for her business. She frequently heard from customers who wanted to purchase some of her key dishes and ingredients for use at home. On one occasion, a group of firefighters brought in a gallon jug and asked if they could buy some of her homemade barbecue sauce. Woods decided to offer a line of canned and bottled products bearing the Sylvia's brand, and they hit store shelves in 1992. That same year, she published her first cookbook, *Sylvia's Soul Food.*

Woods opened a second Sylvia's location in Atlanta, Georgia, in 1997. After a difficult start, the restaurant became a huge success. She published her second cookbook, *Sylvia's Family Soul Food Cookbook,* in 1999. Woods lost her husband Herbert to prostate cancer in 2001, but continued to run the business with her four children and her grandchildren as of 2010.

❖ SOUL FOOD BECOMES PART OF AMERICAN CUISINE

Soul food is a term used to describe African American cuisine that developed primarily in the southern United States. Popular soul food dishes include fried chicken, black-eyed peas, collard greens, and ham hocks. As African Americans migrated out of the South during the early twentieth century, they took with them a taste for soul food that expanded its popularity. There remains debate about whether or not soul food is separate from Southern cuisine, or just a different name for an integrated style of cooking that developed in the South during the nineteenth century.

The origin of soul food stretches back to the time when African slaves were first brought to the United States. They brought with them some ingredients that are recognized parts of African American cuisine. Okra, a plant that produces a green seeded pod eaten as a vegetable, is native to

Ham hocks and collard greens are soul food staples.
© James Nesterwitz/Alamy

West Africa and features prominently in Southern cuisine. Watermelon, a fruit now often identified in the United States with summer picnics and the Fourth of July, was brought from Africa as well.

Slaves living on plantations in the South were often required to grow and prepare their own food, using few resources. They cultivated gardens that included these plants from their ancestral lands, as well as local plants that were abundant and provided easy nutrition. Peanuts, for example, are native to Central and South America, and were adopted by slaves as a food crop because of their high nutritional value. Pecans and corn are also native to the United States, and were used by Native American tribes before being adopted as key parts of a Southern diet. Yams were an important part of many West African diets; they were not successfully transplanted to the United States, so African Americans found a similar vegetable native to their new land—the sweet potato—that served as a replacement in many dishes. Collard greens, another plant native to the American South, were used by African Americans as a replacement for greens from their native regions.

Another, related factor greatly influenced African American cuisine and Southern cooking in general. Because slaves often had to survive on very little, they relied on foods that were easy to cultivate and provided large amounts of protein and fat. The same was also true of poor whites in the South, who raised chickens and pigs rather than cattle because they required fewer resources and matured quickly. Pork and chicken are the staple meats in soul food and in Southern cooking in general. Few parts of the animal were wasted; chitterlings, a popular soul food dish, are made from the cleaned intestines of a pig, while pigs' feet, chicken gizzards, and chicken livers are also popular. Likewise, frying and deep-frying—whether the food is meat, bread, or vegetable—became a common part of Southern cooking because it infused the food with the added fat left over from cooking meat.

Other traditions also played a part in the development of soul food. Pies and cobblers arrived in the United States as imports from England and found a welcome home in the South where abundant fruits like peaches are featured in many desserts. The banana and cayenne pepper were brought by slaves from the West Indies and incorporated into some dishes.

The argument as to whether there is a distinct difference between Southern food and soul food still triggers debate even among food experts. Famous African American chef Edna Lewis refused to call her creations soul food, instead referring to them as country cooking. Writer and civil rights activist Amiri Baraka (1934–) famously argued in favor of the uniqueness of soul food in the 1960s. At that time, the term "soul food" was just becoming popular as an expression of pride in the African American heritage. Whether or not soul food is distinct from other Southern cooking, it is undeniable that African Americans played a key role in the development of a type of cuisine that continues to grow in popularity throughout the United States.

❖ AFRICAN AMERICAN JOCKEYS WIN MAJOR 19TH-CENTURY RACES

Horse racing was a popular sport throughout the South in the years following the Civil War (1861–65). It was also one of the few sports in which African Americans played a dominant role during the nineteenth century. Primarily as jockeys—but also as trainers and owners—African Americans found opportunities in the sport more easily than in other athletic endeavors.

Horses were generally kept and cared for by slaves in the South prior to the Civil War. Plantation owners would sometimes race their horses using slaves as jockeys; the owners believed that the true winning abilities resided in the horse, not its rider. It is no surprise that after the end of slavery

An African American jockey and handler prepare a horse for racing at the Harlem Race Track in 1903. Many of the jockeys in the early days of horse racing were African American until the sport's organizers began to systematically shut them out. *Chicago History Museum/Hulton Archive/ Getty Images*

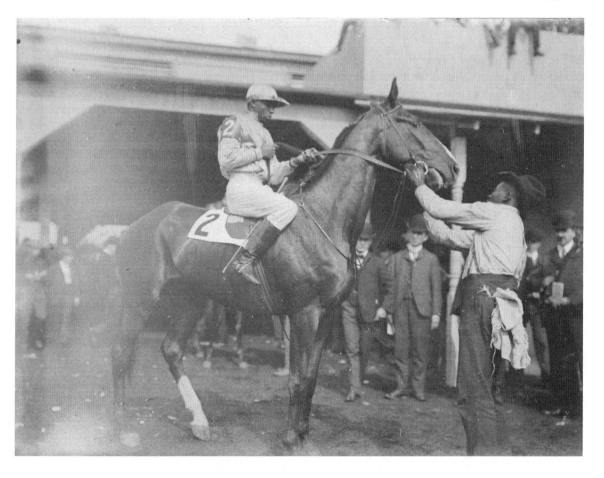

African Americans who had experience working with and riding horses became a part of horse racing as an organized sport.

The first major horse racing events took place in Kentucky. The earliest was the Travers Stakes, which began in 1864. The best-known American race, the Kentucky Derby, began in 1875. Fourteen of the fifteen jockeys who rode in the first Kentucky Derby were African American—including the winner, Oliver Lewis, whose horse Aristides was also trained by an African American. The Kentucky Derby was won by African American jockeys sixteen times during its first twenty-eight years.

One of the most notable jockeys was Isaac Murphy (1861–96), who began riding professionally in 1876 at the age of fifteen. Murphy was the first jockey to garner back-to-back wins in the Kentucky Derby in 1890 and 1891, and won three Derbys total during his career. He won twenty-five major races over a twenty-year period, and hundreds of other races. According to Murphy's own records, he won 44 percent of the races in which he rode. While sports historians can only confirm that he won just over one-third of his races, Murphy's career percentage is still the most successful of any professional jockey. His career was tragically cut short in 1896, when he died of pneumonia at the age of thirty-five.

Drastic changes occurring in American horse racing at the end of the nineteenth century cut short the careers of many African American jockeys. In 1894, the Jockey Club was formed as a way to establish order in the expanding sport. The Jockey Club monitored horse bloodlines, developed an official thoroughbred registry, and instituted rules for licensing jockeys. During this time period, the South was experiencing a backlash against African American advancements, and many states passed laws that effectively limited or denied the rights of black citizens. The Jockey Club set requirements for licensing that many African American jockeys could not possibly meet, and as a result they either left the profession or left the country to race in Europe.

African American jockey Jimmy Winkfield won back-to-back victories in the 1901 and 1902 Kentucky Derby races, but the era of African American dominance in American horse racing quickly ended. Henry King raced as the only African American rider in the 1921 Kentucky Derby, after which seventy-nine years would pass before another black jockey rode in the Derby. That rider was Marlon St. Julian, who in the year 2000 finished seventh in the race.

❖ AFRICAN AMERICAN DANCES FIND MAINSTREAM POPULARITY

Many African American cultural traditions found their way into mainstream American culture after the Civil War (1861–65). One area of African American culture that proved especially popular was dance. At the time, Americans relied mainly on traditional European forms of dance. These dances would probably appear overly stiff and formal to modern spectators. African American dance styles involved freer movement of the body. The social situation of African Americans at the time also made their dances much less formal. These characteristics came to define American dance throughout the twentieth century.

African American dancers perform the cakewalk dance, c. 1901.
Hulton Archive/Getty Images

Plantation Dances Enter the Mainstream

The cakewalk was created by slaves who lived on plantations in the South. It was originally intended to poke fun at the overly formal dances of white Americans. It made use of procession, in which pairs of dancers (or single dancers) marched across the dance floor while the others stood along either side and waited for their turn. This was similar to the promenade tradition in formal dances among whites. The cakewalk involved African American dancers lifting their legs high in exaggerated fashion, and performing broad gestures with a makeshift cane or hat to suggest fancy dress and high social status. These exaggerated movements became more elaborate over time, often involving wild footwork while the dancer's upper body remained rather stiff and formal. The pair of dancers judged to be the best would be awarded a cake as their prize, which is how the dance got its name. Though it originated as a dance mocking white culture, the cakewalk became very popular among white Americans throughout the 1890s. African American stage performers also demonstrated their own versions of the cakewalk with great success, and the dance even made its way to Broadway.

Another type of dance that gained popularity among slave populations on Southern plantations was called the juba dance. It arose when plantation owners forbade their slaves from owning or playing drums. Dancers began to stomp their feet on the ground and pat their bodies with their hands in order to keep rhythm. These sharp, rhythmic movements of the arms and legs gave rise to several different types of dance.

One particular variety of the juba dance became popular in the South, and is believed to have originated in Charleston, South Carolina. The dance involved a twisting inward and outward of the feet to the beat of the music. This move made its way northward to the African American community in Harlem, New York. The step was combined with fast-tempo music and the broad arm gestures of the juba. The first official version of the dance known as the Charleston was performed in the Broadway show *Runnin' Wild* in 1923. It quickly became the most popular dance in the country, though some cities banned the dance for its wild and morally inappropriate movements.

The rhythmic stomping of the juba dance was especially popular in stage performances, as in minstrel shows or vaudeville acts. Other cultures featured similar rhythm dances, such as the Irish step dance. It was the combination of rhythmic foot-tapping and African American jazz music, however, that led to the development and popularity of tap dancing. Tap dancing makes use of metal plates attached to the soles of a dancer's shoes so that the steps are easier to hear. Tap dancing began not as a social dance but as a stage performance, with dancers like Bill "Bojangles" Robinson

(1878–1949) and John W. Bubbles (1902–86) imprinting their own styles on the dance in stage and film work.

Hopping and Swinging Sweep the Nation

A new variation of the Charleston developed a few years after the dance brought black and white Americans into dance halls across the country. The dance became known as the lindy hop in 1928, possibly in honor of aviator Charles Lindbergh (1902–74). Lindbergh, also known as "Lindy," was the first person to fly alone, nonstop, across the Atlantic Ocean in 1928. In the lindy hop, a dancing couple moves from being face to face to standing side by side, where the two perform solo steps that are improvised, or chosen in the moment, by the dancer.

Another important feature that came to be associated with the lindy hop was the aerial. An aerial is a dance move in which a dancer's feet leave the dance floor entirely. This often meant that one dancer was flipped over the back of the other dancer, or was lifted and spun in a circle. Often dancers would come up with increasingly acrobatic moves in an attempt to outdo rivals at local dance halls. One of the most important dance halls in this regard was the Savoy Ballroom in Harlem. The Savoy was integrated at a time when most nightclubs and dance halls were still segregated by race. The cross-cultural effect of having black and white dancers sharing the same floor undoubtedly helped the spread of the lindy hop and its variants across the nation and even around the world.

The main components of the lindy hop were adapted into countless other dances that are collectively known as swing or jitterbug. The many variations went hand-in-hand with the different flavors of jazz music that came to be known as "swing jazz" or just "swing." Dancers incorporated elements from other traditional dances like the waltz and the tango as the popularity of swing grew. Different regions of the country developed their own dance variations, and swing dancing even became popular throughout Europe. Changes in popular music in the 1940s and 1950s were reflected in the dance variations, which included boogie woogie and rock and roll. The root of all these variations remains the basic elements introduced by African Americans in the late nineteenth and early twentieth centuries. In fact, nearly all modern dance forms thought of as uniquely American have roots in African American culture.

❖ BOXER JACK JOHNSON DEFEATS "THE GREAT WHITE HOPE"

African American boxer Jack Johnson (1878–1946) became the first black heavyweight champion of the world when he defeated Canadian fighter Tommy Burns (1881–1955) in 1908. It had been a long road for

Johnson, who had been waiting five years for a chance at the heavyweight title. He was crowned the "colored" heavyweight champion in 1903, but the world heavyweight champion at the time, James Jeffries (1875–1953), refused to fight against a black boxer. Boxing was still largely segregated during this era, so it was unusual for blacks and whites to meet in the ring. This left Johnson with little to do but wait and try to persuade his opponent to meet him in the ring. Jeffries retired from the sport in 1905, and it appeared that the two men would never face off against each other.

Johnson finally got his shot at the world heavyweight title in a fight with Burns in 1908. Johnson won the bout in fourteen rounds to become the champion. Many white fans of the sport—and many whites who had never before cared much about boxing—were appalled at the idea that an African American was now the world champion. Johnson did not attempt to win the affection of white Americans. He was confident and even arrogant about his abilities, often antagonizing his opponents in the ring and shouting back at fans that hurled racist remarks at him. He was extravagant, spending his money on fine suits, prostitutes, automobiles, and even gold caps for his front teeth. He also had a fondness for white women, which was enough for many racists in the South to feel that he deserved to be killed.

The public reaction of whites against Johnson was so extreme that even author and journalist Jack London (1876–1916), known as a supporter of the downtrodden and working class, called for a "Great White Hope" to "remove that smile from Johnson's face." The "Great White Hope" to which he was referring was Jeffries, the former champion who had retired three years before. But facing Johnson meant more than just coming out of retirement for Jeffries. It also meant risking his perfect record of eighteen wins and zero losses. Jeffries had never been knocked out, and had never even been knocked down by another fighter in the ring.

It took a year of constant public pressure for Jeffries to agree to the match, and another year of training and preparation before he would actually face Johnson. The match took place on July 4, 1910, in an outdoor venue built specifically for the occasion in Reno, Nevada. The fight was scheduled to go as many as forty-five rounds if necessary, and the betting odds favored Jeffries.

The two men squared off in front of a crowd of over twelve thousand, with the predominantly white audience clearly favoring Jeffries and many shouting insults at Johnson. Johnson took the offensive early. He landed some devastating shots to Jeffries's face in the sixth round, causing one of his eyes to swell almost all the way shut. Another former heavyweight, James J. Corbett (1866–1933), taunted Johnson from Jeffries's corner in an attempt to distract him, but Johnson just shot back with his own remarks between successful punches.

Jeffries struggled until the fifteenth round, when Johnson knocked him to the canvas for the first time in his professional career. Jeffries slowly got to his feet, and Johnson knocked him down again, and then a third time. Spectators began to cry out for Jeffries's men to stop the fight before Johnson knocked Jeffries out—which would be seen as the ultimate defeat of the living legend. One of Jeffries's coaches entered the ring and ended the fight as the stunned audience sat mostly silent.

African Americans everywhere celebrated when word of Johnson's victory made it across the country. Many cities reported rioting by blacks, but at least some of these were exaggerations made by fearful whites who were seeing, perhaps for the first time, large-scale public demonstrations of African American pride. In some cases, though, whites responded violently, leading to actual race riots and the deaths of dozens of people, almost all African Americans.

Jack Johnson fights James Jeffries in the 1910 title bout. © *Bettmann/Corbis*

The legendary match had been filmed for theatrical showings around the country as a way for the promoter and the boxers to increase their earnings from the bout. Many states—especially in the South—quickly passed laws forbidding the film from being shown. Many whites believed that showing Jeffries's defeat would embolden African Americans in their community, which would lead to further racial violence—even though the race riots that had occurred were prompted by violence from whites, not blacks.

Johnson held the championship for over six years. He defended his title a total of nine times before finally losing to Jess Willard (1881–1968) after twenty-six rounds in Havana, Cuba, in 1915. But it was Johnson's defeat of the previously undefeated Jeffries, America's "Great White Hope," that most boxing historians recognize as his most important bout, calling it the "Fight of the Century."

❖ JOHN TAYLOR BECOMES FIRST BLACK MAN TO WIN OLYMPIC GOLD

John Baxter Taylor (1882–1908) was one of the most notable short-distance runners of the first decade of the twentieth century. He became the first African American to represent the United States in the Olympic Games in 1908. He was also the first African American to win an Olympic gold medal.

Taylor, born in Washington, D.C., moved with his family to Philadelphia at a young age. He excelled in the city's integrated public school system. Taylor joined the track team in high school and quickly earned a reputation as the fastest runner of the quarter-mile sprint in the city. He enrolled at the University of Pennsylvania after graduation and studied to become a veterinarian. Taylor continued to dominate the quarter-mile events in college and served as a reliable team member in relay events. He won the quarter-mile event in the National Amateur Athletic Union championship in 1907. The following year, his strong performance earned him a spot on the U.S. Olympic team for the 1908 Olympic Games in London.

Taylor participated in two events at the Olympics: the 400-meter race, roughly equal to a quarter-mile, and the men's medley race. Taylor won his first-round heat in the 400-meter race by twelve yards over his closest competitor, and he won his second-round heat by five yards. Three of the

American runners John Taylor (far left), William Robbins (far right), and John Carpenter (second from the right), as well as British runner Wyndham Halswelle, compete in the 400-meter race at the 1908 London Olympics. Carpenter was disqualified during the race, prompting teammates Robbins and Taylor to protest by refusing to participate in the event. *Topical Press Agency/Hulton Archive/Getty Images*

four slots in the 400-meter finals were won by members of the U.S. team. In the first running of the final, one of the American runners, John Carpenter, was flagged for obstructing British finalist Wyndham Halswelle during the race. He was disqualified, and Olympic officials ordered that the race be run again. Taylor and the third American finalist, William Robbins, protested Carpenter's disqualification, and chose not to compete in the new running of the event. The only other runner in the final was Halswelle, who ran unopposed and earned the gold medal. If Taylor and Robbins had chosen to run, they would both have earned medals as well.

The final event of the Olympics was the men's medley relay, in which four teammates each ran one segment of a 1600-meter race. Taylor ran in the third slot; this was the 400-meter slot, which was his strongest distance as a runner. His team was already in the lead when Taylor received the baton, but he widened the gap even more before handing it off to Mel Sheppard, who ran the final 800 meters and assured the team's victory. Taylor and his teammates each earned a gold medal. Though the British won the most medals by far during the competition, the United States team had dominated the track and field events.

Taylor's moment of triumph, however, was short-lived. He fell ill with typhoid fever after returning from England. He passed away on December 2, 1908, just four months after winning his gold medal. He was just twenty-six years old. His death was widely reported, and thousands of mourners attended his funeral services. The *New York Times* noted of his funeral, "It was one of the greatest tributes ever paid a colored man in [Philadelphia]."

❖ AFRICAN AMERICANS STRAIGHTEN AND "CONK" THEIR HAIR

African Americans struggled to be accepted as equal members of mainstream American society in the years after the end of the Civil War. One of the ways that African Americans attempted to gain acceptance was through the adoption of fashions and styles that were popular among white Americans. Hairstyles presented a unique challenge; most white Americans had straight hair, while most African Americans had tightly curled hair. Many African Americans attempted to fit beauty standards accepted by whites by using artificial methods to straighten their curled hair. The trend began with African American women, but men also frequently straightened their hair during the 1930s and 1940s.

One popular early method of hair straightening involved the use of hot oil or fat to relax the curly strands, making them easier to comb through and straighten. This was potentially dangerous since it could burn the

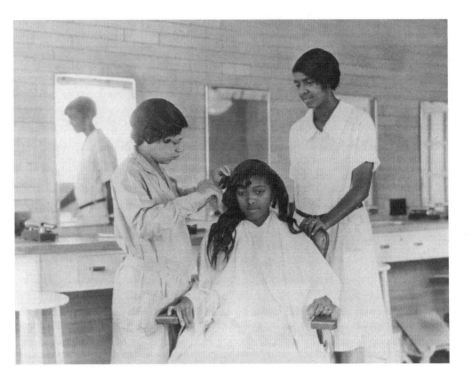

African Americans began to straighten their hair at the beginning of the twentieth century. *Lewis W. Hine/Hulton Archive/Getty Images*

tender skin of the scalp and weaken the strands of hair. African American businesswoman Annie Turnbo Malone (1869–1957) invented a new method of relaxing textured hair in the early 1900s: a comb, heated over an open flame, that warmed the hair as it was brushed through. The biggest advantage of the hot comb was that it essentially eliminated the risk of burning the scalp, though the comb could still burn the hair if allowed to get too hot. Some African American women avoided the trouble of straightening and simply wore wigs that provided the look of straight hair without the risk.

Chemical hair relaxers emerged around 1910 thanks to African American inventor Garrett A. Morgan (1877–1963), who came upon them by accident. While developing a needle lubricant for sewing machines, Morgan discovered that alkaline-based substances such as lye could relax and straighten natural fibers, including hair. Lye still posed the danger of burning a person's scalp because of its corrosive nature. It was usually combined with other ingredients to form a cream that better coated individual hairs and also offered some protection for the scalp.

The discovery of chemical relaxing led to the practice of "conking" among African American men. Conking was the process of chemically straightening hair so it could be styled in ways that were popular among white men. The style was worn by many prominent African Americans, including musicians like Cab Calloway (1907–94) and Nat King Cole (1919–65).

Civil rights activist Malcolm X (1925–65) described his own experiences with conking as a young man in *The Autobiography of Malcolm X* (1965), using a homemade conking solution created from lye, potatoes, and eggs. This formulation, known as congolene, gave the conk its name. Malcolm reflected on the absurd lengths to which he went in an attempt to fit in with white American culture. He eventually came to believe that the process of conking should be condemned as a rejection of African American heritage.

Many African Americans came to agree with this view, particularly as the civil rights movement of the 1950s and 1960s focused on racial pride. Conking and straightening faded in popularity in the 1960s as some African Americans embraced the Afro hairstyle. The Afro haircut was long and curly with a full, bushy, rounded look. It did not require the use of chemicals or tools, and was unique to African American culture. For that reason, it became a symbol of black pride in the 1960s and 1970s. The process of straightening hair did not entirely fade away, however, and many African Americans still use relaxers today as a tool for creating a variety of hairstyles.

❖ THE HARLEM GLOBETROTTERS TEAM IS FORMED

The Harlem Globetrotters are one of the most famous basketball teams in the world, yet they are not part of a professional league. The Globetrotters have entertained fans around the world since the 1920s. The players have been almost exclusively African American, and their longevity and success have made a positive contribution to both sports and entertainment.

The Harlem Globetrotters were formed in Chicago, Illinois, with most of the original members hailing from Wendell Phillips High School. Three players formed their own semiprofessional team after graduating high school. Promoter Abe Saperstein (1902–66) became the team's booking agent and eventually its manager in the late 1920s. It was Saperstein who first suggested that the team—already called the Globe Trotters—be known as the Harlem Globetrotters, even though they were from Chicago. Harlem was considered the center of African American culture, and Saperstein wanted to capture that idea to help market the team.

Saperstein had borrowed the name from another all-black touring basketball team, the Harlem Renaissance (also known as the Rens). They were among the most successful basketball teams of the era. They were not allowed to join the American Basketball League (ABL) when it formed in 1925, despite the quality of their play. The ABL, like most professional leagues in this time period, did not allow black players. African American teams like the Rens and the Globetrotters instead made money by traveling the country and playing exhibition games against other teams. This was known as "barnstorming." To save money, Saperstein drove himself and the five Globetrotters from state to state in a cramped Model T. They often encountered difficulties in finding places to eat and sleep, since many parts of the country were segregated at the time. Some cities in the northern United States did not even offer facilities for African Americans because there were so few in their region.

The Globetrotters played competitive matches like any other basketball team when they first started as a touring team. Their skills earned them victories against some of the top professional teams in the sport. They won the World Professional Basketball Tournament in 1940, and defeated the world champion Minneapolis Lakers in 1948 and again in 1949.

The newly formed National Basketball Association (NBA) integrated its first African American players onto its rosters in 1950. The formation of the NBA marked the decline of the barnstorming basketball era, with NBA teams contracted to play against each other exclusively as part of a set season schedule. Nearly all the professional-level teams that failed to become a part of the NBA eventually disappeared, with one notable exception.

The Harlem Globetrotters playing in a game in 1953. The Globetrotters became known for their clownish antics on the court. *J. R. Eyerman/Time & Life Pictures/ Getty Images*

The Globetrotters could easily gain a large lead against most local teams they played, so they began to perform comic maneuvers and tricks for the audience once they were sure to win. These comic elements became very popular with the audience, and became a formula the Globetrotters followed even after other African American teams were integrated into the NBA. They focused on becoming a successful entertainment franchise rather than trying to succeed as a touring competitive sports team. They also shifted away from trouncing local teams, and began to travel with their own "losing" team, the Washington Generals (whose name was later changed to the New York Nationals). The Generals' skillfully inept performance usually allowed the Globetrotters to perform their signature routines and gags without having to worry about the score. The team did continue to play competitive exhibition games against real challengers on occasion, and their win-loss record remained impressive.

The Losers Win Big

··

The Washington Generals, also known by several other names including the New Jersey Reds, have the longest losing streak in basketball. The exhibition team plays exclusively against the Harlem Globetrotters and has lost thousands of games since their debut in 1953. In fact, according to the official team statistics, they have lost every single game to the Globetrotters except one. Their big win occurred on January 5, 1971, playing as the New Jersey Reds at the University of Tennessee at Martin. The Globetrotters became so focused on entertaining the crowd during this particular game that they allowed the Generals to amass a twelve-point lead with just two minutes left to play. The Globetrotters played hard and fast in an attempt to even the score. Globetrotter Meadowlark Lemon's (1932–) shot to win the game hit the rim and missed as the game clock ran out. The Generals were as shocked as the Globetrotters, and the audience reacted badly. The team owner and coach later stated in an interview for *Sports Illustrated*, "Let me tell you, beating the Globetrotters is like shooting Santa Claus."

The Globetrotters were not without their critics, despite their success. During the struggle for civil rights in the 1950s and 1960s, some criticized the Globetrotters for offering a stereotypical depiction of African Americans. Their clownish behavior for the entertainment of white audiences, the critics argued, reinforced the idea that African Americans are not to be taken seriously. Many prominent civil rights activists defended the Globetrotters, however, pointing to the countless children of all races who have been influenced by their displays of athletics and sportsmanship.

The Globetrotters were the subject of a feature film in 1951, and a sequel in 1954 that starred actor Sidney Poitier (1927–). Two animated television series debuted in the 1970s that focused on the team and its adventures. Team members also starred in a live-action variety series. As of 2009, the Harlem Globetrotters remained popular and continued to play in exhibition matches around the world.

❖ ZOOT SUITS BECOME POPULAR AND CONTROVERSIAL

The zoot suit is a type of garment often associated with jazz culture. A zoot suit consists of a long jacket tailored with wide, padded shoulders and high-waisted pants that drape loosely down the leg, tapering tightly at the ankles. The suit is also known as the drape, which describes the way the amply cut suit hangs loosely on the wearer's body. As part of the "hipster" look, the suit is often accompanied by a wide-brimmed felt hat and a pocket watch on a chain. The suit appears oversized and exaggerated to many people with mainstream fashion tastes, and it is often made in bold or unusual colors. The earliest zoot suits were associated with African American culture and music, though they were later made famous by their connection to Latino culture.

The first zoot suits were created sometime in the late 1930s. American men at the time generally wore two-piece suits, consisting of a tailored jacket and matching pants. The need for a change in this fashion arose with the increasing popularity of jazz-influenced dances like the jitterbug and the lindy hop. The traditional two-piece suit was too constricting for dancers to perform the broad, athletic dance moves that accompanied jazz and swing music. The zoot suit expanded upon the basic two-piece suit design, allowing more freedom of movement and creating a striking shape that could easily identify its wearer as a "hepcat," or culturally sophisticated person. The suit also served as a rejection of traditional fashion rules, much

Bandleader Cab Calloway wears a white zoot suit.
© *Bettmann/Corbis*

like jazz and blues rejected traditional music conventions in favor of a new sound. The zoot suit's popularity spread quickly among African American men, especially those in the music scene. Perhaps the most famous zoot suit was worn by bandleader Cab Calloway in the 1943 film *Stormy Weather*.

Zoot suits became controversial during the early 1940s when the United States was involved in World War II (1939–45). Americans were being asked to cut back on their use of items like fabric and sugar so that these could be put toward the war effort. The zoot suit, which required much more fabric than a traditional suit, was criticized as anti-American by many. New fabric rationing rules issued in April 1942 essentially made the creation of zoot suits illegal.

The zoot suit was at the height of its popularity, however, and had become the garment of choice for many Mexican American men on the West Coast. Throughout 1942 and 1943, general anxiety among the population toward zoot suit wearers led to hundreds of Mexican Americans being arrested and harassed. Tensions continued to rise until June 3, 1943, when a mob of sailors on leave terrorized Mexican American neighborhoods in Los Angeles, beating and stripping down anyone they found wearing a zoot suit. The ensuing five days and nights of chaos are usually described in historical accounts as the Zoot Suit Riots. The event also sparked race riots in other cities across the country. This backlash against the zoot suit destroyed much of its popularity, though it experienced a minor resurgence decades later as part of a revival of swing culture.

❖ THE 1936 BERLIN OLYMPICS DISPROVE NAZI RACIAL MYTHS

The 1936 Olympic Games took place in Berlin, Germany, at a time when German leader Adolf Hitler (1889–1945) and the Nazi Party controlled the country. The Nazis believed in the racial superiority of the Aryan race, or non-Jewish white people. Their hopes of proving Aryan racial superiority to the world at the 1936 Olympics were dashed by the performance of African American track and field legend Jesse Owens (1913–80). Despite competing in a country that officially recognized blacks as undesirable and inferior, Owens won four gold medals and the adoration of German audiences. Many athletes besides Owens also drew attention to the failings of Nazi racial philosophies.

A Racially Charged Atmosphere in Germany

Hitler and his Nazi Party had assumed full control of the German government by 1936, offering Germans a promise that the country would return to the greatness it once exhibited. One of his guiding principles was the elimination of "undesirable" minorities, who he felt had a negative effect on the German economy and on its racial purity. Hitler believed that only members of the "Aryan race"—a term used to refer to early inhabitants of Germany, famously stereotyped as blonde-haired, blue-eyed Caucasians—should be allowed to participate in German society. This idea was disturbing to many, but the Olympic Committee had selected Berlin, Germany's capital city, as the location for the 1936 Summer Olympics back in 1931 before Hitler had come to power. Hitler decided that the Olympics would be a perfect venue for demonstrating the greatness of the German people.

Germany had already instituted laws discriminating against Jewish people and other minorities. It was no surprise when Hitler decreed that only Germans of Aryan lineage would be allowed to participate in the 1936 Olympic Games. The Nazi Party was already riding high on German boxer Max Schmeling's defeat of African American fighter Joe Louis (1914–81) less than two months before the start of the Games. They did not hesitate to

Snubbed by Hitler?

One of the most enduring myths about the 1936 Olympics is that after Jesse Owens won the 100-meter sprint, Hitler left the stadium in disgust and refused to congratulate the athlete. The story spread like wildfire through the American press, primarily in publications that did not actually have reporters in Berlin to witness the event. Owens himself initially denied the story, and several journalists who observed Owens's win stated that Hitler actually exchanged waves with the athlete. It is true that Hitler did not congratulate Owens personally or shake his hand; however, he did not congratulate any athletes after the first day of the Games. He had been criticized by Olympic officials for only shaking hands with German athletes that won on the first day. Rather than shake hands with all the winners—including any African Americans or Jews—Hitler decided instead to withhold his commendations. Hitler did leave the stadium on the first day prior to Cornelius Johnson and David Albritton receiving their medals for the high jump, but German officials insisted that his departure had already been scheduled prior to the event.

describe the match as a demonstration of Aryan superiority. Nazi officials were so determined to make a statement about their racial purity that they dropped Gretel Bergmann, a German Jewish athlete, from the German high jump team even though she held the German record in the sport. (German officials actually did allow a single half-Jewish German, Helene Mayer, to participate on the fencing team, though German journalists were restricted from mentioning her ancestry.)

Many in the United States felt that the country should boycott the Olympics as a statement against Hitler's policies and philosophies. Others argued that American athletes offered the best chance to prove Hitler's theories about Aryan superiority false. Ultimately, eighteen African Americans and two Jewish Americans traveled to Berlin as part of the U.S. Olympic team for the Games, which began on August 1, 1936. The most famous of these athletes was Jesse Owens, who was already a world record holder in the 220-yard sprint and the long jump.

African American Athletes Prove the Nazis Wrong

Athletes from forty-nine countries gathered in Berlin for the 1936 Olympics. Hitler had ordered that the city be made presentable for foreign visitors, which meant the removal of anti-Jewish signs and the arrest of several hundred Jews to keep them from protesting or otherwise communicating with outside journalists. On the first day of competition, African American high jumpers Cornelius Johnson (1913–46) and David Albritton (1913–94) won gold and silver medals, respectively, for the United States, striking the first blow against Nazi claims of racial superiority.

On the second day of competition, Owens won the gold medal in the 100-meter sprint, matching the world record even though he was running on a muddy track. Nazi officials were surely displeased, but the crowd of over one hundred thousand German spectators at the stadium erupted in celebration at Owens's win. Owens went on to win gold medals in the 200-meter sprint and the long jump, and was part of the winning 400-meter relay team.

In all, the United States team won fifty-six medals, second only to Germany's medal count of eighty-nine. African Americans made up less than six percent of the U.S. Olympic team, but won twenty-five percent of the team's medals. Jewish athletes from Eastern Europe had also won many medals, completely discrediting Hitler's beliefs in a superior Aryan race. The cool response Owens and other African American Olympic athletes received from the German government was hardly less disappointing than the response of their own government. Owens, the American hero of the Games, never received any congratulations from President Franklin Roosevelt (1882–1945). He was not even invited to the White House in recognition of his accomplishments until 1956, twenty years later.

American runner Jesse Owens competes with other runners in the 100-meter finals in the 1936 Olympics in Berlin. Owens won the gold medal in the event, eventually winning four. His overwhelming success helped to disprove Nazi beliefs in the racial superiority of German Aryans. *Popperfoto/Getty Images*

❖ BASEBALL AND FOOTBALL ARE INTEGRATED

African American athletes like track-and-field star Jesse Owens and boxer Joe Louis dominated their respective sports as world champions in the 1930s. They were champions, however, in individual sports, as opposed to team sports. Two of the team sports most closely associated with American life—football and baseball—had taken steps backward in terms of openness and integration during this same time period. The professional leagues controlling these sports held to an unspoken agreement to keep African Americans out of their organizations. This discrimination began to dissolve after World War II, leading to the integration of both sports by the late 1940s.

The Major Leagues and the Negro Leagues

The ban on African Americans in baseball occurred during the last decades of the nineteenth century. The game became established as a major pastime and spectator sport at a time when many parts of the country began to enforce segregation laws that kept blacks and whites apart in all areas of life. Baseball followed suit with this discrimination. The few African Americans who had established careers in the sport's early days were shut out according to a "gentlemen's agreement" between team managers and league officials. One notable exception took place in 1916, when Jimmy Claxton—a mixed-heritage pitcher with African American and Native American ancestry—entered the major leagues by hiding his black heritage. He pitched less than three innings of a single game for the Oakland Oaks; within a week his secret was revealed, and he was fired.

A judge named Kenesaw Mountain Landis (1866–1944) was appointed the first commissioner in charge of the major leagues in 1920. Landis was known for maintaining tight control over both the American and National leagues, and he actively resisted any efforts to integrate the sport with African American players. Some of those who resisted integration argued that the races should be kept separate in all aspects of life, including sports. Others simply believed that integrating major league baseball would spell the end of the profitable Negro Leagues, and would ultimately provide fewer opportunities for African Americans.

Landis passed away in 1944, and was replaced as baseball commissioner by Albert "Happy" Chandler (1898–1991), a governor and senator from Kentucky. Chandler was much more open to the possibility of integration. Most of the team managers still favored segregation, but two—Branch Rickey (1881–1965) and Bill Veeck (1914–86)—supported integration. Rickey signed African American player Jackie Robinson (1919–72) to a major league contract that led to his first appearance as a Brooklyn Dodger in April 1947. Veeck signed another black player, Larry Doby (1923–2003),

Branch Rickey speaks with Jackie Robinson as he signs his contract with the Brooklyn Dodgers for the 1948 season. Jackie Robinson integrated major league baseball. *Mark Rucker/Transcendental Graphics/Getty Images*

who debuted as a major leaguer three months after Robinson. Other teams quickly followed suit, spurred on by the outstanding performances of Robinson and Doby. Within five years, the Negro Leagues had all but disappeared, and whites-only minor leagues were limited to areas of the deep South. The final whites-only league had vanished by 1961.

The National Football League Fumbles, Then Recovers

In the 1920s, professional football was not quite as tightly segregated as baseball. The first professional football organization was the American Professional Football Association (APFA), which eventually changed its name to the National Football League (NFL). The league initially featured several African American players and coaches. This changed after George Preston Marshall (1896–1969) took over as manager of the Boston Braves (later known as the Washington Redskins) in 1932. He pressured other managers to exclude African Americans from the league. He was successful, and by 1934 black players had been driven out of the NFL completely.

Public sentiment regarding African American athletes shifted after World War II. Many African Americans had fought and died in the service of their country, and many sports fans and professionals were more willing to accept black participation in mainstream society. The integration of the NFL began, not within the league itself, but from pressure outside the

The Other First African American Pro Baseball Player

Long before Jackie Robinson and the integration of modern baseball, a man named Bud Fowler (1858–1913) was the first known African American professional baseball player. Fowler grew up in Cooperstown, New York, a town traditionally recognized as the birthplace of baseball. Fowler's name appears in recorded statistics as early as 1878 for a minor league team called the Lynn Live Oaks. He went on to play with teams in more than twenty states, as well as Canada, in more than a dozen professional baseball leagues. His career path was not easy; in 1881, he played for the Maple Leafs, an Ontario team, but was cut before the season was over due to complaints about his race from other members of the team. Fowler received notable mentions in *Sporting Life* magazine, including one in 1885 that suggested he was one of the best second basemen in the United States at the time. He was a solid hitter, an excellent base stealer,

Bud Fowler. *Transcendental Graphics/Getty Images*

and even a serviceable pitcher. In 1887, his position with the Binghamton Bingoes ended much like his earlier stint as a Maple Leaf when his own teammates drove him out. It is Fowler who is credited with the invention of shin guards, which he used to protect himself against deliberately vicious slides by opposing players. He continued to move from team to team until opportunities for African Americans in the pro leagues vanished completely, and he finished his career as a player for a Negro League team in 1904.

league. An NFL team called the Cleveland Rams moved to Los Angeles in 1946, and their owner, Dan Reeves, wanted to sign a contract with the Los Angeles Memorial Coliseum to host their games. The committee in charge of the stadium would only agree to the contract if the Rams agreed to sign an African American player to their team. Kenny Washington (1918–71) became the first African American to enter the NFL after the unofficial twelve-year ban on black players. His former teammate Woody Strode (1914–94) was also signed to the Rams, since the team management felt that he would be isolated if he remained the only African American on the

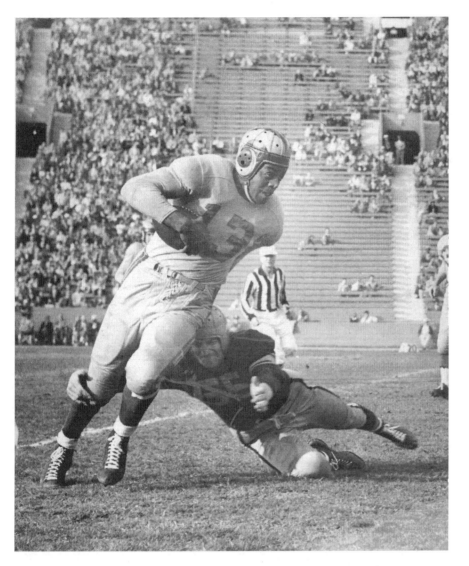

Kenny Washington breaks a tackle in a 1948 football game in Los Angeles. Washington broke a 12-year ban on African American players in the NFL when he signed with the Los Angeles Rams in 1946. *NFL/NFL*

team. They often faced segregation in hotels and restaurants as they traveled, but they also drew many African American fans to each game. Compared to major league baseball, segregation in the NFL began much later and ended a year before Jackie Robinson debuted as a Brooklyn Dodger.

The All-America Football Conference (AAFC) was another professional football organization that became part of the NFL in 1949. The AAFC was even more successful at integrating African American players than the NFL was in its early years. The most successful team of the AAFC was the Cleveland Browns, who signed African American players Bill Willis (1921–2007) and Marion Motley (1920–99) in 1946. The Browns dominated the AAFC for all four years that the league existed, and drew crowds greater than many NFL teams. By 1949, six of the eight teams in the AAFC had signed African American players.

Full integration was slower to come to the NFL, despite the early signing of Washington and Strode. It took thirteen additional years before every other team—minus one—had added African American players to their rosters. That lone holdout was the Washington Redskins, owned by Marshall. Marshall was adamant about keeping African Americans off his team. He was forced to change this policy in 1961. The United States Department of the Interior—who held ownership of D.C. Stadium, which the Redskins planned to use as their home field—told Marshall that the team could not use the stadium unless it ended its discriminatory policies. The Redskins finally integrated with four African American players in 1962.

❖ PAUL ROBESON ENDURES INVESTIGATION FOR COMMUNISM

Paul Robeson (1898–1976) achieved success on so many fronts that he is difficult to classify. He was twice an All-American football player at Rutgers University, where he was the only African American student in attendance at the time. Robeson was also class valedictorian and went on to earn a law degree at Columbia. After college, he gained fame as both a stage actor and as a singer, appearing on Broadway and in films. Robeson used his fame and influence to fight for the rights of the underprivileged of all ethnicities.

It was his work as an activist that brought him attention from the U.S. government. Robeson frequently traveled around the world, visiting the Soviet Union first in 1934. Many Americans were wary of the Soviet Union and its leader, Joseph Stalin (1879–1953). He claimed to be a Communist, in favor of redistributing wealth equally among all members of society. In practice, however, his actions seemed to be more focused on silencing his critics and maintaining power for himself than providing for his citizens.

Robeson supported the basic ideas of socialism, in which the wealthiest members of a society are responsible for helping to provide the essentials for the poorest members. For that reason, he applauded the Soviet Union's efforts to collectively share the country's resources like harvested crops among all its citizens. He also praised the fact that the country made racial discrimination illegal in its constitution—something the United States had yet to do. Robeson himself was never a member of the Communist Party in the United States or elsewhere. His main concerns were the welfare of the oppressed and the opposition to fascism, a political system marked by intense national pride and the rejection of equal rights for all citizens. At the time, Germany, Italy, and Spain were all ruled by fascist leaders.

Paul Robeson responds to questioning by a government committee investigating him as a possible Communist on May 31, 1946. *AP Images*

The spread of communism was feared in the United States at least as much as the spread of fascism. Robeson's praise of many aspects of Stalin's Soviet Union and association with known Communists caused him to be viewed as a threat by some American government officials. He was called to testify before a committee investigating activities they classified as "un-American" in 1946. Robeson pointed out that Americans were free to believe in anything they wanted, including communism, but he also assured the committee that he was not a member of the Communist Party.

Robeson was unafraid to criticize the leaders of his own country. He pointed out the lingering evils of slavery, as well as the ongoing evils of segregation and lynching. He called for America's leaders to right these wrongs. Suspicions of his Communist leanings allowed politicians to dismiss his criticisms as being part of a Communist plot to destroy the United States. Many in the civil rights movement denounced Robeson so that they would not also be labeled as Communist sympathizers.

Robeson visited the Soviet Union again in 1949, after which he held a concert in Peekskill, New York. The concert benefited a civil rights group that some suspected of being a Communist organization, and protestors began rioting after the event. Over one hundred of the concert-goers were beaten by the mob and by police who attacked the victims, claiming that

Stalin's Awful Secret

M any African American intellectuals of the 1920s and 1930s supported the ideals of the Soviet Union. They seemed to match well with the aims of civil rights activists, who also sought support for the working class and equal rights for all citizens. Soviet leader Joseph Stalin was often praised and defended by Robeson and others. Stalin seemed to support the basic ideas of socialism and equality for all on the surface. Yet, it was revealed three years after his death in 1953 that Stalin had terrorized his own people. He had imprisoned anyone who disagreed with his policies. Even worse, his attempts to collectivize agriculture in the 1930s—by requiring all farmers to pool their crops together for equal distribution among all citizens—had failed catastrophically, resulting in a famine that killed approximately ten million people. Robeson no longer defended Stalin's legacy in public after the terrible truth was revealed, but he remained devoted to the Soviet people and the ideals of their constitution.

they had provoked the conflict. The following year, Robeson was denied a passport by the State Department on the basis that his criticisms of the United States posed a threat to the safety of the nation.

Popular opinion against Robeson was so strong that his name was actually stricken from the historical sports records of the 1917 and 1918 All-American college football teams. In 1956, he agreed to testify before the House Committee on Un-American Activities, a group responsible for the blacklisting and intimidation of many celebrities suspected of having Communist sympathies. Robeson's purpose was to argue for the return of his passport, but the committee was only interested in trying to force Robeson to admit that he was a Communist. The committee members questioned the patriotism of Robeson and his friends. Robeson responded by calling the committee un-American. The hearing ended before Robeson was allowed to read his statement regarding his passport.

Two years later, in 1958, the Supreme Court ruled that denying a citizen the right to travel required a legal process. Robeson had received no such trial, and his passport was finally returned to him. Eventually, his name was restored to the rosters of the All-American college football teams of 1917 and 1918. He was finally inducted into the College Football Hall of Fame in 1995, nearly twenty years after his death.

RECIPES FROM THE FIRST SOUL FOOD COOKBOOK (1881)

Soul food was a uniquely African American contribution to American cuisine. People often refer to it by the term "Southern cooking" since it originated in the South and has strong ties to that region. Soul food has its origins in food prepared by African American slaves, who needed to make the most of their meager resources. Soul food, therefore, uses many of the foods that were available to slaves, such as chickens, pigs, peanuts, sweet potatoes, and collard greens. Some of the staple foods in soul food came from Africa, such as okra and watermelon.

The first soul food cookbook was created by former slave Abby Fisher. Fisher was born a slave in Mobile, Alabama. She made her way to San Francisco after the Civil War, where she became a very popular cook. Her food won prizes at county fairs. She won a diploma at the Sacramento State Fair in 1879 and medals for her pickles and jellies at the San Francisco Mechanics Institute Fair in 1880. The women Fisher worked for were so impressed with her food they convinced her to write a cookbook. Fisher was illiterate, so she dictated the cookbook to her employers. They, in turn, formed the Women's Cooperative Printing Office and put her recipes in print in 1881. *What Mrs. Fisher Knows about Old Southern Cooking: Soups, Pickles, Preserves, Etc.* was one of the first cookbooks written by an African American. The following recipes excerpted from Fisher's cookbook are examples of traditional Southern cooking, or what later became known as "soul food."

• •

BREAKFAST CORN BREAD

One tea-cup of rice boiled nice and soft, to one and a half tea-cupful of corn meal mixed together, then stir the whole until light; one teaspoonful of salt, one tablespoonful of lard or butter, three eggs, half tea-cup of sweet milk. The rice must be mixed into the meal while hot; can be baked either in muffin cups or a pan....

CHOW CHOW

Take one cabbage, a large one, and cut up fine. Put in a large jar or keg, and sprinkle over it thickly one pint of coarse salt. Let it remain in salt twelve hours, then scald the cut-up cabbage with one gallon of boiling vinegar. Cut up two gallons of cucumbers, green or pickled, and add to it; cut in pieces the size of the end of little finger. Then chop very fine two gallons more of cucumbers or pickles and add to the above. Seasonings: One pound of brown sugar, one tablespoonful of cayenne pepper, one tablespoonful of black pepper, two gallons of turmerick, six onions, chopped fine or grated. Then put it on to cook in a large porcelain kettle, with a slow fire, for twelve hours. Stir it occasionally to keep it from burning. You can add more pepper than is here given if you like it hot. . . .

SWEET WATERMELON RIND PICKLES

Take the melon rind and scrape all the meat from the inside, and then carefully slice all the outside of rind from the white part of the rind, then lay or cover the white part over with salt. It will have to remain under salt for one week before pickling; the rind will keep in salt from year to year. When you want to pickle it, take it from the salt and put into clear water, change the water three times a day—must be changed say every four hours—then take the rind from water and dry it with a clean cloth. Have your vinegar boiling, and put the rind into it and let it scald four minutes, then take it off the fire and let it lay in vinegar four days; then take it from the vinegar, drain, and sprinkle sugar thickly over it and let it remain so one day. To make syrup, take the syrup from the rind and add eight pounds more sugar to it, and put to boil; boil till a thick and clear syrup. Weigh ten pounds of rind to twelve pounds of sugar; cover the rind with four pounds of it and make the syrup with the remaining eight pounds. While the syrup is cooking add one teacupfull of white ginger root and the peel of three lemons. When the syrup is cooked, then put the rind into the boiling syrup, and let it cook till you can pass a fork through it with ease, then it is done. When cooled put in jar or bottles with one pint of vinegar to one quart of syrup, thus the pickle is made. See that they be well covered with vinegar and syrup as directed. . . .

TERRAPIN STEW

Terrapin

A type of turtle

Always have the female **terrapins,** and put them alive in boiling water. Let them remain for fifteen minutes and then take the shells from them, being careful not to break the galls. Clean the entrails from the meat, and scrape the black skin from the feet with a knife. Half a dozen terrapins will serve twelve persons. After thoroughly cleaning the terrapins, lay them in clear water for ten minutes, and then put them in a kettle to stew with half a pint of water, and stew very slowly for about three hours. Boil half a dozen eggs hard, and rub the yolks to a powder. Then add half a pound of best butter to the eggs and beat together until it becomes a cream. To this cream add one pint of sherry wine and mix it well. Then add this preparation to the stew very gradually, stirring well, so as to thoroughly mix it in. While the stew is cooking, mix a teaspoonful of the best mustard to a tablespoonful of wine and put in. Slice one lemon and add to stew just before dishing it up for table. Three hours is sufficient time to cook it. You had better put the wine in the stew and not mix it with the eggs, for fear you may not mix it in right and that there may be no mistake. With the above directions you have a perfect stew. A teacupful of sweet cream is an improvement, if you like it: also a dozen grains of allspice. Salt and pepper to taste. . . .

A SOUTHERN REMEDY FOR INVALIDS

Take one ounce of cardamom seed, one ounce of Peruvian bark bruised, two ounces of Gentian root bruised, half ounce of dry orange peel, one ounce of aloes, and put the whole into half a gallon of best whiskey or brandy; let it come to a boil, then strain or filter it through a fine cloth or filtering paper.

Dose half wineglassfull three times a day before meals. Will strengthen and produce an appetite....

CHICKEN GUMBO

Salt and pepper chicken before frying it. Take a chicken, separating it from all the joints and breaking the bones, fry the chicken in one and a half tablespoonful of lard or butter. First well mix the chicken in dry flour, then let the fat be hot, put chicken to fry until brown; don't burn the chicken. After fried, put it on in soup kettle with half a gallon of hot water, one and a half quarts of green ochre [okra] cut into thin pieces, throwing the end away, and let the whole boil to three pints; season with pepper and salt. Chop half of an ordinary sized onion fine, and fry it with chicken: chilli pepper chopped fine if added is nice when liked.

◈ JACK JOHNSON'S POST-FIGHT COMMENTS (1910)

Boxer Jack Johnson became the first African American heavyweight champion after defeating white boxer Tommy Burns in 1908. He was a brash, confident fighter who lived an extravagant lifestyle that included marriages to white women. The vast majority of white Americans did not like the fact that Johnson was the champion, and began calling for "The Great White Hope" to take back the heavyweight title. The "Hope" referred to the previous heavyweight champion, James Jeffries, who had retired in 1905 without fighting Johnson. Jeffries came out of retirement to fight Johnson in a heavily publicized fight in Reno, Nevada, on July 4, 1910. Johnson was an underdog to the undefeated Jeffries, but beat him easily in fifteen rounds.

Johnson's comments after the fight are captured in the following *New York Times* article. They reveal the confident nature of Johnson that had so angered the white public. The comments would not be unusual in the modern world of boxing, but the climate of the nineteenth century made such brashness taboo for a black man of the time. The article also includes comments from the fight's promoter and referee that describe the fight from his perspective.

• •

RENO, July 4. —Jack Johnson made the following statement after the fight:

"I won from Mr. Jeffries because I outclassed him in every department of the fighting game. Before I entered the ring I was certain I would be the victor. I never changed my mind at any time.

"Jeffries's blows had no steam behind them. So, how could he hope to defeat me? With the exception of a slight cut on my lower lip, which was really caused by an old wound being struck, I am unmarked. I heard people at the ringside remark about body blows being inflicted upon me. I do not recall a single punch in the body that caused me any discomfort. I am in shape to battle again tomorrow if it were necessary.

"One thing I must give Jeffries credit for is the game battle he made. He came back at me with the heart of a true fighter. No man can say he did not do his best.

"I believe we both fought fairly. There was nothing said between us which was rough. He joked me and I joked him. I told him I knew he was a bear but I was a gorilla and would defeat him.

"For the next few weeks I shall play in vaudeville. Then I shall go to my home in Chicago to rest. I do not think I shall fight for several months, because I do not know a man now who could give me a good battle. No attention will be paid to Sam Langford's challenges by me. I do not consider he could give me a fight that would draw."

Johnson's first words after Jeffries went down were:

"I could have fought for two hours longer. It was easy. Where is my lucky bathrobe? I'm going to give one of my gloves to Jeffries and the other to Corbett. I guess Jeff won't be so grouchy now. Somebody wire to my mother. I wish it was some longer. I was having lots of fun. Not one blow hurt me. He can't hit. He won't forget two punches I landed on him. He was only half the trouble Burns was."

Tex Rickard, the referee and promoter of the fight, said:

"Jack Johnson is the most wonderful fighter that ever pulled on a glove. He won as he pleased from Jeff and was never in danger. I could not help but feel sorry for the big white man as he fell beneath the champion's blows. It was the most pitiable fight I ever saw. As a matter of fact, I thought away down in my heart that Jeffries would be the winner of the fight.

"The fight was won and lost when Jeffries went through the first time. This is official. The other knockdown does not count. It was this way:

"Jeffries was brought to his knees and as he arose, dazed, Johnson hit him with a succession of lefts that sent him through the ropes. As he lay there several of his seconds caught hold of him and helped him to his feet. Under the rules of the game, which I have read thoroughly, while certain people were saying that I would not referee the fight, this disqualified Jeffries, and Johnson was the winner.

"I thought the seconds were going to carry Jeffries to his corner. Instead they shoved him into the ring again to be beaten further, while I was doing all I could during the confusion to stop the fight.

"Jeffries could not hit Johnson and Johnson could hit Jeffries whenever he pleased. Jeffries was not as good as the last time he fought."

◈ TESTIMONY OF PAUL ROBESON BEFORE THE HOUSE COMMITTEE ON UN-AMERICAN ACTIVITIES (1956)

Respected actor, singer, and activist Paul Robeson had his U.S. passport revoked in 1950 due to his criticism of U.S. "imperialism" and his open praise of the Soviet Union. He was suspected of being a Communist, although in reality he was not. The Soviet Union was a Communist country at this time, and the United States was very fearful that the Soviet Union would attempt to spread communism to other countries. The fear of the spread of communism was so powerful that any American suspected of being a Communist could be blackballed, or kept from working. Robeson testified before the House Committee on Un-American Activities in 1956 in the hopes of having his passport returned.

The House Committee on Un-American Activities was an investigative committee of the U.S. House of Representatives charged with the task of rooting out subversive activity, in particular Communist activity in the United States. The committee was notorious for conducting Communist "witch hunts" during the 1950s in which the reputations of many innocent people were damaged by false allegations of communism. The following excerpt from the testimony of Robeson before the committee shows the harsh questioning of committee members as they try to get Robeson to confess that he is a Communist. Robeson repeatedly stresses that his primary concern is the mistreatment of African Americans and the failure of the United States government to protect them. Among the questioners are Richard Arens, director of the committee; Gordon Scherer, congressman from Ohio; and Bernard Kearney, congressman from New York. "The Chairman" refers to the chairman of the committee, Francis Walter, who was a congressman from Pennsylvania.

· ·

The Chairman: The Committee will be in order. This morning the Committee resumes its series of hearings on the vital issue of the use of American passports as travel documents in furtherance of the objectives of the Communist conspiracy. . . .

Mr. Arens: Now, during the course of the process in which you were applying for this passport, in July of 1954, were you requested to submit a non-Communist **affidavit**?

Mr. Robeson: We had a long discussion—with my counsel, who is in the room, Mr. [Leonard B.] Boudin—with the State Department, about just such an affidavit and I was very precise not only in the application but with the State Department, headed by Mr. Henderson and Mr. McLeod, that under no conditions would I think of signing any such affidavit, that it is a complete contradiction of the rights of American citizens.

Affidavit
Sworn written statement

Mr. Arens: Did you comply with the requests?

Mr. Robeson: I certainly did not and I will not.

Mr. Arens: Are you now a member of the Communist Party?

Mr. Robeson: Oh please, please, please.

Mr. Scherer: Please answer, will you, Mr. Robeson?

Mr. Robeson: What is the Communist Party? What do you mean by that?

Mr. Scherer: I ask that you direct the witness to answer the question.

Mr. Robeson: What do you mean by the Communist Party? As far as I know it is a legal party like the Republican Party and the Democratic Party. Do you mean a party of people who have sacrificed for my people, and for all Americans and workers, that they can live in dignity? Do you mean that party?

Mr. Arens: Are you now a member of the Communist Party?

Mr. Robeson: Would you like to come to the ballot box when I vote and take out the ballot and see? . . . Could I ask whether this is legal.

The Chairman: This is legal. This is not only legal but usual. By a unanimous vote, this Committee has been instructed to perform this very distasteful task.

Mr. Robeson: To whom am I talking?

The Chairman: You are speaking to the Chairman of this Committee.

Mr. Robeson: Mr. Walter?

The Chairman: Yes.

Mr. Robeson: The Pennsylvania Walter?

The Chairman: That is right.

Mr. Robeson: Representative of the steelworkers?

The Chairman: That is right.

Mr. Robeson: Of the coal-mining workers and not United States Steel, by any chance? A great patriot.

The Chairman: That is right.

Mr. Robeson: You are the author of all of the bills that are going to keep all kinds of decent people out of the country.

The Chairman: No, only your kind.

Mr. Robeson: Colored people like myself, from the West Indies and all kinds. And just the Teutonic Anglo-Saxon stock that you would let come in.

The Chairman: We are trying to make it easier to get rid of your kind, too.

Mr. Robeson: You do not want any colored people to come in?

The Chairman: Proceed. . . .

Mr. Robeson: Could I say that the reason that I am here today, you know, from the mouth of the State Department itself, is because I should not be allowed to travel because I have struggled for years for the independence of the colonial peoples of Africa, and for many years I have so labored and I can say modestly that my name is very much honored … all over Africa in my struggles for their independence. That is the kind of independence like Sukarno got in Indonesia. Unless we are double-talking, then these efforts in the interest of Africa would be in the same context. The other reason that I am here today, again from the State Department and from the court record of the court of appeals, that when I am abroad I speak out against the injustices against the Negro people of this land. I sent a message to the Bandung Conference and so forth. That is why I am here. This is the basis and I am not being tried for whether I am a Communist, I am being tried for fighting for the rights of my people who are still second-class citizens in this United States of America. My mother was born in your state, Mr. Walter, and my mother was a Quaker, and my ancestors in the time of Washington baked bread for George Washington's troops when they crossed the Delaware, and my own father was a slave. I stand here struggling for the rights of my people to be full citizens in this country and they are not. They are not in Mississippi and they are not in Montgomery, Alabama, and they are not in Washington, and they are nowhere, and that is why I am here today. You want to shut up every Negro who has the courage to stand up and fight for the rights of his people, for the rights of workers and I have been on many a picket line for the steelworkers too. And that is why I am here today. . . .

Mr. Arens: Did you make a trip to Europe in 1949 and to the Soviet Union?

Mr. Robeson: Yes, I made a trip to England and I sang.

Mr. Arens: Where did you go?

Mr. Robeson: I went first to England, where I was with the Philadelphia Orchestra, one of two American groups which was invited to England. I did a long concert tour in England and Denmark and Sweden and I also sang for the Soviet people, one of the finest musical audiences in the world. Will you read what the *Porgy and Bess* people said? They never heard such applause in their lives, and one of the most musical peoples in the world, and the great composers and great musicians, very cultured people, and Tolstoy, and—

The Chairman: We know all of that.

Mr. Robeson: They have helped our culture and we can learn a lot.

Mr. Arens: Did you go to Paris on that trip?

Mr. Robeson: I went to Paris.

Mr. Arens: And while you were in Paris, did you tell an audience there that the American Negro would never go to war against the Soviet government?

Mr. Robeson: May I say that is slightly out of context? May I explain to you what I did say? I remember the speech very well, and the night before in London, and do not take the newspaper, take me, I made the speech, gentlemen, Mr. So and So. It happened that the night before in London before I went to Paris, and will you please listen?

Mr. Arens: We are listening.

Mr. Robeson: That 2,000 students from various parts of the colonial world, students who since then have become very important in their governments and in places like Indonesia and India, and in many parts of Africa; 2,000 students asked me and Dr. [Y. M.] Dadoo, a leader of the Indian people in South Africa, when we addressed this conference, and remember I was speaking to a peace conference, they asked me and Mr. Dadoo to say there that they were struggling for peace, that they did not want war against anybody. It was 2,000 students who came from populations that would range to six or seven hundred million people.

Mr. Kearney: Do you know anybody who wants war?

Mr. Robeson: They asked me to say in their name that they did not want war. That is what I said. There is no part of my speech made in Paris which says fifteen million American Negroes would do anything. I said it was my feeling that the American people would struggle for peace and that has since been underscored by the President of these United States. Now, in passing, I said—

Mr. Kearney: Do you know of any people who want war?

Mr. Robeson: Listen to me, I said it was unthinkable to me that any people would take up arms in the name of an Eastland to go against anybody, and gentlemen, I still say that. What should happen would be that this United States Government should go down to Mississippi and protect my people. That is what should happen.

The Chairman: Did you say what was attributed to you?

Mr. Robeson: I did not say it in that context.

Mr. Arens: I lay before you a document containing an article, "I Am Looking for Full Freedom," by Paul Robeson, in a publication called the *Worker*, dated July 3, 1949. [reading from document] "At the Paris Conference I said it was unthinkable that the Negro people of America or elsewhere in the world could be drawn into war with the Soviet Union."

Mr. Robeson: Is that saying the Negro people would *do* anything? I said it is unthinkable. I did not say it there [in Paris]. I said that in the *Worker*.

Mr. Arens: [reading from document] "I repeat it with hundredfold emphasis: they will not." Did you say that?

Mr. Robeson: I said that in America. And, gentlemen, they have not yet done so, and it is quite clear that no Americans or no people in the world probably, are going to war with the Soviet Union, so I was rather prophetic, was I not?

Mr. Arens: On that trip to Europe, did you go to Stockholm?

Mr. Robeson: I certainly did and I understand that some people in the American Embassy tried to break up my concert, and they were not successful.

Mr. Arens: While you were in Stockholm, did you make a little speech?

Mr. Robeson: I made all kinds of speeches; yes.

Mr. Arens: Let me read you a quotation.

Mr. Robeson: Let me listen.

Mr. Arens: Do so, please.

Mr. Robeson: I am a lawyer.

Mr. Kearney: It would be a revelation if you would listen to counsel.

Mr. Robeson: In good company, I usually listen, but you know people wander around in such fancy places.... Would you please let me read my statement at some point?

The Chairman: We will consider your statement.

Mr. Arens: [reading from document] "I do not hesitate one second to state clearly and unmistakably: I belong to the American resistance movement which fights against American imperialism, just as the resistance movement fought against Hitler."

Mr. Robeson: Just like Frederick Douglass and Harriet Tubman were underground railroaders, and fighting for our freedom; you bet your life.

The Chairman: I am going to have to insist that you listen to these questions.

Mr. Robeson: I am listening.

Mr. Arens: [reading from document] "If the American warmongers fancy that they could win America's millions of Negroes for a war against those countries (i.e., the Soviet Union and the peoples' democracies) then they ought to understand that this will never be the case. Why should the Negroes ever fight against the only nations of the world where racial discrimination is prohibited, and where the people can live freely? Never! I can assure you, they will never fight against either the Soviet Union or the peoples' democracies." Did you make that statement?

Mr. Robeson: I do not remember that. But what is perfectly clear today is that 900 million other colored people have told you that *they* will not, is that not so? Four hundred million in India and millions everywhere have told you precisely that the colored people are not going to die for anybody and they are going to die for their independence. We are dealing not with fifteen million colored people, we are dealing with hundreds of millions.

Mr. Kearney: The witness has answered the question and he does not have to make a speech. . . .

Mr. Robeson: I would say in Russia I felt for the first time like a full human being, and no colored prejudice like in Mississippi and no colored prejudice like in Washington and it was the first time I felt like a human being, where I did not feel the pressure of colored as I feel in this committee today.

Mr. Scherer: Why do you not stay in Russia?

Mr. Robeson: Because my father was a slave, and my people died to build this country, and I am going to stay here and have a part of it just like you. And no Fascist-minded people will drive me from it. Is that clear? I am for peace with the Soviet Union and I am for peace with China, and I am not for peace or friendship with the Fascist Franco, and I am not for peace with Fascist Nazi Germans. I am for peace with decent people.

Mr. Scherer: The reason you are here is because you are promoting the Communist cause in the country.

Mr. Robeson: I am here because I am opposing the neo-Fascist cause which I see arising in these committees. You are like the Alien [and] Sedition Act, and Jefferson could be sitting here, and Frederick Douglass could be sitting here and Eugene Debs could be here. . . .

The Chairman: Now, what prejudice are you talking about? You were graduated from Rutgers and you were graduated from the University of Pennsylvania. I remember seeing you play football at Lehigh. . . .

Mr. Robeson: Just a moment. This is something that I challenge very deeply, and very sincerely, the fact that the success of a few Negroes, including myself or Jackie Robinson can make up—and here is a study from Columbia University— for $700 a year for thousands of Negro families in the South. My father was a slave, and I have cousins who are sharecroppers and I do not see my success in terms of myself. That is the reason, my own success has not meant what it should mean. I have sacrificed literally hundreds of thousands, if not millions, of dollars for what I believe in. . . .

Mr. Arens: Now I would invite your attention, if you please, to the *Daily Worker* of June 29, 1949, with reference to a get-together with you and Ben Davis. Do you know Ben Davis?

Mr. Robeson: One of my dearest friends, one of the finest Americans you can imagine, born of a fine family, who went to Amherst and was a great man.

The Chairman: The answer is "Yes"?

Mr. Robeson: And a very great friend and nothing could make me prouder than to know him.

The Chairman: That answers the question.

Laud

Praise

Mr. Arens: Did I understand you to **laud** his patriotism?

Mr. Robeson: I say that he is as patriotic an American as there can be, and you gentlemen belong with the Alien and Sedition Acts, and you are the nonpatriots, and you are the un-Americans and you ought to be ashamed of yourselves.

The Chairman: Just a minute, the hearing is now adjourned.

Mr. Robeson: I should think it would be.

The Chairman: I have endured all of this that I can.

Mr. Robeson: Can I read my statement?

The Chairman: No, you cannot read it. The meeting is adjourned.

Mr. Robeson: I think it should be, and you should adjourn this forever, that is what I would say. . . .

Research and Activity Ideas

1. Jackie Robinson and Satchel Paige were two Negro League baseball players who were successful in the major leagues. Many other Negro League players never made the transition to the major leagues after the integration of major league baseball. Select a famous Negro League player from the 1930s and 1940s, such as Buck Leonard, "Cool Papa" Bell, Oscar Charleston, or Josh Gibson. Write a report focusing on the player's career. Were his accomplishments comparable to those of major league players? How did the integration of baseball affect his career?

2. Read Malcolm X's famous description of conking from his *Autobiography of Malcolm X*. In it, he describes the painful process of straightening his hair to match prevailing standards of attractiveness that led many African Americans to try to look more "white." Using your library and the Internet, collect at least three other firsthand descriptions by African Americans of cosmetic products or procedures they used to change the natural appearance of their hair or skin. Make sure your accounts come from the period between 1865 and 1965. Share your accounts with classmates, and discuss why such cosmetic changes were popular in the African American community.

3. Edna Lewis and Sylvia Woods are famous for using their Southern roots as inspiration for their cooking. With a small group of classmates, create a menu for a soul food meal, including an appetizer, main dish, side items, and dessert. Each student should contribute to a part of the meal. For your dish, research the ingredients and preparation, and share what you learned with your classmates. Be sure to talk about where the ingredients originated, and how they came to be a part of soul food cooking.

4. The first two African American heavyweight champions of the world, Jack Johnson and Joe Louis, were received by American sports fans in dramatically different ways. There are many different reasons for this, including the boxers' differing personalities, American racial attitudes, and even the unfolding of global conflicts. Write a short essay comparing and contrasting the careers of the two men, explaining how and why their careers developed the way they did.

5. During the 1930s and 1940s, zoot suits became popular with African Americans and Latinos as a reaction against more traditional styles of dress, and also as a way of displaying a wearer's own style and tastes to others. Find pictures of zoot suits in resources in the library and on

the Internet, and create a photo essay on the history of the zoot suit using printed copies or photocopies of the photos you find. Start with the earliest examples you can find and work forward. Include a two- or three-sentence caption with each photo.

6. Nearly every type of popular American dance form since the 1890s has been influenced by African American cultural traditions. Using your library, the Internet, or other available resources, research one of these early dances, such as the cakewalk or the Charleston. Write a report describing the history and popularity of the dance, and then demonstrate how to perform the dance, step by step, for your classmates.

For More Information

BOOKS

Bak, Richard. *Joe Louis: The Great Black Hope.* New York: Da Capo Press, 1998.

Biracree, Tom. *Althea Gibson.* Los Angeles: Holloway House Publishing, 1990.

Cook, Theodore Andrea. *The Fourth Olympiad; Being the Official Report of the Olympic Games of 1908.* London: The British Olympic Association, 1909.

Edmondson, Jacqueline. *Jesse Owens: A Biography.* Westport, CT: Greenwood Publishing Group, 2007.

Gray, Frances Clayton, and Yanick Rice Lamb. *Born to Win: The Authorized Biography of Althea Gibson.* Hoboken, NJ: John Wiley & Sons, 2004.

Haber, Barbara. *From Hardtack to Home Fries: An Uncommon History of American Cooks and Meals.* New York: Simon and Schuster, 2002.

Harris, Wendy Beech. "The Queen and King of Soul Food," in *Against All Odds: Ten Entrepreneurs Who Followed Their Hearts and Found Success.* New York: John Wiley & Sons, 2001.

Kirkham, Pat. *Women Designers in the USA, 1900–2000: Diversity and Difference.* New Haven, CT: Yale University Press, 2002.

Opie, Frederick Douglass. *Hog & Hominy: Soul Food from Africa to America.* New York: Columbia University Press, 2008.

Paige, Satchel, and David Lipman. *Maybe I'll Pitch Forever: A Great Baseball Player Tells the Hilarious Story Behind the Legend.* Lincoln: University of Nebraska Press, 1993.

Roberts, Randy. *Papa Jack: Jack Johnson and the Era of White Hopes.* New York: Simon and Schuster, 1985.

Ross, Charles K. *Outside the Lines: African Americans and the Integration of the National Football League.* New York: New York University Press, 2001.

Schaap, Jeremy. *Triumph: The Untold Story of Jesse Owens and Hitler's Olympics.* New York: Houghton Mifflin, 2007.

Shropshire, Kenneth L. *In Black and White: Race and Sports in America.* New York: New York University Press, 1996.

White, Shane, and Graham White. *Stylin': African American Expressive Culture from Its Beginnings to the Zoot Suit.* Ithaca, NY: Cornell University Press, 1998.

PERIODICALS

Bennett, Lerone, Jr. "Jack Johnson and the Great White Hope." *Ebony,* vol. 60, no. 3 (January 2005): 110–116.

Crothers, Tim. "The General Whose Army Never Wins." *Sports Illustrated,* vol. 82, no. 7 (February 20, 1995): 174–184.

Jones, Thomas B. "Caucasians Only: Solomon Hughes, the PGA, and the 1948 St. Paul Open Golf Tournament." *Minnesota History,* vol. 58, no. 8 (Winter 2003–2004): 383–393.

Major, Gerri. "Dean of American Designers." *Ebony,* vol. 22, no. 2 (December 1966): 137–142.

"Negro Runner Dead; John B. Taylor, Quarter Miler, Victim of Typhoid Pneumonia." *The New York Times* (December 3, 1908): 10.

WEB SITES

"The Fight of the Century." *Unforgivable Blackness: A Film Directed by Ken Burns.* http://www.pbs.org/unforgivableblackness/fight/ (accessed on January 5, 2010).

"Fowler: A 19th-Century Baseball Pioneer." The Official Web Site of Minor League Baseball. http://www.minorleaguebaseball.com/news/article.jsp?ymd= 20060208&content_id;=41022&vkey=news_milb&fext=.jsp (accessed on January 5, 2010).

"Isaac B. Murphy." The National Museum of Racing and Hall of Fame Web site. http://www.racingmuseum.org/hall/jockey.asp?ID=205 (accessed on January 5, 2010).

"Joe Louis (Barrow), Sergeant, United States Army." Arlington National Cemetery Web site. http://www.arlingtoncemetery.net/joelouis.htm (accessed on January 5, 2010).

"The Nazi Olympics (August 1936)." The Jewish Virtual Library. http://www.jewishvirtuallibrary.org/jsource/Holocaust/olympics.html (accessed on January 5, 2010).

"'You Are the Un-Americans, and You Ought to be Ashamed of Yourselves': Paul Robeson Appears Before HUAC." History Matters. http://historymatters.gmu.edu/d/6440/ (accessed on January 5, 2010).

chapter twelve *Religion*

1870 December 16 The Colored Methodist Episcopal Church in America is officially organized in Jackson, Tennessee. It is the first African American denomination organized within the United States.

1880 Henry McNeal Turner, proponent of freed slaves moving to Africa, becomes bishop of the African Methodist Episcopal Church. He follows Bishop Daniel Alexander Payne, who supported missionary work to Africa but did not encourage free blacks to emigrate there.

1885 Sarah Ann Hughes becomes the first woman to be ordained as a deacon in the all-black African Methodist Episcopal Church. A backlash from male deacons causes her ordination to be revoked just two years later.

1895 September 24 Three different African American Baptist groups come together in Atlanta, Georgia, to form the National Baptist Convention, the country's largest African American religious body.

1900 The African Methodist Episcopal Zion Church becomes the first African American church to declare a policy of gender equality in the ministry when it upholds the ordinations of Julia A. J. Foote and Mary Jane Small as church elders.

1901 Reverend Florence Spearing Randolph goes to London to represent the African Methodist Episcopal Zion Church at a conference of Methodists.

1905 William Joseph Seymour moves to Houston, Texas, where he studies with Charles Parham. Both men are credited as forefathers to the modern Pentecostal faith.

1906 The federal Bureau of the Census reports that the number of African American Baptists in the United States has grown to more than 2.2 million, up from approximately 1.3 million in 1890.

1906 Reverdy Cassius Ransom gives his speech "The Spirit of John Brown," credited by African American leader W. E. B. Du Bois with influencing the formation of the National Association for the Advancement of Colored People (NAACP).

1906 April William Joseph Seymour begins the Azusa Street Revival, which is often credited as a key development in the growth of the Pentecostal faith. The Azusa Street Revival is the longest-running continuous revival in United States history.

1913 The plant, equipment, and copyrights of the National Baptist Publishing Board are valued at $350,000, making it one of the largest black-owned businesses anywhere in the United States.

1919 Sweet Daddy Grace opens his first house of prayer, a nondenominational Pentecostal church.

1929 Wallace Fard joins the Moorish Science Temple, a group that teaches that African Americans were descended from the Muslim Moorish people and that Islam is therefore the proper religion for African Americans.

1930 Wallace Fard, inspired by the teachings of the Moorish Science Temple, founds the Nation of Islam in Chicago, Illinois.

1931 Father Divine achieves national fame when a judge who sentenced him to a year in prison mysteriously drops dead several days later.

1932 Wallace Fard disappears, sparking a struggle over who will lead the Nation of Islam.

1932 Elijah Muhammad becomes leader of the Nation of Islam. He will lead the organization for more than forty years.

1935 Howard Thurman meets with Mohandas Gandhi, a leader of the Indian independence movement. Gandhi urges Thurman to imagine religious faith as a tool to overcome oppression.

1944 Howard Thurman founds the first interracial, multifaith church in the United States, Church for the Fellowship of All Peoples in San Francisco, California.

1947 Gospel singer Mahalia Jackson achieves national recognition for her recording of "Move on Up a Little Higher." The recording makes her one of the first two gospel singers ever to achieve gold-record status.

1951 Ralph Abernathy becomes a pastor at First Baptist Church in Montgomery, Alabama. In Montgomery, he establishes a close relationship with fellow minister Martin Luther King Jr. in the fight for civil rights and justice.

1953 Malcolm X is released from prison and begins to recruit followers for the Nation of Islam.

1953 Howard Thurman becomes the first African American dean of a chapel at a major white institution of higher education when he accepts a position as dean of Marsh Chapel at Boston University.

1954 The Colored Methodist Episcopal Church changes its name to the Christian Methodist Episcopal Church because of the increasingly negative, Jim-Crow associations with the term "colored."

1956 Benjamin L. Hooks, future leader of the National Association for the Advancement of Colored People (NAACP), is ordained as a Baptist minister.

1957 Reverends Martin Luther King Jr. and Ralph Abernathy co-found the Southern Christian Leadership Conference (SCLC), a group that teaches the use of nonviolent direct action to protest injustice and promote civil rights for African Americans.

1959 The documentary "The Hate that Hate Produced" is produced by Mike Wallace and African American journalist Louis Lomax and aired on national television. The documentary causes widespread anxiety among white Americans about the Nation of Islam.

1960 Sweet Daddy Grace dies and is succeeded by Sweet Daddy McCullough, who brings the Pentecostal United House of Prayer into more mainstream acceptance.

1964 **March** Malcolm X leaves the Nation of Islam and founds his own religious organization, the Organization of Afro-American Unity, built on a belief in world brotherhood.

1965 **February 21** Malcolm X, while attending a meeting in Harlem, is shot dead by three members of the Nation of Islam.

The abolition of slavery brought about numerous important changes in the religious lives of African Americans in the South. Slaves had been prohibited from holding religious services without any whites present. Freedom from slavery after the Civil War ended in 1865 allowed former slaves throughout the South to join churches of their choice. The vast majority joined all-black churches. As a result, the number of African American churches in the South increased. These new churches became the center of many African American communities.

The formation of the Colored Methodist Episcopal Church in 1870 was a particularly important development. The Colored Methodist Episcopal Church, known simply as the CME, was an all–African American church that emerged out of the mixed-race Methodist Episcopal Church South (MECS). Many African Americans who had converted to Christianity while they were slaves had been members of MECS. Many of them left that church after the Civil War to join single-race churches. The CME became the first major all-black denomination to be organized in the South. It grew steadily in size and had expanded through the United States by the early 1900s.

Many African American churches in the South were financially dependent on white churches in the North in their first few years of existence after the Civil War. As black churches in the South grew in number and in size, many began to seek ways to become more independent and self-sufficient. The founding of the National Baptist Publishing Board (NBPB) by R. H. Boyd (1843–1922) in 1896 was a crucial development in this area. The NBPB provided Sunday school lessons, prayer books, hymnals, and other printed materials to black Baptist churches throughout the South. The NBPB would go on to become one of the largest, most successful black-owned businesses in the United States.

Some African American churches became strong enough to focus their attention outward to missionary work. Particularly notable was the African Methodist Episcopal Church's missionary work in Africa. First under the leadership of Bishop Daniel Alexander Payne (1811–93), the church began a strong campaign to establish missions in Africa. The next bishop of the church, Bishop Henry McNeal Turner (1834–1915), continued work in Africa. He made many trips to Africa and continued Payne's efforts to establish schools and spread Christian ideas there.

The Azusa Street Revival was another important development in African American religion during the segregation era. It is notable because it was the longest-running continuous revival in all of American history. It lasted day-in and day-out, with several prayer meetings and services a day, seven days a week, for three straight years beginning in 1906. The revival was also important because it is considered to be an important precursor to the modern Pentecostal faith.

An aspect of African American religious practice, and the revivalist tradition in particular, that had a particularly strong influence on American culture was gospel music. Gospel music is a combination of traditional church hymns with popular African American musical forms like blues, jazz, spirituals, and ragtime. Gospel music quickly became part of the liturgy, or ritual of worship, in African American churches across the country. The Fisk Jubilee Singers, a vocal group from Fisk University in Nashville, Tennessee, first brought gospel and African American spirituals to worldwide attention during their historic world tour in the 1870s. But it was the growth of radio in the 1920s and 1930s that brought African American gospel music mainstream popularity. From the 1940s onward, gospel music was also popularized by performers who recorded albums and songs with famous jazz artists.

Most African Americans in the period beten 1865 and 1965 were Christians. Many went to all-black churches that had distinctly African American practices and customs, but these churches were part of mainstream Christian denominations. The Nation of Islam, a church founded in Detroit in 1930 by Wallace Fard, was a departure from this tradition. The Nation of Islam taught its followers that African Americans were descended from the Moorish people of the African continent, and that the proper religion for African Americans was Islam, not Christianity. The Nation of Islam's teachings were not part of orthodox (traditional) Islam, however. Instead, the church combined parts of Islam with a philosophy of black nationalism. After Fard mysteriously disappeared in 1934, Elijah Muhammad (1897–1975) took over as the leader of the church. The Nation of Islam grew and flourished under Muhammad's leadership. Its belief in segregation of the races made it controversial, but it was also commended for its teachings of temperance, self-respect, self-reliance, and clean living for its followers. The Nation of Islam was responsible for establishing numerous black Muslim businesses during this era, creating economic opportunities for African Americans where few existed before.

It is difficult to point to an African American religious figure or movement without strong ties to politics and activism during the period between 1865 and 1965. This is because religion was, and remained even into the twenty-first century, a primary vehicle for civil rights activism. As African Americans began to fight for civil rights and equal social and political opportunity in the United States, religion became an important part of that battle. Religion brings people together in regular meetings, important for any kind of activism or political organizing. Also, many religions emphasize a theme of freedom from bondage. This theme was appealing to African Americans in the wake of slavery. By using Bible stories and biblical themes in their public speeches, important civil rights leaders such as Martin Luther King Jr. (1929–68) and Ralph Abernathy (1926–90) were able to convince many white religious leaders and white Christians of the righteousness of their struggle for equal rights. One of the most important civil rights organizations of the 1950s and 1960s, the Southern Christian Leadership Conference (SCLC), was founded by about sixty black southern ministers in 1957. The SCLC was dedicated to nonviolent protest as a means of political action. This Christian organization was enormously successful in pushing the civil rights agenda and bringing about change in America. The SCLC organized sit-ins and protests to force desegregation in Birmingham in 1963. The same year, the SCLC helped organized the famous March on Washington for Jobs and Freedom. The passage of the Civil Rights Act of 1964 and the Voting Rights Act of 1965 was in large part due to the consistent, nonviolent pressure of African American church leaders.

★ *Headline Makers*

★ RALPH ABERNATHY
(1926–1990)

Ralph Abernathy was one of the most prominent leaders of the civil rights movement. He was a close associate of Martin Luther King Jr. (1929–68) and one of the organizers of the Montgomery bus boycott. Abernathy continued his work after King's assassination, becoming head of the Southern Christian Leadership Conference (SCLC) leading the nonviolent resistance movement for equality in the United States.

Ralph Abernathy was born in Linden, Alabama. He was the tenth of twelve children in a prosperous, or wealthy, family. Although his family was well-to-do, they lived frugally, not spending much money. His father stressed the importance of church and education and donated money generously. Abernathy was still in high school when he was drafted into the military to serve in World War II (1939–45). He returned home after his service and earned a general equivalency diploma (GED), the equivalent of a high-school diploma. He then enrolled at Alabama State College in Montgomery, Alabama, which was the first state-supported university for African Americans in U.S. history.

Ralph Abernathy.
© *Bettmann/Corbis*

Joins the Ministry

Abernathy had long been concerned with justice and fairness. He was president of the student body in college, and led a huge protest at the school during his sophomore year. The students thought it was unfair that the faculty was served different, and better, food than the students were. Abernathy led the student body on a boycott of the school dining hall, which meant that the students refused to eat there. The boycott was a success, and the quality of food served in the cafeteria improved. Abernathy also led a protest aimed at improving living conditions in the school dormitories. His interactions with teachers and staff at the university also encouraged his commitment to social justice. He learned in his classes about the importance of voting rights for African Americans. He also learned that religion could be a tool for working toward social justice.

Abernathy's college years influenced his decision to become a minister. He was a student religious leader as the superintendent of the student Sunday school. After he graduated from college, he enrolled at Atlanta University to pursue a master's degree in sociology. It was during his days at Atlanta University that he first met Martin Luther King Jr. after he heard King give a sermon at Ebenezer Baptist Church in Atlanta.

The two men developed a close relationship after they both became pastors in Montgomery, Alabama. Abernathy became a pastor at First Baptist Church in Montgomery, Alabama, in 1951. Shortly thereafter, King became pastor at Dexter Avenue Baptist Church, also in Montgomery. Both became respected leaders in the African American community in Montgomery. The men gained national prominence in 1955 when they led a boycott of the Montgomery bus system. Their boycott was in response to the arrest of Rosa Parks (1913–2005), a black woman who was arrested for refusing to give up her seat on the bus to a white man. King and Abernathy, along with a group of other activists, convinced many African Americans in Montgomery to refuse to use the bus system. The city lost so much revenue, or money, from the boycott that it was eventually forced to lift the segregationist rule on city buses.

Plays Central Role in the Civil Rights Movement

The Montgomery bus boycott was only the beginning of Abernathy and King's civil rights efforts together. The men co-founded the Southern Christian Leadership Conference (SCLC) in 1957. King was the president and Abernathy was the secretary-treasurer. The purpose of the SCLC was to use nonviolent direct action to promote civil rights for African Americans. King convinced Abernathy to give up his post at First Baptist and move to Atlanta in 1961. There, Abernathy became the pastor at West Hunter Baptist Church. Four years later, Abernathy became the vice president of the SCLC, prompting people to speculate, or guess, that he would replace King one day as president.

King and Abernathy's partnership was cut short by King's assassination. The two had been planning a massive march of poor people on Washington, D.C. They wanted to demand more economic opportunities. King was shot to death on April 4, 1968, before the march happened. Abernathy delivered the eulogy, or speech in remembrance, at King's funeral. He recalled his long friendship with King and the struggles for justice they had undertaken together. He said he was proud to have worked closely with King but never jealous of the fact that King had received more of the spotlight. The Poor People's Campaign later took place in Washington, D.C. Some fifty thousand people attended the protest.

Abernathy succeeded King as the president of the SCLC after King's assassination. Under his leadership, the organization's mission shifted somewhat. Initially, it had been focused on achieving equal rights for African Americans under the law. But by 1968, African Americans mostly had the same legal status as whites. Still, many found that they were unable to get ahead financially. Accordingly, the SCLC began to focus more on economic rights for African Americans. This push involved several aspects, like equal educational resources, access to health care, and quality job opportunities. These struggles continued into the twenty-first century.

Abernathy did experience some controversy later in his career. He resigned from the SCLC in 1977 amid accusations that he had mismanaged the organization's finances. He also angered many African Americans by supporting Republican presidential candidate Ronald Reagan (1911–2004) in the 1980 election. His autobiography, published in 1989, was also a source of controversy. The book included information about King cheating on his wife with other women. Abernathy insisted that he had only intended to show King as a human who also made mistakes. He died of a heart attack several months after the book was published.

★ M. J. DIVINE
(1879–1965)

M. J. Divine, known as Father Divine, is a controversial figure about whom little is definitively known. He founded the Peace Mission movement and had thousands of followers who gave him all of their possessions. He preached a radical message of racial and gender equality. To some, he is remembered as a dangerous cult leader. To others, he is remembered as a role model and hero for his vision of racial unity and his work on behalf of poor, inner-city African Americans.

Little is known about Divine's early life. Many believe that he was born George Baker. George Baker was the son of former slaves who was born in 1879 in Maryland, though some believe he was born further south. He did not have much formal education, but he loved to read religious writings. He moved to Baltimore, Maryland, in 1899 at the age of twenty. In Baltimore, he worked as a gardener and began teaching Sunday school. It was there, too, that he renamed himself Father Major Jealous Divine.

Develops Unorthodox Religion

Divine developed unorthodox (nonstandard or unusual) religious views. He read widely about Catholicism, Methodism, and Pentecostalism.

He dabbled in Eastern philosophy and psychology. He is said to have received his religious calling from Reverend William Joseph Seymour (1870–1922) at the Azusa Street Revival, a Pentecostal movement in California in the early twentieth century. In 1906, he met a black preacher named Samuel Morris, who had a controversial message. Morris was kicked out of several churches for saying that he himself was God. He believed that God lived within everyone, and so everyone was divine. Divine believed that he, too, was a living incarnation of God.

M. J. Divine. *The Library of Congress*

Divine traveled around for several years preaching his message that involved his being God. His message combined elements of many religions and philosophies. He found people to follow him, and he moved to New York in 1915. His followers gave all of their money and possessions to his ministry, and they lived together in a communal house in the suburbs of New York. He took care of his followers and helped them find work. He managed their communal resources. He eventually married one of his disciples, a woman named Pinninnah who was much older than he. She became known as "Mother Divine," and was second in command of his organization.

Divine taught his disciples the importance of hard work. He used his talents as a businessman to create job opportunities for his followers and successfully invest their money. Also central to Divine's beliefs were racial equality and justice. He reasoned that if all people had God within them, it was not possible that blacks were inferior to whites. He also taught his followers to abstain from alcohol, tobacco, drugs, and swearing.

Peace Mission Thrives

Divine's following was known as the "Peace Mission," and it thrived in its early years. It became all the more successful when the Great Depression struck in 1929. The Great Depression was the period following a devastating stock market crash in 1929 when the economy was bad and there was high unemployment. Divine was generous with his followers and with the poor in general. Each Sunday, he hosted an all-day feast that was open to the public. He did not charge people to come eat at his home, but he forbade alcohol or un-Christian behavior. Hundreds of poor people attended each week. During the poverty-stricken Depression, people believed that Divine's feasts were nothing short of a miracle. Divine's followers, who still pooled all of their money to be managed by Divine, had a prosperous lifestyle during these difficult years.

Divine's unorthodox message, coupled with the fact that he had begun to attract a number of white followers, raised the suspicions of the authorities. Police sent an undercover informant to live in the house in 1930. They believed she would find the house full of immoral practices and sexual deviance. The informant reported back that she saw nothing illegal going on in the house. Even so, she did not believe that the community could live such an affluent lifestyle from the members' work alone. Divine was eventually arrested for "disturbing the peace" in 1931.

Divine achieved widespread fame around the time of his trial in 1931. He was found guilty, and the judge sentenced him to a year in prison. Several days later, the judge unexpectedly dropped dead. This prompted widespread rumor and speculation, or guessing, that Divine had some kind of supernatural powers and had caused the judge's death. Divine's prison sentence was eventually reversed, and he moved his operations to Harlem in New York City.

Divine's Peace Mission movement grew rapidly during the 1930s. Soon, there were numerous branches in New York and New Jersey, and even some as far away as California. The organization also prospered financially. Divine's followers had to donate all of their worldly possessions to the Mission, so it eventually was an organization with substantial holdings. By some estimates, the organization was worth over $15 million by the end of the Great Depression. Divine used much of that money to buy property. He had white followers buy property in white areas for use by the Mission to further his goal of racial equality. These properties included an estate across the street from President Franklin D. Roosevelt's property and a beachfront hotel in Atlantic City, New Jersey.

The end of the Depression brought the beginning of the decline of the Peace Mission movement. World War II brought prosperity to the country, and Divine's message of simple, frugal living became less popular. His wife died in 1943, which deeply distressed him and made him question his divinity. He was sued by a former follower over a failed investment. He retired to Pennsylvania, where he lived a quiet life. He remarried a young, white Canadian woman in 1946. He died in 1965, and his widow, called "Mother S. A. Divine," took over as spiritual leader of the movement.

★ BENJAMIN L. HOOKS
(1925–)

Benjamin L. Hooks fought for justice on multiple fronts. He was a Baptist minister, but he was also a lawyer, an activist, and a government servant. He served for years as the executive director of the National Association for the Advancement of Colored People (NAACP), the largest civil rights organization in the United States.

Benjamin Lawson Hooks was born in Memphis, Tennessee, in 1925. He was the fifth of seven children of a relatively wealthy family. His family owned a photography business that was very popular with the African American community in Memphis. Hooks's family was high-achieving in general. In addition to the successful family business, his grandmother had been the second African American woman ever to graduate from college in the United States. Times grew harder for the family in 1929, when the Great Depression began. People could no longer afford the luxury of a professional photographer, so the family business struggled. During these times of struggle, Hooks's parents taught their children to be hard-working.

Becomes Both Lawyer and Minister

Hooks's passion for justice grew strong after he graduated from college. He attended LeMoyne College in Memphis. After graduating from college, he served the United States in World War II, where he was stationed in Italy. He was angered by the fact that the prisoners he guarded had more civil rights than he did. When he returned from the

Benjamin L. Hooks.
Diana Walker/Time & Life Pictures/Getty Images

war, Hooks decided to attend law school. He went to law school at DePaul University in Chicago, Illinois. He graduated in 1948 and returned to Memphis to practice law. He faced racism and discrimination as a lawyer in Memphis, where he was not allowed to join white bar associations.

Hooks had always been interested in joining the ministry in addition to his career as a lawyer. His father discouraged it, though. He did not want to see Hooks become a minister. His father did not have much respect for organized religion. Hooks could not ignore his call to serve as a minister despite his father's objections. He was ordained (or officially made a minister by the church) as a Baptist minister in 1956. He became the pastor at Middle Baptist Church in Memphis. He would preach there until 1972. He also preached at Greater Mount Moriah Baptist Church in Detroit, Michigan, where he began preaching in 1964. He preached at the two churches on alternating Sundays.

Hooks also worked for a long time as a civil servant. He became a public defender in 1961 for Shelby County, Tennessee, meaning that he represented clients who were too poor to pay for their own attorneys. He was appointed to be a judge for the Shelby County Criminal Court in 1965. He was the first black judge of a criminal court in Tennessee or the South since the time shortly after the Civil War. Hooks began serving in the federal government in 1972. President Richard M. Nixon (1913–94) appointed him to be the first black member of the Federal Communications Commission (FCC). The FCC is a government agency that regulates the radio and television industries.

Leads NAACP

Hooks stepped down from the FCC in 1976 to become the executive director of the NAACP. He faced several challenges. The NAACP had been a pioneering organization during the civil rights movement in the 1950s and 1960s. But in the 1970s, the organization faced the challenge of declining membership and depleted resources. When Hooks took the helm at the NAACP, the organization was about one million dollars in debt. It also was challenged by other, more militant organizations. These groups said that the NAACP was too conservative. Other critics said that the NAACP only served the interests of the middle class. Hooks was determined to address these challenges facing the organization.

Hooks's vision for the NAACP was to shift some of the organization's focus from politics to the everyday challenges facing African Americans. He forged relationships between the NAACP and the business community. He fought for economic justice by backing the 1978 Humphrey-Hawkins bill. That bill required the federal government, through its financial policies, to encourage the creation of jobs and to lower the unemployment rate. Hooks also sought to expand the reach of the NAACP's mission. Instead of focusing solely on civil rights, Hooks led the organization to fight for justice in the effects of environmental problems, the inner cities, health insurance, and improvement in the criminal justice system. Hooks also looked to advance the NAACP's causes and goals across the political spectrum. In 1980, Hooks became the first African American to address both the Republican and Democratic presidential conventions.

Hooks retired from the NAACP in 1992, but remained busy and active. He reconnected with his work as a minister and began preaching again at Middle Baptist Church in Memphis on a full-time basis. He continued another job he had begun while at the NAACP: chairman of the Leadership Conference on Civil Rights (LCCR). The LCCR was a coalition, or alliance, of various civil rights organizations. He became president of the National Civil Rights Museum, which is also located in Memphis. Hooks worked as a college professor, teaching classes at Fisk University. In 2000, he was honored by the University of Memphis, which named a civil rights institute after him.

★ **ELIJAH MUHAMMAD**
(1897–1975)

Elijah Muhammad was the leader of the Nation of Islam from 1934 to 1975. The organization was founded by Wallace Fard (1877–1934), Muhammad's mentor, who only led the organization for a few years. Muhammad led the organization to national prominence. The Nation of Islam remained a strong religious and cultural African American organization into the twenty-first century.

Elijah Muhammad was born with the name Elijah Poole in 1897. He was born in Sandersville, Georgia, a rural community. His parents were former slaves. They worked as sharecroppers, as did many former slaves. Share-cropping was a system where former slaves worked land owned by a farmer. The sharecroppers had to give half of their crops to the landowner in return for using the land. This system kept many sharecroppers living in extreme poverty. Elijah received some formal education before he had to drop out of school to help his family on the farm.

There was not much of a future for Elijah's family in Georgia. He was one of thirteen children. He left home when he was sixteen years old and married a woman named Clara. Eventually, the family decided to move to the North, something a number of former slave families did after finding little economic opportunity in the South. This was known as the "Great Migration," which took place after World War I (1914–18). Elijah and

Elijah Muhammad. *Hulton Archive/Getty Images*

Clara moved their family north in 1923 to Detroit, Michigan. Elijah found several jobs in Detroit, including work on an assembly line in an auto-manufacturing plant.

Becomes Leader of the Nation of Islam

Elijah became acquainted with Wallace D. Fard, founder of the Nation of Islam, in 1930. Elijah came to agree with Fard's teachings that Islam ought to be the black man's religion and decided to join the Nation of

Islam. When joining the Nation of Islam, people had to write a letter to Fard asking for an original name to replace the "slave name" given to their ancestors by whites. Fard gave Elijah the name Elijah Karriem. Elijah quickly became one of Fard's most loyal followers. Fard rewarded him for his loyalty by renaming him Elijah Muhammad. He made Elijah his chief minister.

Police were looking closely at Fard's organization in 1932. They were concerned about his radical teachings. That year, they arrested Fard in connection with a murder committed by someone with loose ties to the Nation of Islam. The police could not tie him to the murder, however. He was released and ordered to leave Detroit. Fard went into hiding, and it was at this time that he made Muhammad the chief minister of the Nation of Islam and prepared him to take over. Fard then mysteriously disappeared, which caused confusion and unrest within the organization.

Divisions within the organization caused Muhammad to relocate to Chicago, Illinois, where Nation of Islam Temple Number Two was located. Muhammad established Temple Number Two as the official headquarters of the Nation of Islam in 1934. He did not stay long in Chicago. Divisions within the organization caused Muhammad to fear being killed by an alternate faction of the Nation of Islam. He fled to Milwaukee, Wisconsin, and then to Washington, D.C. There, he spent many hours reading books recommended to him by Fard. He also established Temple Number Four there in 1939.

Muhammad's activities in Washington, D.C., brought him to the attention of law enforcement authorities. Undercover officers investigated the group. The United States was preparing to enter World War II, and there was a fear that the Nation of Islam would attempt to weaken the country's war effort. Authorities were alarmed by the refusal of the members of the Nation of Islam to join the armed forces. Muhammad himself was arrested in 1942 for failing to comply with the draft. Muhammad was convicted and spent four years in federal prison. During this time, law enforcement also closed Temple Number Two in Chicago.

Law enforcement pressure did not succeed in slowing the movement. Instead, Muhammad came out of prison a hero to his followers. Disputes over whether he was the rightful leader of the movement stopped. Followers of the Nation of Islam were more loyal than ever. Muhammad moved to Chicago and began to expand the Nation of Islam. No longer simply a religious organization, the Nation of Islam began to open businesses, including a restaurant and bakery in Chicago.

The Nation of Islam grew rapidly throughout the 1950s. Muhammad wrote a popular newspaper column, which he had syndicated, or published widely, in black newspapers and publications throughout the United States. The growth was also in large part due to the emergence of Nation of Islam leader Malcolm X (1925–65). Originally named Malcolm Little, Malcolm X joined the movement while serving time in prison in Massachussetts. Malcolm X was in many ways more charismatic and a better speaker than Muhammad. Muhammad made him the national spokesman for the Nation of Islam, and Malcolm succeeded in bringing many more followers into the organization.

Rift with Malcolm X

Malcolm X brought the Nation of Islam publicity and increased membership, but he also brought controversy. In 1963, he gave a speech about the assassination of President John F. Kennedy (1917–63) that many thought was a justification of the president's killing. Malcolm X referred to the assassination as the "chickens coming home to roost," in the sense that white America was being punished for its sins against black Americans. Muhammad publicly reprimanded him for his comments. Some believed that Muhammad's real dissatisfaction was the fact that Malcolm had begun to overshadow Muhammad as the most prominent leader of the Nation of Islam.

Soon after Muhammad's public reprimand, Malcolm X left the Nation of Islam and formed his own black Muslim group. In 1965, Malcolm X was assassinated not long after his defection. This tragedy sparked tremendous controversy as his followers wondered who was to blame. The three gunmen directly responsible for the attack were Nation of Islam members, but questions remained about who had "ordered" the killing. Louis Farrakhan (1932–), a loyal follower of Muhammad who would eventually take over leadership of the organization, had written a newspaper column denouncing Malcolm X, which made some suspect him. There was some speculation that disgruntled, or upset and angry, followers of Muhammad were responsible for the assassination. Some even speculated that Muhammad himself ordered the attack. Nothing was ever proved.

Elijah Muhammad continued to be the target of considerable controversy in his final years leading the Nation of Islam. It was revealed that he had fathered thirteen children outside of his marriage. He was criticized as hypocritical for these extramarital affairs, given that the Nation of Islam preached faithfulness to one's spouse. There were also allegations of abuse of organization funds by Muhammad and his family members. Critics said Muhammad did not live the disciplined life he required of his followers. He was said to have a $150,000 diamond-studded hat, wear other expensive clothes and jewelry, and travel by private airplane.

Muhammad died of heart failure in 1975. Upon his death, the Nation of Islam divided between two leaders: Muhammad's son W. D. Muhammad and Louis Farrakhan. Muhammad's son became leader of the Nation of Islam, which he renamed the World Community of Al-Islam in the West. He led the organization away from the black separatism preached by his father. Farrakhan refounded the Nation of Islam in 1978. Farrakhan and Muhammad's son led competing factions for years, but they eventually agreed in 2000 to work together in the best interest of the organization. Farrakhan remained the national leader of the Nation of Islam organization as of 2010.

★ FLORENCE SPEARING RANDOLPH (1866–1951)

Florence Spearing Randolph was a prominent African American female minister, activist, and organizer in the late nineteenth and early twentieth centuries. She was inspired to go into the ministry in part because of her involvement with the temperance movement, an activist movement aimed at keeping people from drunkenness and immoral behavior. As a minister and activist, she tirelessly campaigned for equal justice for men and women of all races.

Florence Spearing Randolph. *Fisk University Libraries. Reproduced by permission.*

Florence Spearing Randolph was born on August 9, 1866, in Charleston, South Carolina. She had an extremely privileged upbringing for an African American at the time. Unlike many blacks born then, she was not descended from former slaves. African Americans in her family had been free for generations before the Civil War. Her father was a wealthy cabinetmaker who enjoyed a high social status. Randolph was educated at local public schools and received further education at what was called a normal school, which was a school for the training of teachers. Her education and her family's social status gave Randolph more choices for work than most African Americans at the time, few of whom had much formal education.

Randolph moved to New Jersey to live with her sister and work as a dressmaker in 1885. She had more opportunities in New Jersey than she did in South Carolina. She was able to make about three times as much money as a dressmaker in New Jersey as she could in South Carolina. Randolph also met her husband in New Jersey. Hugh Randolph was a cook who worked in a dining car on a railroad. Florence Randolph had her first and only child in 1887, Leah Viola Randolph. Randolph started her own dressmaking business and enjoyed great success.

Becomes a Minister

Randolph's early inspiration to become a minister came from helping her blind grandmother. When Randolph was a young girl in Charleston, her grandmother would visit people's homes to minister to those who were ill or could not make it to church. Randolph's grandmother brought her along on many of these visits, and they were a major inspiration for her to become a minister. Another factor that led Randolph toward the ministry was her involvement in the temperance movement in the late 1880s and in the 1890s. Temperance means not drinking alcoholic beverages, and it was a popular cause among reformers in the late nineteenth century, especially women. Randolph joined the Women's Christian Temperance Union (WCTU), a prominent temperance activist group. The organization's Christian philosophy was another inspiration to Randolph.

Randolph first went to get a license to preach in 1897. She wanted to preach at churches that were part of the African Methodist Episcopal Zion (AMEZ) Church. Bishop Alexander Waters, one of the future founders of the National Association for the Advancement of Colored People (NAACP), supported her bid to become a minister. In 1900, the AMEZ Church held a conference in Atlantic City, New Jersey. The American ministers at that conference selected people to represent them at a conference in 1901 in London, England, which was the Third Methodist Ecumenical Conference. They selected Randolph as one of those delegates, or representatives. While she was in London, she was invited to preach at the Primitive Methodist Church of Mattison Road.

When she returned from overseas, Randolph was selected to be the pastor of Pennington Street Church in Newark, New Jersey. She eventually served as a pastor of five different churches in New Jersey. She was consistently assigned to "problem" churches, ones that were struggling to remain financially afloat or churches with few members. She managed to create big changes at these churches. But time after time, once Randolph led a church to success, church elders would replace her with a male pastor and send her to the next struggling church. Throughout her career, Randolph faced some criticism from church members and elders who did not think it was proper for a woman to be a minister.

Fights for Equality and Justice

A big part of Randolph's ministry involved missionary work, ministerial work with a humanitarian focus. Her missionary work at the AMEZ Church was directed at Africa. She traveled extensively in Africa in the early 1920s. She first went to Liberia, on the west coast of the continent. She made many trips into the interior of Africa to minister to people and learn about living conditions there. When she returned to the United States, she went on a tour to educate people about life in Africa. She held missionary-related leadership positions in the AMEZ and worked hard to raise money for missionary work in Africa. She eventually extended her fund-raising efforts to raise money for missionary work in South America as well.

Randolph also labored as an activist for gender and racial equality in the United States. She was actively involved with the National Association of Colored Women's Clubs (NACWC), a coalition of women's groups throughout the United States. Randolph founded the New Jersey Federation of Colored Women's Clubs, a subgroup of the NACWC. The New Jersey Federation was a coalition of women's groups within the state of New Jersey. The federation became involved with local, state, and national politics. One of the federation's causes under Randolph's leadership was a campaign against lynching, which is an execution of a person by a mob without opportunity for legal protection or a fair trial. A close family friend of Randolph's was lynched in South Carolina, which led her to rally the federation to campaign against lynching. The federation, along with other women, presented an appeal to President Woodrow Wilson (1865–1924) for racial harmony and racial equality in the United States.

In 1925, Randolph became pastor of the Wallace Chapel African Methodist Episcopal Zion Church in Summit, New Jersey. Her leadership led to an increase in membership in the church. Randolph continued to focus on equal rights for women and minorities. In 1933, she was awarded an honorary doctorate of divinity from Livingstone College in North Carolina. She retired in 1946, and died five years later at the age of eighty-five.

★ WILLIAM JOSEPH SEYMOUR
(1870–1922)

William Joseph Seymour is widely credited with the growth and success of the Pentecostal movement. The Pentecostal faith emphasizes personal and direct experience with the Holy Spirit, including speaking in tongues, or speaking verbal utterances that may sound unintelligible to others. This is said to be the Holy Spirit speaking through a person. Seymour led the Azusa Street Revival from 1906 to 1909. It remains the longest-running continuous revival in U.S. history.

Seymour was born on May 2, 1870, in Centerville, Louisiana. His parents, Simon Seymour and Phyllis Salabarr, were recently freed slaves. His family was very poor when he was growing up. His parents were religious and had associations with both the Baptist and the Catholic churches. Seymour was baptized in the Catholic faith at a church called Church of the Assumption in Franklin, Louisiana. Growing up, Seymour had visions of God.

Joins Pentecostal Movement

Seymour moved to Indianapolis, Indiana, in 1895 at the age of twenty-five. There, he worked as a waiter and joined the Simpson Chapel Methodist Episcopal Church. It was a predominantly African American church. The Methodist Episcopal Church was a stronghold among African Americans during segregation times. In 1900, Seymour moved to Cincinnati, Ohio. While there, he joined a new congregation, the Evening Light Saints. This was a Holiness group. The Holiness movement believed that people are inherently sinful, but that their sinful nature can be cleansed by God. The members believed in faith healing and total sanctification, meaning a state of divine grace after being baptized or coming into the Christian faith.

Seymour began his career as a minister not long after moving to Ohio. He became an ordained minister in the Church of God in 1902. After that, he became a traveling evangelist, or person who preaches the gospel, making trips to Illinois, Mississippi, Georgia, and Louisiana.

Seymour eventually found his way to Houston, Texas. His family had relocated there from Louisiana. Seymour decided to settle there as well. He became the pastor of a Holiness church in Houston in 1905. He was to be a temporary replacement for Lucy Farrow, a Holiness minister who was also the niece of Frederick Douglass (c. 1818–95). Douglass was a famous black abolitionist.

Farrow introduced Seymour to the practice of speaking in tongues and also to Charles Parham. Parham was a minister who established the first Pentecostal Bible school in Topeka, Kansas. He also ran a Pentecostal school in Houston. Seymour wanted to join Parham's school, but he disagreed with Parham's belief in segregation. His affiliation with him did not last long, but some cite his association with Parham as a major influence in developing his Pentecostal ideas.

Azusa Street Revival

Seymour moved to Los Angeles, California, in 1906. He was inspired to go there by a woman he met in Houston named Neeley Terry. Terry told him about new kinds of religious practices in Los Angeles, which Seymour wanted to experience for himself. He first was invited to preach at a church in Los Angeles that had been established by Julia Hutchins. Hutchins had been expelled from her Baptist church for her Holiness views.

At Hutchins's church, Seymour gave a sermon about the importance of interracial unity for religion and also about speaking in tongues as a sign of the Holy Spirit. Hutchins did not believe in speaking in tongues, and she banished Seymour from her church. Seymour soon moved to the home of Mr. and Mrs. Richard Asberry. He began preaching at their home. It was there, too, that Seymour himself first spoke in tongues. Word quickly spread about the events going on at the Asberry home, and soon there were so many worshippers that they could not fit in the house.

Seymour moved his preaching from the Asberry home to a building at 312 Azusa Street in Los Angeles. The building was an unused African Methodist Episcopal church. It was being used as a warehouse. Seymour and his congregation converted the space into a makeshift church for their services. The congregation quickly grew as the word spread about Azusa Street. The *Los Angeles Times* ran a story about Azusa Street on April 18, 1906. That same day, there was a very powerful earthquake in California. The earthquake, which began near San Francisco, killed three thousand people and could be felt as far south as Los Angeles. Rumors began to spread that there were connections between the things happening at Azusa Street and the earthquake. This brought even more followers to the church.

By May 1906, the church on Azusa Street was attracting close to one thousand people a day. There were round-the-clock prayer meetings. The media paid attention, and stories ran in many major publications about the events at Azusa Street. The church was officially renamed the Azusa Street Apostolic Faith Mission of Los Angeles in 1907. The church grew and grew. Seymour ordained more ministers, and new branches of the church were started. The church also had its own publication, *The Apostolic Faith*. The publication would eventually reach a circulation, or readership, of twenty thousand.

Seymour's mission began to splinter in 1909. His teacher, Charles Parham, disapproved of Seymour's church and started his own rival mission that attracted many of Seymour's followers. Seymour also lost access to his mailing list for the church publication (though details about how this happened are unclear). Further rivalries with other religious leaders caused Seymour's influence to dwindle until his death in 1922.

★ HOWARD THURMAN
(1900–1981)

Howard Thurman was a minister and teacher who founded a theology of liberation and nonviolence. Thurman, influenced early on by Mohandas Gandhi (1869–1948) and the struggle for Indian independence, himself influenced civil rights leaders in the United States like Martin Luther King Jr. It is said that his thinking was a foundational influence for King's nonviolent style of civil disobedience. Thurman also founded the first interracial and multi-faith church in the United States.

Thurman was born in Daytona, Florida, in 1900. Daytona, like other Southern cities at the time, was segregated. The city was somewhat unique in that it became a haven in the winter for wealthy Northerners looking to escape the cold. For that reason, Thurman would remember, the city was perhaps more relaxed when it came to race than other Southern cities. Thurman's mother and grandmother nurtured him and taught him early about spirituality. They were both devout Christians who taught him that religion can be a source of comfort and security when life becomes difficult. They also taught him the importance of education.

Howard Thurman. *Mark Kauffman/Time & Life Pictures/Getty Images*

Influenced by Education and Religious Leaders

Educational opportunities were severely limited for African Americans in Daytona. Schools were segregated, and the black schools only taught up through the seventh grade. It was impossible for African Americans to get beyond a seventh-grade education in Daytona public schools. The fact that black children could not complete eighth grade also meant that they could not go to high school. High-school attendance was not mandatory like it is today. The principal of Thurman's school was so impressed with him, he taught him the eighth-grade material privately so that he could take the high school entrance exam. Thurman passed the exam, but he could not attend high school in Daytona since there were no black high schools there. He was able in the end to attend a high school for African Americans in Jacksonville, Florida, where he lived with a relative. Thurman could not live with the relative after the first year, so he had to get his own apartment and work for money to pay rent. He struggled and often went hungry, but he managed to graduate in 1919 as valedictorian of his class.

Thurman received a scholarship to attend Morehouse College, a historically black college in Atlanta, Georgia. He did not think that he would become a minister when he entered college. Instead, he majored in economics. Religion became a passion for Thurman, however, and he found himself taking many religion and philosophy classes while at school. During his senior year, he decided to attend seminary, which is graduate school for people who want to become ministers. He was admitted to Colgate-Rochester Theological Seminary in upstate New York, where he was one of only two black students in his class.

Thurman became pastor of Mt. Zion Baptist Church in Oberlin, Ohio, after graduation. While there, he met Rufus Jones, who would be a great influence on Thurman's ministry. Jones was a Quaker mystic who was the leader of the Interracial Fellowship of Reconciliation. Jones also taught religion classes at Oberlin College. Thurman studied with Jones, taking his classes and working with him at Oberlin. After that, Thurman became a professor of religion. He first taught at Morehouse College, where he had attended school. He joined the faculty at Howard University in Washington, D.C., in 1931. He was a professor of religion there. He was made dean of the Rankin Chapel at Howard after just one year.

Develops His Theology

In 1935, Thurman had an opportunity to travel that would change his life and philosophy. He was the chair of a group of African Americans who traveled to India, Burma, and Ceylon. This trip reinforced for Thurman the idea that religion could be a tool for racial unity and a tool to fight oppression. While on this trip, he met with the Hindu leader Mohandas Gandhi, a leader of the Indian independence movement. Gandhi was famous for using civil disobedience and nonviolent action to fight oppression. He inspired Thurman to think of faith as a tool to overcome segregation and oppression of African Americans in the United States.

Thurman was so inspired by his visit with Gandhi that he wanted to pass Gandhi's principles on to others. He shared the experience with people like Martin Luther King Jr. and James Farmer (1920–99), who founded the Congress of Racial Equality. He also wrote about it in his famous book, *Jesus and the Disinherited,* which was published in 1949. That book contained an interpretation of the New Testament that would serve as a foundation and inspiration for the nonviolent civil rights movement. Thurman argued that the goal of Jesus's life was to help and empower the oppressed and disinherited all over the world to overcome oppression. He wrote of a "deep river of faith" that could help people overcome oppression. The river, he said, "may twist and turn, fall back on itself and start again, stumble over an infinite series of hindering rocks, but at last the river must answer the call to the sea."

Thurman left his post at Howard University in 1944 and moved across the country to San Francisco, California. There, he founded the first truly racially integrated, multicultural church, the Church for Fellowship of All Peoples. The idea of the church was that people of all racial backgrounds, and even of different religious faiths, could be united by their common belief in God. Thurman's unique ministry attracted the attention of Harold Case, the president of Boston University. He recruited Thurman to be the dean of the Marsh Chapel at Boston University and to join the theology staff there in 1953. Thurman became the first African American to head a chapel at a major white university.

Thurman was featured in *Life* magazine as one of the twelve most important religious figures in the United States in 1953. Thurman served as dean until 1965, then devoted himself to the running of the Howard Thurman Educational Trust in San Francisco for the remainder of his life. He died in San Francisco in 1981.

❖ BLACK CHURCHES FLOURISH IN THE RECONSTRUCTION SOUTH

The end of the Civil War in 1865 brought about a whirlwind of changes in the lives of former slaves. Slaves' ability to follow the religion of their choosing had been severely limited during slavery. A major change that came about during Reconstruction (the period from 1865 to 1877, when the North actively tried to rebuild the South after the Civil War) was the rapid growth of African American churches in the South. These churches provided former slaves and other African Americans with an opportunity to express a unique vision and form of Christianity. Black churches also became important centers of political activity. African American churches thrived throughout the South into the twenty-first century. They are one of the most lasting and valuable legacies of Reconstruction.

African American members of the First Congregational Church in Atlanta pose outside their building c. 1899. Black churches flourished during the Reconstruction period after the Civil War. *Buyenlarge/Hulton Archive/ Getty Images*

The End of Slavery Brings Religious Freedom

African American slaves were denied their right to religious freedom. Slaves were forbidden from holding non-Christian religious beliefs. Even those slaves who converted to Christianity faced severe restrictions. White slave owners refused to allow large groups of slaves to gather without white supervision. They believed that such gatherings could brew rebellions and resistance by slaves. Slave owners also refused to allow African Americans to serve as ministers. Ministers occupy powerful positions of leadership, and slave owners believed it was dangerous for their slaves to view anyone but a white person as a leader. As a result, slaves could only attend white-run churches, and they were denied the opportunity to participate meaningfully in those churches. They were required to sit in the back rows and remain silent during worship services.

A robust and distinctive form of Christianity emerged among African American slaves despite these restrictions. This African American Christianity featured beliefs and practices that were different from the Christianity practiced in white churches. Many white Christians in the United States in the 1800s believed the country was God's chosen land, akin to Israel in the Bible. By contrast, many slaves viewed the United States as a land of captivity, akin to Egypt in the Bible. Slaves' Christian beliefs centered on a vision of redemption and salvation. Slaves' Christian worship practices differed from those of whites because they drew on African traditions of song, dance, and public speaking. These practices were discouraged by white slave owners and largely remained underground.

The Civil War and the end of slavery brought about significant changes in the religious lives of African Americans in the South. Many slaves viewed their emancipation as proof that their religious beliefs were correct. They believed the end of slavery was a form of divine reward brought about by years of faith and prayer. As a result, many African Americans in the South believed that Christianity needed to play a central role in their lives and communities as free citizens. They began creating their own churches. A small number of newly freed slaves chose to join white or mixed-race congregations, but most African Americans became members of African American churches.

Black Churches Open Throughout the South

Several factors contributed to these new churches' ability to attract all–African American congregations. One of the most important was the evolution of segregation. As soon as slavery ended, whites in the South began passing laws and adopting social customs designed to force African Americans into an inferior social position. The Black Codes and eventually

Black Denominations Grow and Expand During Reconstruction

A frican American churches grew rapidly in number throughout the South in the years following the end of the Civil War. Only a small number of these new African American churches chose to become part of Christian denominations that were majority-white. The vast majority joined all-black denominations. Some of these African American denominations had been founded in the North before the Civil War. Others were established in the Reconstruction South. By the early twentieth century, the vast majority of African Americans were members of one of six major, independent African American denominations. Below is a list showing the name, place of founding, and date of founding for each of these six denominations.

1. **African Methodist Episcopal Church:** Philadelphia, Pennsylvania—1816
2. **African Methodist Episcopal Zion Church:** New York, New York—1821
3. **Colored Methodist Episcopal Church:** Jackson, Tennessee—1870
4. **National Baptist Convention, USA:** Atlanta, Georgia—1895
5. **The Church of God in Christ:** Jackson, Mississippi—1897
6. **National Baptist Convention of America:** Nashville, Tennessee—1915

Jim Crow laws required racial segregation, which means the law forced members of different races to remain separated from each other. By the late 1800s, there were two distinct societies and cultures in the South. Blacks and whites were apart from each other in housing, education, transportation, and employment. Religion was no exception. Racial segregation played a major role in the evolution of distinctively African American churches.

These new all-black churches were appealing to African Americans for many reasons. African Americans were able to hold leadership positions as ministers and in other capacities in these new churches. In addition, African Americans were able to give voice to their unique religious beliefs and openly practice their religion the way they wanted. Some of these churches joined existing African American denominations (groups of churches or congregations with shared religious beliefs and practices), while others branched out and established new denominations (see sidebar).

Churches Become Centers of African American Communities

The number of African Americans attending all-black churches in the South grew at an explosive rate in the years after the Civil War. For example, the African Methodist Episcopal Church (AMEC)—an all-black denomination founded in Philadelphia in 1816—gained 50,000 new members in the South during the first year after the Civil War. More than 250,000 African Americans in the South had joined the AMEC by the time Reconstruction ended in 1877. Approximately 1.35 million African Americans were members of Baptist churches in 1890. That number had grown to more than 2.2 million by 1906. Other denominations experienced similar levels of growth in their membership. In addition, the number of church buildings increased dramatically. African Americans built churches in cities, towns, and communities throughout the South.

These churches played a number of important roles in the African American communities they served. Church-run and church-supported schools provided the best educational opportunities for black students in the late 1800s. Black churches also provided important social services. They operated orphanages, old folks' homes, homeless shelters, and emergency medical care facilities. In addition, African American churches became important centers of political life and activity. Many recently freed slaves did not know how to read, so black ministers and preachers took it upon themselves to educate their congregations on the important political issues of the day. Many of the first African Americans to hold elected office in the South were ministers, including Hiram Rhoades Revels (1827–1901), the first African American ever to serve in the United States Senate.

Most historians believe that by the end of the 1800s, the church was the single most important institution in the lives of African Americans in the South. Churches were the centers of religious, political, and community life in many African American communities. By 1913, there were nearly forty thousand African American churches in the United States.

❖ FORMER SLAVES FORM COLORED METHODIST EPISCOPAL CHURCH

The Colored Methodist Episcopal Church, often referred to simply as the CME, was organized on December 16, 1870, in Jackson, Tennessee. The CME was organized by a group of former slaves who had been members of a different Methodist Episcopal church. On several previous occasions, new branches of the Methodist Church in the United States had been formed in response to different racial attitudes and beliefs among the church's members. The former slaves who founded the CME were interested in having an independent church that catered to the beliefs, practices, and situation of African Americans in the South. The CME grew rapidly and spread throughout the United States. It was still in operation in the twenty-first century.

The Methodist Church Reaches Out to Slaves

All Methodist churches in the United States are descendents of the original Methodist Church of England, which began in the 1730s. Many of the Pilgrims and other early British settlers in places that later became part of the United States were Methodists. These American Methodists organized their own church, called the Methodist Episcopal Church, in 1784. Disagreements about whether slavery was morally acceptable and compatible with the Christian faith began causing divisions within the Methodist Episcopal Church in the early 1800s. Those divisions came to a head in 1845, and the church split in two. Methodists who opposed slavery formed a denomination called the Methodist Episcopal Church South (MECS).

The CME eventually emerged out of the missionary work of the MECS. Missionary work is the practice of trying to spread religious beliefs to other people. The MECS sent white missionaries to speak to slaves in the South during the mid-1800s. These missionaries explained that one fundamental belief of the Methodist faith was that suffering in this life would be rewarded in the next. In other words, people such as slaves who were trapped in difficult situations could take comfort in the knowledge that they could find an eternal reward in heaven.

The MECS's missionary work among slaves was very successful. Slaves in the South began joining the MECS in large numbers. Specifically, nearly half of the more than four hundred thousand slaves who were members of the Christian faith at the time the Civil War started in 1861 were members of the MECS. However, the number of African Americans who belonged to the church began to decline once the Civil War ended. This was because most former slaves wanted to belong to churches with all-black memberships. There were only 76,000 African Americans who still belonged to the MECS by 1866.

Former Slaves Seek a Church of Their Own

The idea that African American members of the MECS should branch out and form a church of their own came from Isaac Lane (1834–1937). Lane was an African American preacher in the MECS. He believed former

slaves needed a church of their own. Lane attended the MECS's annual conference in New Orleans in 1866. He proposed that the MECS allow African Americans to form their own church. The MECS approved the idea, and preparations began for the establishment of the CME.

The MECS trained and ordained hundreds of African American preachers between 1866 and 1870. An administrative and organizational structure for the new church was created. Ownership of the churches attended by former slaves was transferred to the new church. The Colored Methodist Episcopal Church was officially organized in Jackson, Tennessee, on December 16, 1870. It was the first major all-black denomination to be organized in the South.

The CME quickly became one of the largest and most influential black churches in the South. One key to its growth was its view that social justice—responding to and improving the social welfare and meeting the political concerns of African Americans—was a cornerstone of the church. The CME took on a prominent role in educating African American children, organizing political and civil rights movements, and providing social services to the poor, elderly, and ill. As large numbers of African Americans left the South for points north and west during the Great

Migration of the early 1900s, the CME went with them. By the early 1920s, the CME had established a nationwide presence.

The CME became actively involved in opposing racial segregation and supporting the civil rights movement in the mid-twentieth century. The CME changed its name to the Christian Methodist Episcopal Church in 1954 because it believed the term "colored" was outdated and carried negative connotations about African Americans. The CME remained in operation under that name as of 2010. It was the third largest African American Methodist body in the United States. As of the early 2000s, the CME included more than three thousand churches and served more than eight hundred thousand members in the United States and several African and Caribbean nations.

❖ AFRICAN AMERICAN WOMEN PLAY A PROMINENT ROLE IN RELIGION

African American women became heavily involved in religion in the late 1800s, yet they were barred from leadership positions in their churches. Some African American women fought for the right to be ordained as priests or ministers. Eventually three such women—Sarah Ann Hughes (1849–unknown), Julia A. J. Foote (1823–1901), and Mary Jane Small (1850–1945)—were ordained by their churches. Other African American women became important participants in the temperance movement. The temperance movement was a religious and political movement in the 1800s that aimed to curb or eliminate the consumption of alcohol. The temperance movement provided many African American women with an opportunity to exercise leadership in the religious arena.

A Fight Is Waged for Spiritual Equality

An enormous number of African American churches were founded throughout the South after the Civil War ended in 1865. Hundreds of thousands of former slaves converted to Christianity and began attending church on a regular basis. The church became the cornerstone of many African American communities. Women typically made up a very high percentage of the congregation at African American churches. Even so, African American women were not allowed to serve as ministers, pastors, preachers, or deacons, or in other leadership positions in their churches. Sexism, the belief that women are inferior to men, was to blame. Many men believed that women were not intelligent or charismatic enough to serve as religious leaders.

Some African American women responded by exerting their leadership in ways other than as ministers and deacons. For example, many African American women joined missionary societies. Missionary societies are

An African American female pastor leads her congregation in prayer c. 1939. African American women had very few opportunities in church leadership in the early twentieth century. *Buyenlarge/Hulton Archive/ Getty Images*

religious groups dedicated to converting nonbelievers to their faith. Missionary work allowed African American women to preach their faith in a less formal setting. Other African American women became teachers and educators in church-sponsored schools. This, too, put African American women in a position to speak authoritatively about the basic beliefs and principles of their religion.

Other African American women fought back against the sexist view that they were not suited to serve as ordained officials (persons who have officially been granted ministerial or priestly authority by a church). For example, Sarah Ann Hughes was a member of the African Methodist Episcopal (AME) Church in North Carolina in the 1880s. She traveled throughout the state conducting informal religious exercises in the early 1880s despite not being an ordained official of the church. Hughes felt a deep calling to serve as an ordained minister. The AME Church had never ordained a woman, but Hughes had built a reputation as a gifted, eloquent preacher. Bishop Henry McNeal Turner (1834–1915) finally ordained Hughes as a deacon in 1885. She only served in that position for two years, however. A group of male deacons and pastors forced the AME Church to revoke her ordination in 1887. The AME Church would not ordain another woman until 1948.

The church in which African American women made the most headway as ordained officials was the African Methodist Episcopal Zion Church. The AME Zion Church was one of the largest African American churches of the late 1800s. It had 300,000 members in 1884, and by 1896, that number had grown to 350,000. Julia A. J. Foote became the first woman to be ordained as a deacon by the AME Zion Church in 1894. Mary Jane Small joined her the next year. Both women were later ordained as elders, or full priests: Small in 1898 and Foote in 1900.

Foote and Small's ordination as elders made them the first women, black or white, to be fully ordained as ministers in any Methodist church. Just as Sarah Ann Hughes faced resistance to her ordination from the male deacons in her church, so too did some male priests of AME Zion argue that Small's and Foote's ordinations should be revoked. However, AME Zion upheld their ordinations in 1900. It thereby became the first African American church ever to adopt a policy of gender equality in the ministry. Many African American churches would not follow suit for another fifty years or more.

The Temperance Movement Takes Off

These stories of African American women as ordained officials turned out to be the exception rather than the rule. Most African American women who were looking for a way to give voice to their religious convictions were forced to turn to other avenues. One such avenue was the temperance movement. The temperance movement was a religious and political movement that aimed to restrict or eliminate the consumption of alcohol. It was founded on the idea that alcohol caused moral weakness and physical illness, and reduced the drinker's ability to resist the temptations of sin. The temperance movement started in the North many years before the Civil War. At that time, most of its adherents (people who believed in it) were middle-class white women.

Many African American women in the South, particularly those who were recently freed from slavery and lived in extreme poverty, became involved in the temperance movement after the Civil War. The movement had previously advocated temperance, which means limited or moderate intake. It changed course after the war and began advocating abstinence, which means absolutely no drinking at all.

Historians believe that two main factors drew African American women to the temperance movement. First, it gave them an opportunity to serve as religious leaders at a time when they were excluded from more formal leadership roles such as ministers and deacons. Second, and relatedly, the temperance movement was an opportunity for African American women to become involved in politics, where they were barred from holding elected office, voting, sitting on juries, or otherwise participating in civic and political life.

Some African American women who participated in the temperance movement argued that the sobriety and self-control that came along with abstaining from alcohol would help African Americans gain acceptance by whites. Others argued that drinking alcohol promoted laziness and thereby prevented hard work, which was an important aspect of religious virtue. Alcohol's negative effects on the family were also stressed. African American women worked through their churches and through religious reform societies to convince their husbands and other family members to pledge to give up drinking. In this way, the temperance movement helped African American women exercise moral authority and influence.

The temperance movement ultimately culminated (came to its most successful point) in 1919 with the addition of the Eighteenth Amendment to the Constitution. The Eighteenth Amendment prohibited all manufacture and sale of alcohol throughout the United States. It was repealed by the Twenty-First Amendment in 1933.

❖ AFRICAN AMERICAN MISSIONARIES MINISTER TO AFRICA

During the 1800s, the African Methodist Episcopal Church was heavily involved with missionary work in Africa. Some of this involved traditional missionary work: traveling to other countries, setting up schools, providing humanitarian services, and teaching the people there about one's religion. The African Methodist Episcopal Church's missionary work had a particular flavor during the 1900s. Some church leaders, including influential bishop Henry McNeal Turner, wanted their missionary efforts to result in African Americans moving "back" to Africa. African American missionaries from other religious denominations also achieved notable successes in the early

Henry McNeal Turner set up missionary efforts in Africa with the goal of encouraging African Americans to move there. *Time & Life Pictures/ Getty Images*

twentieth century. However, African Americans were actively discouraged from missionary work for much of the twentieth century.

Henry McNeal Turner Pushes Vision of Emigration

Henry McNeal Turner (1834–1915) was a bishop of the African Methodist Episcopal Church who is best known for his efforts in Africa. He was born before African Americans were freed from slavery. Turner was born to a family of free blacks, so he himself was free his whole life. He joined the African Methodist Episcopal Church as a teenager, and the church offered him a job as a traveling preacher. His experiences during this period leading up to the Civil War would have a profound effect on him. He traveled around the country, particularly the American South, and he was horrified by the practice of slavery.

Turner was successful and rose quickly through the ranks of the African Methodist Episcopal Church. He also became a political leader, elected to the Georgia legislature in 1868. He lost his post after the Georgia lawmaking body passed a law forbidding African Americans from holding public office. The experience disillusioned Turner, who came to believe that the United States held little opportunity for African Americans.

Turner was elected bishop of the African Methodist Episcopal Church in 1880. He was increasingly hopeless about the state of affairs for African Americans in the United States. He began preaching that African Americans needed to find a new homeland for themselves outside of the United States. For Turner, Africa seemed the natural solution.

Turner used his position as bishop of the African Methodist Episcopal Church to direct many of the church's efforts toward Africa. He traveled extensively in Africa, making four trips there in 1891 alone. He established schools in the African countries of Liberia, Sierra Leone, and South Africa. He also began to push his vision of emigration (leaving one's country to move to another) to Africa. He encouraged the U.S. federal government to fund African American emigration. He traveled and spoke passionately to African Americans, encouraging them to emigrate to Africa.

Turner was by no means alone in his commitment to mass emigration to Africa. Many newly freed slaves and their children felt an understandable connection to Africa after the Civil War. Many agreed with Turner that African Americans should move to Africa. Other members of the African Methodist Episcopal Church felt it was their duty to offer Africans the benefits of Western civilization along with spiritual enlightenment.

Colonial Africa and African American Missionaries

The African Methodist Episcopal Church was the main force in missionary work by African Americans after 1865, but African American missionaries did have some success through other organizations in the 1890s and early twentieth century. The Presbyterian Church sponsored two young African Americans, Samuel Lapsley and William Henry Sheppard, to establish the Presbyterian Congo Mission in 1890. The two men worked together in the mission in the village of Luebo in the Congo until Lapsley died in 1892. Sheppard continued his mission work in the Congo for twenty years.

Emma Delaney was a widely respected African American Baptist missionary who built schools in central and western Africa. She worked in Africa from 1902 to 1905, then returned to Africa in 1912. She worked in Liberia from 1912 to 1920. Delaney was one of many African American missionaries to serve in Liberia. Liberia is an African nation with a unique history that made it particularly open to African American missionaries. It was founded as an American colony by freed slaves in 1822 with the help of the American Colonization Society, a group of American abolitionists. It became an independent nation in 1847. It was never colonized by European powers, unlike the rest of Africa.

The domination of Africa by European colonial powers in the nineteenth and twentieth centuries created obstacles for African Americans interested in missionary work. Most white churches were unwilling to send African American missionaries to Africa. Colonial governments tended to be suspicious of African American missionaries. They did not treat them as equal with white missionaries, which made it difficult for black missionaries to make progress with their work. Colonial governments were concerned that African Americans would encourage Africans to throw off European rule. White churches were reluctant to risk offending colonial governments despite the successes of missionaries such as Lapsley, Sheppard, and Delaney. They stopped sending African American missionaries to work in Africa by the 1920s. African American churches that tried to send missionaries were discouraged from doing so in a variety of ways. The U.S. government cooperated with colonial governments by refusing to grant passports to African Americans seeking to do missionary work in Africa. Colonial governments themselves withheld visas from African American missionaries.

African nations began to achieve independence from colonial rule in the middle of the 1950s. The pace of decolonization increased rapidly through the 1960s. As decolonization continued, African American Christians showed renewed interest in missionary work. Even in the twenty-first century, however, African Americans made up only about one percent of the total number of American missionaries in Africa.

❖ SWEET DADDY GRACE ESTABLISHES NEW PENTECOSTAL BRANCH

Most churches were segregated after freedom from slavery permitted African Americans to form their own congregations. Denominations tended to divide along color lines. An important exception was the Pentecostal, or revivalist, church tradition. Pentecostal churches brought the races together in a shared, powerful religious experience in the early twentieth century. Sweet Daddy Grace (1881–1960) was an important figure in the development of this religious movement.

Sweet Daddy Grace was born Marceline Manoël de Graça. He was born in the Cape Verde Islands. His heritage was mixed; he was part Portuguese and part African. Grace moved to the United States around 1908, settling in New Bedford, Massachusetts. There, he worked odd jobs for some time.

Sweet Daddy Grace, founder of the United House of Prayer, was known for his flamboyant image. © *Corbis*

A trip to the Holy Land, what is now Israel, planted in Grace a desire to found a church. Grace opened his first house of prayer in West Waltham, Massachusetts, in 1919, naming himself bishop. A series of religious revivals in Charlotte, North Carolina, in the mid-1920s recruited thousands of followers to his unique brand of Pentecostalism. He incorporated the church as the United House of Prayer for All People of the Church on the Rock of the Apostolic Faith in 1926.

Grace's house of prayer was based on the Pentecostal tradition. Pentecostals believe in the direct experience of God during worship through the Holy Spirit. Pentecostal worship services often involve such practices as faith healing and speaking in tongues. The daily services at Grace's house of prayer included emotional worship that was a unique characteristic of Pentecostalism.

Grace commanded his congregation with a great deal of authority. There were rumors that Grace believed that he was God, although Grace did not make that claim. Grace believed that he bridged the gap between God and his followers. Many people outside the church were skeptical of his quirky personality. He wore brightly colored suits and grew his fingernails long and painted them. He wore expensive jewels and kept his hair long. He also had some unusual practices. He baptized new converts with fire hoses, for instance, and encouraged church members to buy specially-blessed products bearing his name.

Over time, Grace's church grew large in scope. He traveled constantly, establishing eleven different houses of prayer all over the country. Grace gradually became less involved with day-to-day religious worship services and focused on the church's businesses. He used donations from church members to make investments and open businesses for the church. He acquired several manufacturing businesses for the church, and also engaged in real-estate investments. These investments paid off and increased the wealth of the church. The church owned businesses from New York to Los Angeles to Cuba. The church held a valuable real-estate portfolio, or range of properties, in New York City.

When Grace died in 1960, the United House of Prayer continued to thrive. There was momentary confusion over who would succeed, or come after, Grace as leader of the church. He was eventually replaced by Sweet Daddy Walter McCollough (1915–91). By the time Grace died, the church was a multimillion-dollar organization with over one hundred branches. McCollough was not the charismatic leader that Grace was, but he was also not nearly so controversial. Under McCullough's leadership, the church's business focus shifted to services that helped members, such as finding housing. The church continued into the twenty-first century as a strong presence in African American religious life.

❖ GOSPEL MUSIC BECOMES PART OF CHURCH LITURGY

Gospel music has long been an important part of the African American religious tradition. It is also an important African American contribution to popular culture. Gospel music emerged in the early 1900s. It was a blend of popular music like rhythm and blues and religious themes and messages. The word "gospel" comes from the Old English word for "good news." "Gospel" is also a word used to refer to the first four books of the New Testament in the Bible, which tell the story of the life of Jesus. Like the New Testament, gospel music is full of themes of freedom from oppression, joy, hopefulness, and salvation.

Thomas Dorsey poses with his gospel quartet in 1934. Dorsey composed around 800 gospel songs and popularized the music genre in the mid-twentieth century. *Frank Driggs Collection/ Getty Images*

Dorsey Becomes "Father of Gospel Music"

Many songs and strains of African American religious music can be considered precursors, or forerunners, to gospel music. But Thomas A. Dorsey (1899–1993) was the first person to write true gospel songs. He was a jazz musician, a pianist who played with some of the most famous jazz singers of the early twentieth century. These included Ma Rainey (1886–1939) and Bessie Smith (1894–1937). He was also a religious man, a Baptist. He began writing songs that combined religious themes with some of the musical conventions of jazz and blues music in 1930. He also combined elements of spirituals and ragtime music, as well as other diverse musical influences.

Dorsey wrote some eight hundred gospel songs. Some of the best-known include "(There'll Be) Peace in the Valley (for Me)," "I'm Going to Live the Life I Sing About in My Song," and "Take My Hand, Precious Lord." Reactions to

Dorsey's music were mixed at first. Some people even called it "devil's music." They did not think there was a place for popular music in church worship services.

Despite some disagreement, gospel music grew in popularity as church choirs made it part of their regular worship music. Dorsey founded many gospel choirs that came to sing in black churches all over the United States. In 1931, Dorsey founded the nation's first gospel choir at Ebenezer Baptist Church in Chicago, Illinois. The choir was so popular that similar choirs quickly sprung up all over Chicago. Dorsey also founded the National Convention of Gospel Choirs and Choruses (NCGCC). Based in Chicago, the NCGCC trained choirs from all over the country to sing gospel music.

Jackson and Cleveland Win National Acclaim

Another person who did much to advance gospel music was Mahalia Jackson (1911–72). Jackson grew up in New Orleans, Louisiana. She was raised in a religious household. She, like Dorsey, was influenced by religious worship and music as well as popular musicians like Ma Rainey and Bessie Smith. She moved to Chicago in 1927. First she became the lead singer of a gospel group called the Johnson Singers, but she soon became a solo artist. Her powerful, rich voice also attracted the attention of Thomas Dorsey. From 1935 to 1945, she was his "official song demonstrator."

Jackson also had a celebrated career as a solo recording artist. She began recording songs in 1937. In 1947, she became nationally known for her recording of "Move on Up a Little Higher." For that song, she won one of the first two gold record awards ever given to a gospel artist. Jackson also recorded a song with superstar jazz artist Duke Ellington (1899–1975).

Jackson also made some famous public appearances, which strengthened the place of gospel music in American culture. She was invited to sing in 1961 at an inauguration party for President John F. Kennedy (1917–63). In 1963, she performed at the March on Washington at which Martin Luther King Jr. (1929–68) delivered his famous "I Have a Dream" speech. She appeared in several movies: *St. Louis Blues* (1958), *Imitation of Life* (1959), and *Jazz on a Summer's Day* (1958).

James Cleveland (1931–91) grew up in Chicago, where he attended Pilgrim Baptist Church and sang in the choir. Thomas Dorsey was choir director at that time, and set Cleveland on the path to musical success. Cleveland began composing his own songs starting in the late 1940s. By the 1960s, Cleveland was including the sounds of popular African American music known as soul and R&B (rhythm and blues) into his gospel songs, just as Dorsey had used jazz and blues sounds in his compositions. Cleveland won five Grammy Awards for his gospel recordings. Cleveland's voice was rough and gravely, but very expressive. He was a popular, engaging performer.

Gospel's Wider Influence

Cleveland's music showed how closely related African American church and popular music had become by the 1960s. The soul and R&B music of that period evolved from gospel music. Many popular African American singers and groups got their earliest training singing in gospel choirs and started their careers recording gospel music. Aretha Franklin (1942–), Sam Cooke (1931–64), and Al Green (1946–) are just a few examples. As these artists achieved mainstream success, the sounds of African American gospel music became more familiar—and more popular—with white audiences.

Gospel music became big business in the 1960s. It moved out of its traditional church setting and became more like popular music. Gospel music recordings continued to prove very successful in the twenty-first century, with albums by artists such as Kirk Franklin (1970–) regularly topping popular music rankings. Nevertheless, church-based gospel choirs remain a distinctive feature of most African American houses of worship.

❖ THE NATION OF ISLAM IS FOUNDED

The Nation of Islam played a tremendous role in the civil rights era and contributed to the rise of the black power movement. But it was founded, grew, and began to thrive during the segregation era, decades before African Americans achieved civil rights.

Wallace Fard Lays the Foundation

The Nation of Islam was founded by a man named Wallace Fard (1877–1934). He served a prison term in California in the 1920s, after which he moved to Chicago, Illinois. Fard joined the Moorish Science Temple in Chicago, where he learned things that would inspire him to found the Nation of Islam. The Moorish Science Temple taught that African Americans were descended from the Moors in Africa. The Moors were a Muslim culture, so the Moorish Temple taught that Islam was the proper religion for blacks in the United States. The Moorish Science Temple also taught that African Americans were superior to whites. It preached a message of black nationalism, a message of economic and cultural independence from white culture in the United States.

Fard moved to Detroit, Michigan, inspired by what he had learned in Chicago. Fard became a street peddler in Detroit, selling cloth and sewing supplies in black neighborhoods. The charismatic Fard became well

Nation of Islam Teachings

The Nation of Islam taught that blacks were the original race of humans on Earth, which makes them superior to other races. It taught that the Earth and Moon had once been one unit but that they had been divided by an explosion. At that time, it was said, the black tribe of Shabazz was created, the original humans on Earth. Whites, by contrast, had been created by an evil magician named Yakub. For this reason, whites were evil and degraded. The Nation of Islam sought to lift up blacks, who had been taken from Africa and enslaved in America.

known. He told people that he was the prophet of a new religion based on the teachings of the Moorish Science Temple. Fard took the teachings of the Moorish Science Temple and added some of his own personal philosophy. The result was a religion he called the Nation of Islam.

In 1930, Fard met a young man who would become the Nation of Islam's leader. His name was Elijah Poole (1897–1975). Poole was interested in Fard's teachings, which included the idea that African Americans should renounce their "slave names," the names that whites gave their ancestors when they came to the United States. Poole soon became Fard's closest lieutenant, and Fard gave him the name Elijah Karriem. He changed Elijah's name again to Elijah Muhammad when it became clear that he would become the new leader of the organization.

Fard became the target of police scrutiny, or close watchfulness, in 1932. One of his followers had committed a brutal murder. When the man was arrested, he cited Fard's teachings as his reason for the killing. This made the police turn their attentions to Fard himself. They did not charge him with the murder. But they did warn him that he must stop preaching the message that they believe caused the murder. Fard obeyed initially, but then he started to preach once more. He was again arrested. After this arrest, Fard left town and disappeared permanently.

Nation of Islam Flourishes Under Elijah Muhammad's Leadership

When Fard disappeared, the Nation of Islam devolved into bitter battles over who would take his place. Some thought his heir should be Elijah Muhammad, whom Fard had given the title "chief minister of Islam."

Nation of Islam members stand on the steps of Muhammad's Temple No. 2 with bundles of the organization's newspaper *Muhammad Speaks* under their arms, Chicago, Illinois, 1965. *Robert Abbott Sengstacke/Hulton Archive/Getty Images*

He had groomed Muhammad to be his successor. But other ministers believed that they were the rightful heir to Fard, and bloody battles ensued. Muhammad was forced to flee Detroit to avoid threats against his life.

After he fled Detroit, Muhammad went to Chicago, Illinois, in 1936. There he set up the Nation of Islam's "Temple Number Two," which would become the headquarters for the Nation of Islam. Muhammad continued Fard's teachings, which were loosely based on the Islamic faith. He taught that African Americans descended from a black tribe from the African continent. He taught that they owed no loyalty to the white power structure of the United States, which had for years enslaved and oppressed them.

The Hate that Hate Produced?

Television commentator Mike Wallace (1918–) produced a television documentary in 1959 called "The Hate that Hate Produced." He made the documentary with African American journalist Louis Lomax (1922–70). The documentary profiled the rise of the Nation of Islam. It contrasted the Nation of Islam with the integrationist ideas of the National Association for the Advancement of Colored People (NAACP) and other civil rights groups. The documentary was critical of the Nation of Islam's teachings, criticizing them as hatemongering.

Around the same time, the Nation of Islam received criticism from other corners, too. Thurgood Marshall (1908–93), who would become the first African American justice to sit on the United States Supreme Court, publicly criticized the Nation's teachings. At the time, he was chief legal counsel for the NAACP. He said the Nation of Islam was run by "thugs" from prisons and jails. Various publications ran critical articles as well. Many of these publications, including *U.S. News & World Report* and the *Chicago Daily News,* called the Nation of Islam a "black supremacy cult." The Nation of Islam's separatist teachings became the subject of much national anxiety when they were publicized. People were especially anxious at the "white devils" label Muhammad and Fard had given to the white power structure in the United States.

But supporters of leaders like Elijah Muhammad and Malcolm X believed that their teachings were necessary to unify the black community and help African Americans rise above their often dismal circumstances during the segregation era. The nonviolent Christian strategies advocated by leaders like Martin Luther King Jr. were not working, they said. Rather than teaching its followers to turn the other cheek, the Nation of Islam taught self-defense. Rather than teaching its members to seek acceptance in white society, the Nation of Islam taught African Americans to strengthen their own communities and seek success outside of white culture.

The motto of the Nation of Islam under Muhammad's leadership was "Do for Self." The idea was that African Americans should not rely on the white power structure for their emancipation and civil rights. They needed to lift up their own communities and create their own opportunities.

Although Muhammad's teachings were quite radical, the lifestyle he preached for his followers was very conservative. He taught his followers to rely on themselves, and to avoid debt and excessive spending. He preached a conservative morality as well: that people should avoid adultery, that women should dress extremely modestly, and that men should place their families first. Followers of the Nation of Islam were to avoid pork, fatty foods, drugs, alcohol, and tobacco. Clean living was important. The Nation of Islam also emphasized education as a means to black advancement.

Perhaps the most important development under Muhammad's leadership was the idea that his followers should create their own economic opportunities. Hundreds of black-owned businesses sprung up in black neighborhoods with the help and support of the Nation of Islam. There were "Black Muslim" bakeries, grocery stores, and restaurants. Muhammad encouraged his followers to pool their resources and open bigger businesses, like farms and factories. These businesses provided economic opportunities for African Americans in cities across the United States that were otherwise not available to them in many places during the segregation era.

Muhammad's controversial teachings attracted the attention of law enforcement in many cities. By the beginning of the 1940s, he was living in Washington, D.C., where he had established a Nation of Islam temple. The federal government, suspicious of possible un-American or treasonous activities going on in the Nation of Islam, sent an undercover operative to investigate the organization. The individual did not uncover un-American activities, but did discover that many members of the Nation of Islam opposed U.S. involvement in World War II, and many refused to serve in the armed forces.

Muhammad was eventually arrested in 1942 for failing to register for the draft, or mandatory military service. He served four years in federal prison for refusing to comply with the nation's selective service laws. Muhammad emerged from prison the undisputed leader of the Nation of Islam. Other competitors by this point more or less gave up their claims to head the organization.

Malcolm X Helps the Movement Flourish

Another factor in the rise of the Nation of Islam to the powerful civil rights organization that it became was the leadership of Malcolm X (1925–65). Malcolm X was born Malcolm Little. He had a rocky childhood and went on to serve time in prison in Massachusetts. It was in prison, between 1947 and 1952, that Malcolm Little converted to Islam.

Malcolm X speaks at a rally in Harlem in 1963. Malcolm X was the Nation of Islam's most dynamic representative until he left the organization in 1964. *AP Images*

Malcolm X was a powerful public speaker, and upon his release from prison, he became a spokesman for the Nation of Islam. He was extremely successful at recruiting young new members to convert and join the Nation of Islam. During the 1950s, Malcolm X increasingly became the public face of the Nation of Islam, while Muhammad focused his energies on building the organization's strong economic network.

The Nation of Islam began to splinter in the mid-1960s. Malcolm X broke from the group, in part because he was disillusioned by what he saw as the moral failings of Muhammad and in part because he had been inspired by a more inclusive form of Islam he had encountered during travels in the Middle East. Shortly after forming his own religious organization, he was assassinated by members of the Nation of Islam in February 1965. Muhammad's own son, W. D. Muhammad, was eager to move away from the radical separatism preached by his father. When Elijah Muhammad died in 1975, his son took over and renamed the Nation of

Islam as the World Community of Al-Islam in the West. The Nation of Islam was re-founded in 1978 by Louis Farrakhan (1933–). The church had about ten thousand members as of 2009, far below its peak of more than fifty thousand in the late 1960s and early 1970s.

❖ MINISTERS MOVE TO THE FOREFRONT OF ACTIVIST LEADERSHIP

Many African American religious leaders during the period between 1865 and 1965 fought for social justice, particularly civil rights for African Americans. African American religious leaders also fought for gender equality, temperance, and justice for the poor, among other social causes. By the early twentieth century, the potential of African American religious groups to force social change became clear. Churches had the organization, structure, and funding necessary for effective action. Church members hold regular meetings, have established leaders, and have uniting principles.

Martin Luther King Jr. leads a protest march in 1963. King is the most famous of the many minister-activists who actively worked for African American civil rights. *National Archives and Records Administration (NARA)*

The fact the Christian teachings stress equality, brotherly love, and liberation from bondage made it natural for African American churches to apply their religious beliefs to the quest for equal rights.

The African Methodist Church and the Early Push for Equal Rights

The African Methodist Episcopal Church (AME Church) was established in 1816 by black abolitionists. The cause of freedom for slaves and equality for African Americans were the church's founding principles, and remained its focus into the twentieth century. Some leaders of the AME Church, including Reverdy Cassius Ransom (1861–1959), were involved with activist W. E. B. Du Bois's Niagara Movement. The Niagara Movement was formed to directly oppose the politics of early civil rights leader Booker T. Washington (1856–1915). Washington believed that African Americans should focus on self-improvement rather than actively seek inclusion and integration in white society. The Niagara Movement was based on the idea that blacks should not wait for civil rights, but should demand them. The movement disbanded in 1910, but its offshoot, the National Association for the Advancement of Colored People (NAACP), would become highly influential. The NAACP continued to be an important force in politics into the twenty-first century.

Christian Leaders Lead the Civil Rights Movement

African American religious leaders were active in the fight for equal rights throughout the early part of the twentieth century, but took a national stand against discrimination and injustice during the civil rights movement of the 1950s and 1960s. The most famous African American minister-activist was Martin Luther King Jr. King worked with a network of other religious leaders, inspired by faith to fight for civil rights. In 1955, King, Ralph Abernathy (1926–90), and other religious and community leaders came together to organize one of the first major acts of protest of the modern civil rights era: the Montgomery bus boycott. The boycott of the Montgomery, Alabama, public bus system was organized after Rosa Parks (1913–2005), an African American woman, was arrested for refusing to give up her seat on a bus to a white person. King, a young minister at the Dexter Avenue Baptist Church in Montgomery, was chosen to lead the boycott. It was an enormous success. The boycott had widespread support, not just in Montgomery's African American community, but in African American communities across the country. It attracted national media attention. The loss of fares from black riders had immediate, direct impact on the city of Montgomery's finances. The boycott continued for more than a year, until the Alabama Supreme Court upheld a district court ruling that declared bus segregation unconstitutional. A new city ordinance officially desegregated public buses.

Their success with the Montgomery bus boycott inspired King and Abernathy to co-found the Southern Christian Leadership Conference (SCLC) in 1957. The SCLC was a coalition of dozens of African American religious and community leaders who joined together with the common goal of advocating for integration. King, Abernathy, and the SCLC used nonviolent direct action to put pressure on the government and private businesses to give rights to African Americans. The SCLC enjoyed a dramatic, hard-won success in 1963 in their attempts to force the desegregation of stores in downtown Birmingham, Alabama. Boycotts of downtown merchants began in 1962, causing a sharp decline in business. Sit-ins at lunch counters, libraries, and even churches followed. King and Abernathy, along with dozens of other protestors, were arrested in April 1963 for disobeying a sheriff's order against protesting. While jailed, King wrote his famous "Letter from Birmingham Jail" calling on white clergymen to recognize the importance of the civil rights struggle.

The Birmingham campaign reached a frightening climax on May 2 and 3. On May 2, about a thousand African American schoolchildren skipped school in order to participate in what was later called the "Children's Crusade." They were told by protest organizers to move into downtown Birmingham in groups and integrate into pre-selected buildings. Most of the children were arrested. Another group of about a thousand children gathered on May 3, but Birmingham's sheriff Bull Connor ordered fire hoses turned on them. The blasts from the hoses knocked the children off their feet and sent them rolling down the street. German shepherd attack dogs were then used against protestors. Images of the incident on May 3 made international headlines and outraged the American public.

Violent outbursts continued through May, but by July, Birmingham had overturned most of its segregation ordinances. The Birmingham campaign made King a national figure and a hero to the African American community. In the summer of 1963, King delivered his famous "I Have a Dream" speech at the March on Washington for Jobs and Freedom. This major political rally was organized by the SCLC, the NAACP, the Urban League, and African American labor organizations. King won the Nobel Peace Prize for his efforts on behalf of civil rights in 1964.

Leaders of the Nation of Islam Also Press Civil Rights Issues

Not all African American religious leaders agreed with King's approach to civil rights. A prominent young leader in the Nation of Islam, Malcolm X (1925–65), directly criticized the use of children during the SCLC's Birmingham campaign and called King's philosophy of nonviolence ineffective.

The Nation of Islam was founded in Detroit in 1930. It combined elements of traditional Islam with a philosophy of black separatism. Leaders of the Nation of Islam were active as activists and political leaders. Elijah Muhammad (1897–1975), the long-time leader of the organization, taught his followers to respect themselves and their communities. He told followers that Islam, not Christianity, was the natural religion of African Americans. He preached a lifestyle of temperance: abstaining from alcohol, tobacco, drugs, even fatty and unhealthy foods. He also fought for business and economic opportunities for African Americans. The Nation of Islam and its members opened numerous businesses that would serve and provide economic opportunity for African Americans.

It was the inspiring leadership of Malcolm X, however, that brought tens of thousands of followers to the Nation of Islam and attracted national media attention. Malcolm X had converted to Islam in prison. He became active in the Nation of Islam after his release from prison in 1952. He spread its message of self-reliance and self-respect for African Americans. He also focused unflinchingly on the effects of racism in the United States, past and present, and called whites "inferior" and "devils." Malcolm pushed for African Americans to separate from white society and move to Africa if possible. By 1964, his view changed somewhat. He converted to traditional Sunni Islam and traveled throughout Africa and Europe. His experiences led him to revise his negative views of white people and seek cooperation with other civil rights leaders. He was assassinated in 1965 before he could put his new philosophy into action.

Both Christian and Muslim African American church leaders continued their social activism after the deaths of Malcolm and, in 1968, Martin Luther King Jr. Abernathy took over leadership of the SCLC after King's assassination, and he led the Poor People's Campaign in Washington, D.C., in 1968 to bring the plight of the poor to the attention of President Lyndon B. Johnson (1908–73). After Malcolm's death, Minister Louis Farrakhan (1933–) became one of the Nation of Islam's most prominent leaders. In 1995, he organized the Million Man March on Washington, in which hundreds of thousands of African American men gathered together in an effort to combat negative stereotypes of black men and call attention to the challenges still facing the African American community. Jesse Jackson (1941–), a major SCLC leader who went on to found his own social activism groups, was a speaker at the Million Man March. His presence at the event is evidence that the activist traditions of Martin Luther King Jr. and Malcolm X eventually did come together.

AZUSA STREET REVIVAL SERMON (1906)

The Azusa Street Revival was the longest continuously running revival in U.S. history, starting in 1906. "Revival" refers to a series of religious meetings, often marked by strong emotion. The series of meetings led by African American preacher William Joseph Seymour on Azusa Street lasted for three years and are credited with starting the Pentecostal movement. The Pentecostal religious movement is a branch of Christianity that emphasizes direct experience of God through the Holy Spirit. The following excerpt is from a sermon Seymour gave in 1906 called "River of Living Water." In it, Seymour explains the significance of an encounter Jesus had with a Samaritan woman at a well, and how that encounter relates to the modern believer's experience with the Holy Spirit.

．．．．．．．．．．．．．．．．．．．．．．．．．

In Jesus Christ we get forgiveness of sin, and we get sanctification of our spirit, soul and body, and upon that we get the gift of the Holy Ghost that Jesus promised to His disciples, the promise of the Father. All this we get through the **atonement.** Hallelujah!

The prophet said that He had borne our griefs and carried our sorrows. He was wounded for our **transgressions,** bruised for our **iniquities,** the chastisement of our peace was upon Him and with His stripes we are healed. So we get healing, health, salvation, joy, life—everything in Jesus. Glory to God!

There are many wells today, but they are dry. There are many hungry souls today that are empty. But let us come to Jesus and take Him at His Word and we will find wells of salvation, and be able to draw waters out of the well of salvation, for Jesus is that well.

At this time Jesus was weary from a long journey, and He sat on the well in Samaria, and a woman came to draw water. He asked her for a drink. She answered, "How is it that thou being a Jew asketh drink of me who am a woman of Samaria, for the Jews have no dealings with the Samaritans?" Jesus said, "If thou knewest the gift of God, and who it is that saith to thee, give me to drink, thou wouldest have asked of Him and He would have given thee living water."

O, how sweet it was to see Jesus, the Lamb of God that takes away the sin of the world, that great sacrifice that God had given to a lost, dying and benighted world, sitting on the well and talking with the woman; so gentle, so **meek** and so kind that it gave her an appetite to talk further with Him, until He got into her secret and uncovered her life. Then she was pricked in her heart, confessed her sins and received pardon ... was washed from stain and guilt of sin and was made a child of God,

Atonement
Christian belief in reconnection with God brought about by Jesus's death

Transgressions
Sins

Iniquities
Sins

Meek
Obedient

and above all, received the well of salvation in her heart. It was so sweet and joyful and good. Her heart was so filled with love that she felt she could take in a whole lost world. So she ran away with a well of salvation and left the old water pot on the well. How true it is in this day, when we get the baptism with the Holy Spirit, we have something to tell, and it is that the blood of Jesus Christ cleanseth from all sin. The baptism with the Holy Ghost gives us power to testify to a risen, resurrected Saviour. Our affections are in Jesus Christ, the Lamb of God that takes away the sin of the world. How I worship Him today! How I praise Him for the all-cleansing blood. . . .

Above all, let us honor the blood of Jesus Christ every moment of our lives, and we will be sweet in our souls. We will be able to talk of this common salvation to everyone that we meet. God will let His anointing rest upon us in telling them of this precious truth. This truth belongs to God. We have no right to tax anyone for the truth, because God has entrusted us with it to tell it. Freely we receive, freely we give. So the gospel is preached freely, and God will bless it and spread it Himself, and we have experienced that He does. We have found Him to be true to His promise all the way. We have tried Him and proved Him. His promises are sure.

◈ EXCERPT FROM MARTIN LUTHER KING'S "LETTER FROM BIRMINGHAM JAIL" (1963)

Martin Luther King Jr. had been leading a protest of segregation practices in Birmingham, Alabama, in 1963. The protest had sparked violent confrontations between Birmingham police and the demonstrators. The police initiated the violence by attacking peaceful demonstrators with clubs, police dogs, and fire hoses. A court had ordered that there be no more protests because of the violence. King continued to lead the protests in defiance of the court order, and was arrested.

The violent result of the protest and King's willingness to break the law to continue the protest caused white clergymen to ask the black community to stop their demonstrations. They felt that the actions of King and the demonstrators were unwise and untimely. King responded to their criticism from his jail cell with a famous letter known as "Letter from Birmingham Jail" in August 1963. The letter defended the nonviolent tactics used by the demonstrators and framed them in terms of Christian principles. The following excerpt from King's letter shows the influence that Christianity had on the civil rights movement.

· ·

My Dear Fellow Clergymen:

While confined here in the Birmingham city jail, I came across your recent statement calling my present activities "unwise and untimely." . . . [S]ince I feel that

Two pages of a
handwritten copy of
Martin Luther King Jr.'s
"Letter from Birmingham
Jail." *AP Images*

you are men of genuine good will and that your criticisms are sincerely set forth, I want to try to answer your statement in what I hope will be patient and reasonable terms.

I think I should indicate why I am here in Birmingham, since you have been influenced by the view which argues against "outsiders coming in." . . .

I am in Birmingham because injustice is here. Just as the prophets of the eighth century B.C. left their villages and carried their "thus saith the Lord" far beyond the boundaries of their home towns . . . .

We have waited for more than 340 years for our constitutional and God given rights. The nations of Asia and Africa are moving with jetlike speed toward gaining political independence, but we still creep at horse and buggy pace toward gaining a cup of coffee at a lunch counter. Perhaps it is easy for those who have never felt the stinging darts of segregation to say, "Wait." But when you have seen vicious mobs lynch your mothers and fathers at will and drown your sisters and brothers at whim; when you have seen hate filled policemen curse, kick and even kill your black brothers and sisters; when you see the vast majority of your twenty million Negro brothers smothering in an airtight cage of poverty in the midst of an affluent society; when you suddenly find your tongue twisted and your speech stammering as you seek to explain to your six year old daughter why she can't go to the public amusement park that has just been advertised on television, and see tears welling up in her eyes when she is told that Funtown is closed to colored children, and see ominous clouds of inferiority beginning to form in her little mental sky, and see her beginning to distort her personality by developing an unconscious bitterness toward white people; when you have to concoct an answer for a five year old son who is asking: "Daddy, why do white people treat colored people so mean?"... I hope, sirs, you can understand our legitimate and unavoidable impatience. You express a great deal of anxiety over our willingness to break laws. This is certainly a legitimate concern. Since we so diligently urge people to obey the Supreme Court's decision of 1954 outlawing segregation in the public schools, at first glance it may seem rather paradoxical for us consciously to break laws. One may well ask: "How can you advocate breaking some laws and obeying others?" The answer lies in the fact that there are two types of laws: just and unjust. I would be the first to advocate obeying just laws. One has not only a legal but a moral responsibility to obey just laws. Conversely, one has a moral responsibility to disobey unjust laws. I would agree with St. Augustine that "an unjust law is no law at all."...

Civil Disobedience
Refusing to obey the government for philosophical reasons

Academic Freedom
The idea that scholars should be free to study whatever they want without being directed by the government or university officials

Zeitgeist
The general intellectual, moral, and cultural climate of an era

Latent
Existing but not visible or apparent

Of course, there is nothing new about this kind of **civil disobedience**.... It was practiced superbly by the early Christians, who were willing to face hungry lions and the excruciating pain of chopping blocks rather than submit to certain unjust laws of the Roman Empire. To a degree, **academic freedom** is a reality today because Socrates practiced civil disobedience. In our own nation, the Boston Tea Party represented a massive act of civil disobedience....

Oppressed people cannot remain oppressed forever. The yearning for freedom eventually manifests itself, and that is what has happened to the American Negro. Something within has reminded him of his birthright of freedom, and something without has reminded him that it can be gained. Consciously or unconsciously, he has been caught up by the **Zeitgeist**, and with his black brothers of Africa and his brown and yellow brothers of Asia, South America and the Caribbean, the United States Negro is moving with a sense of great urgency toward the promised land of racial justice. If one recognizes this vital urge that has engulfed the Negro community, one should readily understand why public demonstrations are taking place. The Negro has many pent up resentments and **latent** frustrations, and he must release them. So let him march; let him make prayer pilgrimages to the city hall; let him go on freedom rides and try to understand why he must do so. If his repressed emotions are not released in nonviolent ways, they will seek expression through violence; this is not a threat but a fact of history. So I have not said to my people: "Get rid of your discontent." Rather, I have tried to say that this normal and healthy discontent can be channeled into the creative outlet of nonviolent direct action. And now this approach is being termed extremist. But though I was initially disappointed at being categorized as an extremist, as I continued to think about the matter I gradually gained a measure of satisfaction from the label. Was not Jesus an extremist for love: "Love your enemies, bless them that curse you, do good to them that hate you, and pray for them which despitefully use you, and persecute you."...

I hope this letter finds you strong in the faith. I also hope that circumstances will soon make it possible for me to meet each of you, not as an integrationist or a civil-rights leader but as a fellow **clergyman** and a Christian brother. Let us all hope that the dark clouds of racial prejudice will soon pass away and the deep fog of misunderstanding will be lifted from our fear drenched communities, and in some not too distant tomorrow the radiant stars of love and brotherhood will shine over our great nation with all their scintillating beauty.

Yours for the cause of Peace and Brotherhood,
Martin Luther King, Jr.

Clergyman
Minister

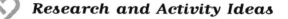

Research and Activity Ideas

1. Many African American ministers during segregation times were ardent activists and community organizers. For many, religion and social issues like equality and desegregation were not separate issues at all. Instead, many believed that their religious moral values also required them to advocate for social change and justice. Choose one of the ministers profiled in this chapter and find one of their sermons on the Internet. Can you see connections between the person's religious beliefs and commitments to equality and social change? Write an essay exploring the connections you see. Be sure to use at least three specific examples from the sermon.

2. Followers of the Nation of Islam in the pre–civil rights era tended to oppose the integration of the white and black races. By contrast, many black Christians, like members of the Southern Christian Leadership Conference, supported integrationist policies. Research the views of Elijah Muhammad, leader of the Nation of Islam, and Martin Luther King Jr., leader of the Southern Christian Leadership Conference. Write an essay comparing and contrasting their views on segregation and separatism. Be sure to use three different examples for each person. Then, analyze how the men's religious views influenced their views on integration versus segregation.

3. Choose one of the religious sects discussed in this chapter, like Pentecostalism, the Nation of Islam, or the African Methodist Episcopal Church. Do some research to find out more about that sect's views on God and the relationship between religious and daily life. Then think about why that sect's particular viewpoint might have made it attractive to African Americans during the segregation era. Is there anything about the sect's teachings that might have been particularly appealing to African Americans in the decades after the end of slavery? Have a discussion with your classmates where you present your research and theory. Then, see if others have different ideas about what might have made that sect popular with African Americans during this time period.

4. Women played different roles and had different degrees of involvement with various religious movements during the pre–civil rights era. For instance, many women were ministers of Pentecostal churches around the turn of the century. By contrast, many criticized the Nation of Islam for being less inclusive of women. Father Divine, a mystic leader, believed strongly in gender equality. Choose three religious sects or leaders from the pre-civil rights period and consider their views

on the proper role of women in society and also in the religion itself. Compare and contrast their views on things like: Did women hold leadership roles? Did they have speaking roles in church or temple? Then consider why these differences might exist. Write an essay discussing your findings.

For More Information

BOOKS

Battle, Michael. *The Black Church in America: African American Christian Spirituality.* Oxford: Wiley-Blackwell, 2006.

Collier-Thomas, Bettye. *Jesus, Jobs, and Justice: African American Women and Religion.* New York: Knopf Publishers, 2010.

Lincoln, C. Eric, and Lawrence H. Mamiya. *The Black Church in the African-American Experience.* Durham, NC: Duke University Press, 1990.

Lovett, Bobby L. *A Black Man's Dream: The First 100 Years (Richard Henry Boyd).* Nashville, TN: Mega Corporation, 1993.

Mitchell, Henry H. *Black Church Beginnings: The Long-Hidden Realities of the First Years.* Grand Rapids, MI: William B. Eerdman Publishing Co., 2004.

Phillips, Charles Henry. *The History of the Colored Methodist Episcopal Church in America: Comprising Its Organization, Subsequent Development and Present Status.* Jackson, TN: C.M.E. Church, 1925. Also available online at http://docsouth.unc.edu/church/phillips/menu.html (accessed on December 14, 2009).

Raboteau, Albert J. *African-American Religion.* New York: Oxford University Press, 1999.

Robeck, Cecil M., Jr. *The Azusa Street Mission and Revival.* Nashville, TN: Thomas Nelson, Inc., 2006.

Stowell, Daniel W. *Rebuilding Zion: The Religious Reconstruction of the South, 1863–1877.* Oxford, England: Oxford University Press, 1998.

Thurman, Howard. *Howard Thurman: Essential Writings.* Maryknoll, NY: Orbis Books, 2006.

WEB SITES

This Far by Faith: African-American Spiritual Journeys. http://www.pbs.org/thisfarbyfaith/ (accessed on December 14, 2009).

chapter thirteen ## Science and Technology

1872 Railroad worker Elijah McCoy invents an automatic lubricating cup for machine parts, which soon becomes a standard part on many kinds of machinery.

1875 Furniture maker David Fisher invents the joiner's clamp, which holds two pieces of wood together tightly so they can be glued without requiring a great deal of human effort.

1876 Physicist Edward Bouchet becomes the first African American in the United States to earn a Ph.D., awarded at Yale University.

1876 Lewis Latimer, a draftsman for a patent attorney in Massachusetts, assists Alexander Graham Bell with his patent application for a new device, the telephone.

1881 Lewis Latimer creates a more durable filament for incandescent lightbulbs, greatly improving the durability and practicality of electric lighting.

1883 Inventor Jan Ernst Matzeliger creates a shoe lasting machine that dramatically decreases the amount of time required to assemble shoes.

1884 Willis Johnson invents an eggbeater that serves as the basis for modern kitchen mixers.

1885 Sarah Goode becomes the first African American woman to earn a patent with her design for a bed that folds away into a desk.

1891 Albert Richardson invents the butter churn.

1891 Philip Downing invents the first drop mail box for the United States Postal Service.

1892 Inventor Granville T. Woods patents a method for supplying electricity to moving trains from stationary blocks situated along the train's tracks.

1893 Thomas Stewart invents the modern mop.

1896 Charles Brooks invents the automated street sweeper.

1897 George Washington Carver launches the Agricultural Experiment Station at the Tuskegee Institute.

1897 John Love invents the first mechanical pencil sharpener.

1897 Lloyd Ray invents the dustpan, the design of which remains largely unchanged into the twenty-first century.

1899 Avid golfer George Grant invents the golf tee.

1909 Inventor Garrett Morgan discovers a chemical relaxer capable of straightening textured hair.

1909 **April 7** Explorer Matthew Henson accompanies Robert Peary on the first human expedition to reach the geographic North Pole (though some experts have since disputed this claim).

1914 March 24 Garrett Morgan patents a safety hood that serves as a prototype for future gas masks.

1915 Biologist Ernest E. Just becomes the first recipient of the Spingarn Medal, presented by the National Association for the Advancement of Colored People (NAACP) for outstanding achievements performed by an African American.

1915 George Washington Carver publishes *How to Grow the Peanut and 105 Ways of Preparing It for Human Consumption.*

1921 January George Washington Carver testifies before the House Ways and Means Committee regarding the usefulness of peanuts, an appearance that earns him fame.

1921 June 15 Bessie Coleman becomes the first African American woman to earn an international pilot's license.

1923 November 20 Garrett Morgan invents an automobile traffic signal that becomes the model for traffic signals around the world.

1932 Pilots James Herman Banning and Thomas C. Allen become the first African Americans to travel across the United States by plane.

1937 Willa Brown becomes the first African American woman to earn a pilot's license in the United States.

1939 Ernest E. Just publishes *The Biology of the Cell Surface,* an important work in the field of cell biology.

1945 The Tuskegee Institute opens its School of Veterinary Medicine, one of fewer than a dozen such veterinary schools in the country.

1952 Biochemist Harold Dadford West becomes the first African American president of Meharry Medical College in Nashville, Tennessee.

1955 Mathematician David Blackwell is hired as the first African American tenured professor at the University of California at Berkeley.

1956 Perry Young becomes the first African American to earn a helicopter pilot's license.

1960 Pilot and surgeon Vance Marchbanks is selected as the medical specialist for the Mercury space program; he is responsible for monitoring vital signs and health information of astronauts while they are in space.

1961 Aeronautical engineer O. S. Williams begins working for NASA, where he designs the small-rocket propulsion system used to land the Apollo lunar module on the surface of the Moon.

1965 **March** Marlon Green is hired as the first African American pilot for a major airline.

1967 Pilot and scientist Robert H. Lawrence is selected to become the first African American in space as part of the Manned Orbital Laboratory project; he dies six months later in a plane crash before getting his chance to travel into space.

1968 Microbiologist Harold Amos is chosen as the chairman of the Department of Bacteriology and Immunology at Harvard, making him the first African American to serve as a department chair at the university.

1972 A moon-based observatory designed and built by astrophysicist George R. Carruthers is put into operation by Apollo 16 astronauts.

Overview

The African American presence in the areas of science and technology was fairly limited at the end of the Civil War (1861–65). Aside from a few notable intellectuals, African Americans had been largely excluded from receiving advanced educations. This began to change in the years immediately following the Civil War. There was a push to increase educational resources for African Americans, particularly in the South, where many freed blacks had never before received any sort of schooling. The emphasis was on basic education. The colleges built throughout the South were called "normal schools," and their focus was generally to offer basic education and to train students to provide a basic education to other African Americans. Some schools like the Tuskegee Institute focused on training in other practical trades as well. None, however, focused on education in the sciences.

African American physicist Edward Bouchet (1852–1918) was a rarity for his time. He grew up near Yale and attended the university just after the Civil War, when public sentiment favoring African American education was high. Yale was also one of the few colleges in the United States to offer a Ph.D. in the sciences. Bouchet earned his Ph.D. in physics in 1876, but discovered a painful truth that would continue to affect African American scientists for decades: Even universities willing to admit African American students would not hire them as teachers. Since no African American colleges had programs in advanced sciences like physics, Bouchet found himself teaching at the Institute for Colored Youth. More than forty years passed between Bouchet's achievement and the next Ph.D. in physics for an African American, Samuel Elmer Imes (1883–1941).

African Americans seeking advanced training in the sciences found themselves locked into an unfortunate system. Many, like Imes, could not attend colleges or universities in the South because the training was simply not available. Those who achieved advanced degrees at the few willing universities that existed in the North found that the only jobs they could get were at African American universities, many of which did not offer advanced science programs. This slowly began to change as highly educated scientists entered universities like Howard University and the Tuskegee Institute, and began their own advanced science programs.

Still, many of these scientists found themselves without the resources they needed to conduct research. Ernest E. Just (1883–1941) was a prominent biologist who worked at Howard University, but did not have basic laboratory equipment to allow him to study cells. For that reason, he began spending his summers at the Marine Biological Laboratory (MBL) at

Woods Hole, Massachusetts. It was for work completed at the MBL that Just received the very first Spingarn Medal, an award given by the National Association for the Advancement of Colored People (NAACP) for outstanding achievements by an African American. Like Just, many African American scientists who took teaching positions in the South spent their free time back in the North at universities that offered better laboratory resources.

This lack of resources slowly began to change during the first half of the twentieth century. The Tuskegee Institute became the first African American school to receive its own Agricultural Experiment Station in 1897, which was overseen by George Washington Carver (1864–1943). The university also became home to the first veterinary school for African Americans in 1945. At the time, it was one of fewer than a dozen veterinary schools in the United States, and offered programs as advanced as any other veterinary college.

Even as many African Americans struggled to achieve an education in the sciences, many others found their way to success through inventions. Submitting a patent for a new invention required no special schooling, and the patent office did not discriminate against inventors based on their race. This led to a huge surge in inventions by African Americans during the last decades of the nineteenth century. Inventors like Granville T. Woods (1856–1910), Lewis Latimer (1848–1928), and Garrett Morgan (1877–1963) had a profound impact on various fields, including electrical science, fire safety, and traffic control. Many more inventors offered improvements to existing devices that made life easier for all Americans.

These pioneers seldom became known to the general public, who still viewed African Americans as incapable of technological or scientific accomplishments equal to those of whites. This began to change when Matthew Henson (1866–1955) accompanied explorer Robert Peary (1856–1920) on his expedition to the North Pole in 1909. When the team returned from their historic journey, Henson enjoyed some popular success, giving lectures and writing a book. This success did not readily lead to a job, and Peary went out of his way to downplay Henson's role in the expedition.

Bessie Coleman (1892–1926) captured media attention when she became the first African American woman to earn her pilot's license in 1921. Her ideas about African American participation in the field of aviation were carried on in her honor after her tragic death at age thirty-four, when William J. Powell (1897–1942) founded the Bessie Coleman Aero Club and flight school dedicated to African American pilot training. Another event in 1921 played a key role in shifting American perceptions about African Americans in the sciences. George Washington Carver was invited to speak before the House Ways and Means Committee regarding the many uses of the peanut. His intelligence and charm won over the members of Congress, and he became a media sensation as the best-known African American scientist of the early twentieth century. Carver showed Americans that old perceptions about African Americans were wrong.

African American scientists became prominent in nearly every field of study in the decades that followed. David Blackwell (1919–) helped to define the area of statistics known as game theory. Emmett W. Chappelle's (1925–) work in biochemistry led to significant advances in fields as wide-ranging as disease detection and the search for extraterrestrial life. And scientists from various fields, including Vance Marchbanks (1905–88), O. S. Williams (1921–), and Robert Shurney (1921–2007) made key contributions to the American space program during the Mercury and Apollo space missions—regarded by many as humankind's greatest scientific and technological achievement.

Headline Makers

★ HAROLD AMOS
(1919–2003)

Harold Amos was one of the most distinguished microbiologists in the United States, and was the first African American to serve as a department chair at Harvard Medical School. He used his time at Harvard to promote the sciences to minority students. He also worked to increase the number of African Americans on faculty at medical schools across the country.

Amos was born in 1919 in Pennsauken, New Jersey, just across the Delaware River from Philadelphia, Pennsylvania. He was the second of what would be nine children in the family. His father was a postal worker who did not graduate from high school. He wanted more for his children than a career similar to his own. Amos was able to overcome the educational limitations that were typically associated with growing up in a segregated society. He finished high school and earned a scholarship to attend Springfield College, a private institution in Massachusetts. He graduated from that institution with a bachelor's degree in chemistry in 1941.

Harold Amos.
© *Bettmann/Corbis*

Amos's continuing education was interrupted by World War II. He became a member of the U.S. Army Quartermaster Corps, the branch in charge of ensuring that troops receive food, fuel, and other materials. This branch of the Army also deals with handling the bodies of soldiers killed in action.

Amos returned to his education after the war, earning a master's degree from Harvard University in 1947. He went on to earn his doctorate in bacteriology and immunology in 1952. Amos received a Fulbright scholarship to study abroad from 1951 to 1952. He chose the Pasteur Institute in France, known for its studies of microbiology and cell biology as they relate to infectious diseases. He returned to the United States to continue his studies at Harvard Medical School. He began teaching at Harvard Medical School in 1954 in the department of bacteriology and immunology. He was the only African American instructor working at Harvard, which would be the case for many years.

Amos was selected as the chairman of the department of bacteriology and immunology in 1968, making him the first African American to serve as a department chair at Harvard. He served in that role until 1971, and again from 1975 to 1978. He actively promoted African American scientists as a founding member of the Hinton-Wright Society in 1983; the society served as a place where nonwhite scientists in the Boston area could find support and exchange ideas with peers. He worked to expand the ranks of African American and other minority faculty members at medical schools through the Minority Medical Faculty Development Program of the Robert Wood Johnson Foundation, which was later renamed the Harold Amos Faculty Development Program in his honor. His efforts to promote diversity at Harvard led to his being awarded the first Harold Amos Faculty Diversity Award in 1999. Amos served on the President's Cancer Panel under President Richard M. Nixon (1913–94), and was also active in leadership with the American Cancer Society.

Amos's work generated a number of honors over the years, including the Charles R. Drew World Medical Prize from Howard University and the Public Welfare Medal of the National Academy of Sciences. He became a professor emeritus at Harvard in 1988. Amos died in 2003 due to complications from a stroke.

★ DAVID BLACKWELL
(1919–)

David Blackwell was the first African American tenured professor for the University of California at Berkeley when he accepted a professorship in statistics in 1955. He made significant contributions to the field of mathematics. Blackwell's statistical theories have been used in various real-world applications, and his early work on game theory was instrumental in shaping that field of academic study.

Blackwell was born in Centralia, Illinois, to Grover and Mabel Blackwell, an inn manager and his wife. Grover had not attended school past the fourth grade, but he and Mabel provided a stimulating educational environment for their son. David's grandfather, a former teacher and store owner, possessed a mathematical mind, and David's first encounter with algebra was in one of his grandfather's books. Blackwell attended an integrated school, and his high school math teacher encouraged the students to work out the solutions to mathematical "puzzles" printed in a magazine called *School Science and Mathematics*. Blackwell excelled in solving the problems, and one of his solutions was printed in the magazine. He graduated from high school in 1935 at the age of sixteen.

David Blackwell. *Jon Brenneis/Time & Life Pictures/ Getty Images*

Blackwell attended college at the University of Illinois at Urbana-Champaign. He knew that he wanted to major in mathematics, but had planned on using his degree to become an elementary school teacher after college. This career course changed as he discovered his love for advanced math like probability. He blazed through his course work in college, completing not just a bachelor's degree but a master's and a doctorate by the time he was twenty-two. Blackwell then received a Rosenwald fellowship that allowed him to study at Princeton for a year.

Blackwell was exposed to the harsh reality of racism he had not known as a child when he sought a job as a mathematics professor. The only colleges willing to hire him were African American colleges. Jerzy Neyman (1894–1981), a mathematician who worked at the University of California at Berkeley, interviewed Blackwell for a teaching position at his school, but racial attitudes at the time prevented him from offering Blackwell a job. Blackwell ended up taking a position teaching at Southern University in Louisiana in 1942. He moved to Clark College in Atlanta, Georgia, a year later, and then to Howard University in Washington, D.C., in 1944. While living in Washington, he attended a lecture by Abe Girshick that constituted Blackwell's first real exposure to statistics—the field for which he later became known.

Blackwell began his own studies in statistics, and began to publish many articles in mathematics journals discussing various elements of estimating and decision-making, topics that applied to many other areas like economics and accounting. He was especially interested in game theory, a branch of math that involves strategic choices made by one or more participants in a specific situation where the choice made by each participant affects the outcome for other participants. His work in this area resulted in the book *Theory of Games and Statistical Decisions* (1954), co-authored with Girshick.

Blackwell remained at Howard for ten years, becoming the head of the mathematics department in 1947. His developing reputation in the mathematics community finally broke down racial barriers at Berkeley in 1954. Blackwell received an offer from Jerzy Neyman to become a visiting professor at the school. He became the first African American tenured professor at the university in 1955. He also served as president of the Institute of Mathematical Statistics that year.

Blackwell became chairman of the department of statistics at Berkeley in 1957. He became an emeritus professor for the university in 1989. His long career generated many honors, including numerous honorary doctorates and the Berkeley Citation, which is the highest honor given by the university. The Committee of Presidents of Statistical Societies awarded him the R. A. Fisher Award, the most prestigious award in statistics, in 1986. He was the first black mathematician to be elected to the National Academy of Sciences.

⭐ GEORGE WASHINGTON CARVER (1864–1943)

George Washington Carver is one of the best-known African American scientists in American history. He is famous for coming up with hundreds of different uses for Southern crops like the peanut and the sweet potato. His accomplishments are not as easy to pinpoint as with other scientists, however. He did not write scientific papers, nor did he open his labs for others to observe his methods and findings. Still, his modest charm and obvious intelligence captured the imagination of Americans of all colors during the first half of the twentieth century, and no doubt inspired many young African Americans to pursue their own scientific interests.

An Integrated Childhood in a Segregated World

Carver was born in Diamond, Missouri, to slave parents Giles and Mary. His actual birthday is unknown. He often claimed later in life that he was born in 1864, but could have been born as late as 1865. His father was killed in an accident either before George was born or soon after. His

George Washington Carver. *The Library of Congress*

mother Mary was the slave of Moses and Susan Carver, white farmers who opposed the idea of slavery but needed help taking care of the farm and household. The Carvers, like a majority of Missourians at the time, supported the Union during the Civil War.

When George was just an infant, he and his mother Mary were kidnapped by Confederate marauders and taken away to Arkansas. A local Union scout searched for them and was able to return with George. Mary was never seen again. The Carvers then raised George, as well as his older brother Jim, as their adopted children. George never knew his biological mother or father, though as an adult he kept the original bill of sale from the Carvers' purchase of his mother as a treasured memento.

George was frail and in poor health throughout much of his childhood, the result of a chronic respiratory illness. The physical labor involved in farm work was too much for him to handle, so Moses and Jim took care of that while George was allowed to pursue his own interests. He became curious about the plants, animals, and minerals he found around the farm, and eventually showed a special skill for caring for plants. George and Jim were schooled at home by the Carvers, since some whites in the town objected to allowing the children to attend the local school. It did not take long before George's desire for education surpassed his parents' abilities to teach him. At around the age of twelve, George was given permission to move to Neosho, the nearest town with a school for African American students.

He quickly grew disappointed by the level of education available in Neosho, and decided to accompany another family who was moving to Fort Scott, Kansas. Kansas was known at the time for its generally accepting attitude toward African Americans. Carver was again disappointed; he witnessed the vicious lynching of a young black man accused of raping a white girl in 1879. He moved to Olathe, Kansas, and later to Minneapolis, Kansas, attending school and performing odd jobs for money and a place to live. He sent an application to a college in Highland, Kansas, and was accepted. The school denied him admission, however, when school officials realized that he was black.

A Farmer, a Teacher, and an Inventor

Unable to continue his education, Carver moved west, purchased a plot of land, and became a farmer. He was remarkably successful in growing a number of different crops and plants, and his knowledge of soil and agriculture continued to grow. His desire to further his education never left him, however. He left Kansas and ended up at Simpson College in Indianola, Iowa, in 1890. While there, he excelled in nearly every subject, and even became a successful painter. He also earned the friendship and respect of his fellow students, who were mostly white. Many provided anonymous donations to help him pay for his schooling.

After just a year, Carver was encouraged to enroll at Iowa State College to study horticulture, the science of cultivating plants. He was the only African American on campus, and his reception was at first chilly. He ultimately won over both students and staff, and earned both his bachelor's and master's degrees at the school by 1896. His success did not go unnoticed. Booker T. Washington (1856–1915), founder of the Tuskegee Institute in Alabama, invited Carver to work at the school as the head of the department of agricultural research.

Carver kept a busy schedule at Tuskegee, but was free to perform any research he wished. One of the problems that interested him most was the depleted soil found throughout the South. Where gigantic cotton fields

George Washington Carver conducts an experiment in his laboratory, January 25, 1921. © *Bettmann/Corbis*

had once grown abundantly, many farmers were having difficulty getting any crops to grow. Carver's own experience as a farmer taught him that planting the same crop year after year in the same soil—a type of farming known as monoculture—tended to rob the soil of its nutrients. This is exactly what had happened throughout the South, since cotton was the most profitable crop to grow.

Carver discovered that this sort of farming depleted the nitrogen from the soil. This problem could be reversed by switching between various kinds of crops. Carver recommended growing legumes such as peanuts, which were excellent at replenishing nitrogen in the soil. He released this information in a bulletin put out by the Tuskegee Experiment Station, *How to Build Up Worn Out Soils,* in 1905. He hoped that poor farmers in the region, especially African American farmers, could use the information to improve crop yields. Carver also recommended growing sweet potatoes, which performed well even in poor soil. He created a traveling wagon in 1906 that visited farms and spread word of his discoveries to help educate local farmers.

The Peanut Man

Carver dedicated himself to finding many different uses for peanuts as a way to encourage farmers to plant the crop. It was already clear that peanuts were useful as food; they contain a great deal of protein, and growing them was much cheaper than buying or raising animals for meat. Carver used his labs at Tuskegee Institute to invent other uses for the peanut, as well as for sweet potatoes and other nitrogen-fixing crops like soybeans. He published his most famous bulletin, *How to Grow the Peanut and 105 Ways of Preparing it for Human Consumption,* in 1916. Despite the title, Carver did not limit his imagination to nutritional uses for peanuts. He also came up with ways to use them in face cream, glue, ink, insecticide, and dozens of other products. He showed the same inventiveness with the sweet potato, which he used to make dyes, synthetic cotton, and even alcohol.

It was his inventiveness with peanuts that earned Carver an appearance before the United States Congress in 1921. He was called to speak before the Ways and Means Committee regarding the issue of tariffs, or additional taxes, on imported peanuts. His purpose was to illustrate the many uses for peanuts, which he did by providing samples of various creations to the committee members. At least one of the committee members treated Carver with disrespect because of his race, but he won the attention and praise of other members, and was allowed to continue speaking long past his allotted time of ten minutes. The appearance earned him both fame and respect, and he was often called upon to promote the Tuskegee Institute.

Carver received the Spingarn Medal from the National Association for the Advancement of Colored People (NAACP) in recognition of his beneficial research in 1923. He continued publishing bulletins on his agricultural findings until his death in 1943. A museum in his honor was founded on the institute campus in 1941. Carver did little to document his many experiments and creations over the years. This frustrated many scientists of his day; it also kept others from making or using many of the useful products he had created from peanuts, sweet potatoes, and other crops.

Carver's health began to fail in the 1930s. He died on January 5, 1943, as a result of complications from anemia. A national monument in his honor was created and opened to the public in 1953. He was the first African American to be honored with a national monument by the United States government.

★ EMMETT W. CHAPPELLE (1925–)

Emmett W. Chappelle is one of the most versatile and successful biochemists of the twentieth century. His research has helped astronauts breathe safely and search for alien life, and has helped doctors screen patients for infections of the urinary tract, spinal fluid, and other areas. Chappelle followed his own curiosity and spirit of exploration into several different fields of study, nearly all of which led to important discoveries and advances in humankind's understanding of living things.

Chappelle was born in Phoenix, Arizona, the third of four children raised by poor farmers. The family house did not even have electricity for much of Chappelle's youth. He was educated in segregated schools even though there were few African Americans in the area. His poor and modest upbringing did not stop him from graduating from high school in 1942 at the top of his class.

World War II Service and College

Chappelle could not go straight to college because the United States had just entered World War II. He entered the U.S. Army and received some training in engineering. Chappelle was placed on the front lines in an African American infantry division. The military segregated its soldiers at the time, and many African Americans fought and died to protect freedoms that they were not fully granted themselves. Chappelle's division fought against Nazi forces in Italy, and he was wounded twice in action. Chappelle and his division remained in Italy after the fighting ended to maintain peace and order until early 1946.

Chappelle returned to the United States and began taking engineering classes at Phoenix College. The federal government covered the cost of his education through the GI Bill of 1944. He completed the courses offered in Phoenix, and moved to California to pursue an engineering degree at the University of California at Berkeley. However, Chappelle switched his major to biology after enjoying some classes on the subject. He graduated in 1950 and moved to Nashville, Tennessee, where he worked as a biochemistry teacher at Meharry Medical College, renowned as the first medical college for African Americans in the United States. The position allowed him time and resources to perform his own research when he was not busy teaching the college's nursing students.

He developed a reputation as a biomedical researcher while at Meharry. He wrote papers on his studies of how the human body recycles iron for use in red blood cells, and on the biological processes involved in allergic shock. He left Meharry to continue his education at the University of Washington, where he earned a master's degree in biochemistry in 1954. He then returned to California, working at the Research Institute of Advanced Studies at Stanford University while continuing his studies. His work at Stanford focused largely on amino acids, a class of molecules found in living things that link together to form proteins.

Works with NASA

Chappelle moved to Baltimore, Maryland, in 1958 to work as a research scientist for an aerospace company, the Martin Marietta Corporation. The company was working on spacecraft design for the National Aeronautics and Space Administration (NASA). Chappelle's research led him to the discovery that algae, tiny organisms similar to plants, can transform potentially deadly carbon monoxide into carbon dioxide, a common and safe chemical found in the air. This discovery proved useful to the space program, since carbon monoxide accumulation in a spacecraft could pose a serious threat to astronauts.

Chappelle went to work for Hazelton Laboratories in Virginia, another company heavily involved with NASA, in 1963. His work centered on ways to detect certain types of cells in very low concentrations. To do this, he measured the amount of light given off by different types of cells under certain conditions. This work was intended to aid in the search for life on other planets, but his research led him to invent a way to detect bacteria in a liquid sample. This led to improved methods of testing for urinary tract infections and other types of infections.

Chappelle began to work for NASA directly in 1966 at the Goddard Space Flight Center in Maryland. He continued to use light to study minute changes in different living things, including plants. This led to several innovations in crop and soil monitoring, some of which are used by the United States Soil Conservation Service. Chappelle later worked with the United States Department of Agriculture on similar research.

Over the course of his career, Chappelle used his knowledge of biology and chemistry to achieve significant advances in several different fields, from space exploration to medical testing to agriculture. By the time he retired in 2001, Chappelle had earned fourteen patents for his various innovations. He was inducted into the National Inventors Hall of Fame in 2007.

★ JEWEL PLUMMER COBB
(1924–)

Jewel Plummer Cobb's research as a cell biologist focused on the relationship between pigment in skin cells and skin cancer. She published dozens of scientific papers on the subject, and her work helped doctors and researchers better understand the dangers posed by prolonged skin exposure to ultraviolet radiation. In addition, Cobb used her power and influence as an administrator to increase the ranks of minority students and women in the sciences.

Jewel Plummer Cobb.
Reproduced by permission of Jewel Plummer-Cobb

Cobb was born in Chicago, Illinois, to a family with a rich and diverse educational history. Her father, Frank Plummer, was a medical doctor educated at Cornell, and her grandfather was a pharmacist who attended Howard University. Her mother, Carriebel Plummer, was a dance instructor who studied physical education at a prestigious college. Cobb grew up surrounded by books, medical journals, and family friends with expertise in many different fields.

She first attended elementary school in an integrated classroom, surrounded by white students. She was soon forced to change to another public school where African American students were the majority. She fell in love with the field of biology in high school after she had an opportunity to look at the world in an entirely new way: through the lens of a microscope. She studied the subject, and was particularly intrigued by the book

Microbe Hunters (1926) by Michigan microbiologist Paul De Kruif. The book features chapters devoted to history's most important bacteriologists.

Cobb graduated from high school in 1941 and selected the University of Michigan to pursue a degree in biology. The university's segregated living quarters and harsh racial attitudes drove her to leave after only one year. She moved to Alabama to attend Talladega College, a respected African American university, but had to retake many courses because her previous work at the University of Michigan could not be transferred. She still managed to earn her degree in less than four years and, on the recommendation of one of her professors, she applied to New York University to continue her studies.

Cobb attended New York University from 1944 until 1950, earning both a master's degree and a doctorate in cell physiology. One of her main areas of study was pigment in cells, which is caused by a substance called melanin. In addition to coloring the skin, melanin protects skin cells from the potentially damaging radiation of the sun's rays. This damage can lead to skin cancer. Cobb's work focused on identifying potentially cancerous pigment cells and on analyzing different possible treatments for skin cancer. Cobb also worked as a teacher for the school, and later was awarded a fellowship by the National Cancer Institute to continue her studies at the Harlem Hospital Cancer Research Foundation.

Cobb went to work for the University of Illinois as the head of its Tissue Culture Laboratory in 1952. She moved back to New York two years later and established the Tissue Culture Research Laboratory for New York University. She continued her own research into skin cancer and pigment cells as she worked as a professor for the university. In 1960, Cobb relocated to Sarah Lawrence College, also in New York, where she remained until 1969.

Cobb next moved on to Connecticut College, serving as dean of the school, professor of zoology, and director of the school's cell biology lab. Despite her hectic schedule and numerous responsibilities, Cobb still made time to continue her research each morning in the lab. She remained at Connecticut College for seven years.

In 1976, she accepted a position as dean of Douglass College in New Jersey, a women's college affiliated with Rutgers University. Cobb also worked as a biology professor at the school. She found that her duties required so much of her attention that she could no longer continue her research into pigment cells. She switched her focus to encouraging more minority and female students to pursue careers in the sciences.

Cobb was able to achieve success in this regard when she was selected as president of California State University, Fullerton, in 1981. In addition to expanding campus housing and science facilities, she increased scholarships for women and minorities attending the school. She remained president of the college until 1990. She then continued her crusade to recruit minority students into the sciences by working with the Southern California Science and Engineering ACCESS Center and Network, as well as the Science Technology Engineering Program (STEP) Up for Youth program. In 1993, Cobb was honored by the National Academy of Sciences with a Lifetime Achievement Award for her research and for her dedication to promoting the sciences among minorities and women.

★ BESSIE COLEMAN
(1892–1926)

Elizabeth "Bessie" Coleman became the first licensed female African American pilot in the world in 1921. She had to train and earn her pilot's license in France because of the limited opportunities offered to African Americans in the United States at the time. Although she died in a tragic plane accident at a young age, her talent and tenacity have earned her a place in aviation history.

Eager to Leave Her Mark on the World

Coleman was the tenth of thirteen children born to Susan and George Coleman, sharecroppers living in the small town of Atlanta, Texas. Bessie was just two when the family moved to Waxahachie, a town south of Dallas. Her father was able to purchase a piece of land there and build a house. Bessie had to walk several miles each day to the nearest segregated, one-room schoolhouse, where she performed well. There were no local libraries, but she borrowed books from a traveling wagon that visited the area twice each year.

George Coleman was three-quarters Native American, and left his family in 1901 to live on a reservation in Oklahoma. Susan Coleman went to work as a housekeeper, and Bessie took over responsibility for her younger siblings. She still found time to attend school, and completed her education through the eighth grade. This was the highest level taught for African American students in the area. She got a job as a laundry worker and slowly saved up money to pay for additional schooling. She used her savings to attend the Colored Agricultural and Normal University in Langston, Oklahoma, in 1910. She had to return home after one semester when she ran out of money.

Bessie Coleman. *Fotosearch/ Hulton Archive/Getty Images*

She moved to Chicago, Illinois, in 1915, where her older brothers had already moved. This was during the period known as the Great Migration, when millions of African Americans moved from the oppressive, segregated conditions of the South to urban areas in the North, which offered greater economic opportunities and relatively more freedom. Coleman lived with her brothers and began working as a manicurist. Soon the rest of her family moved to Chicago from Texas. Both of her older brothers fought in France during World War I (1914–18). One of Coleman's brothers told her that in France there were women who had learned to fly planes. She loved the idea and vowed that someday she too would fly.

Earning Her Wings

The first manned airplane flight had taken place less than twenty years before, when the Wright brothers managed to keep their craft in the air for just under one minute. Thérèse Peltier, a French woman, became the first female pilot in 1908 by flying a short distance in Turin, Italy. The industry grew rapidly, and several countries used planes as part of their military strategy in World War I. Still, there were very few people in the world capable of flying airplanes, and nearly all of them were men.

Coleman investigated the possibility of learning to fly in the United States, but learned that it was not just her gender that posed a problem. African Americans were excluded from many types of advanced or specialized education at the time. Flight schools for African Americans had not yet been created. The first African American pilot—Eugene Bullard (1894–1961)—was trained in and flew for France, not the United States, in 1917 during the war. Coleman decided that if she wanted to become a pilot, she would have to go to France, where women and African Americans were treated as equals on the airfield.

Coleman sailed for France in 1920. She attended flight training at the Fédération Aéronautique Internationale (International Aeronautic Federation), and received her international pilot's license on June 15, 1921. She was the first African American woman in the world to be licensed as a pilot. When she returned to the United States, she was greeted with enthusiasm and press coverage, but did not have a way to earn money by flying. The airline industry did not yet exist, and even crop dusting would not become a profitable enterprise for several years. Coleman discovered that to earn a living as a pilot, she would have to perform stunts for crowds of spectators.

Stunt flying required special skills and training, so Coleman returned to France in 1922 and trained at Nieuport, an airplane manufacturer that specialized in racing planes. Upon returning to the United States, she began appearing at air shows around the country, earning fame wherever she went. She could not yet afford her own plane, so she had to borrow one for her performances. She dreamed of owning her own plane and opening a flight instruction school.

A Dream Fulfilled Becomes a Tragedy

Her dream of owning a plane came true in 1923, but was short-lived. Soon after buying the plane, she crashed during a flight to Los Angeles, plummeting several hundred feet to the ground. She was seriously injured and required months of hospitalization. She returned to Chicago to regroup amidst her family and friends. She delivered lectures on her experiences as a pilot, and awaited another opportunity to fly. She got a chance after eighteen months when she received an offer to fly in a series of exhibitions across her native state of Texas. She proved wildly popular, and soon put a down payment on another plane.

Coleman continued to fly, and added parachute jumping to her performance. She also opened a beauty shop in Florida to help pay for her plane and to finance her dream of opening an aviation school. She finally paid off the plane in 1926, just in time to have it delivered to Jacksonville, Florida, for a performance at a May Day celebration there. On April 30, she and another pilot took the plane up for a test flight. Coleman flew as the passenger so she could observe the layout of the field onto which she would be parachuting for the show, which was to take place the following day. She was not wearing her safety restraint because she needed to lean over the side of the plane to see below. Approximately ten minutes into the flight, the pilot lost control of the plane, and Coleman was thrown out of her seat, falling several hundred feet to her death. She was just thirty-four years old. The pilot, unable to regain control of the plane, was also killed in the crash.

Thousands attended Coleman's memorial service and funeral in Chicago. In 1929, William J. Powell (1899–1942), a pilot who faced challenges much like Coleman's when he wanted to learn to fly, decided to open his own school in Los Angeles. He called it the Bessie Coleman Aero Club, in honor of the legendary female pilot's final, unfulfilled dream.

★ MATTHEW HENSON
(1866–1955)

Matthew Henson was the longtime assistant to famed explorer Robert Peary (1856–1920), generally recognized as the first explorer to reach the North Pole. Henson was with him on that momentous trip, and even holds the distinction of arriving at the location first. Although some doubt Peary's claim of reaching the Pole, no one can doubt Henson's loyalty and dedication in assisting Peary on his historic journey.

Henson was born just three years after the end of the Civil War, but his parents, Lemuel and Caroline Henson, had lived as free blacks their

Matthew Henson. *Apic/ Hulton Archive/Getty Images*

entire lives in the North. Henson's first written account of his life, published in 1912, explains that his mother died when he was just seven, and he was left in the care of an uncle in Washington, D.C. A later account, cowritten by Henson in 1955, suggests that Henson's mother died when he was much younger, and his father died when he was eight, leaving him in the care of his stepmother. Henson completed elementary school, which was the highest educational level most African Americans were expected to achieve at the time. He then ran away to Baltimore and signed on as a cabin boy for a merchant ship. He was just thirteen.

Henson spent years traveling around the world, visiting Asia, Africa, and Europe. He learned a great deal about the world and about exploration, including seamanship. He eventually returned to Washington, D.C., and took a job working in a hat store. There, in 1888, Henson met Commander Robert Peary of the U.S. Navy. Peary was impressed by Henson, and hired him as his personal assistant. Henson first accompanied Peary to Nicaragua, and later was a member of Peary's team on his expeditions to the Arctic region.

Journey to the North Pole

Peary's expeditions in the Arctic were the most successful of the era, at least in part because he chose to adapt to the environment much like the native Inuit people did. His exploration team carried less equipment and built igloos, for example, allowing them to move faster and cover more ground. Several of his expeditions were dedicated to exploring northern Greenland, and Peary was the first to map portions of the island's north coast. Henson served in a variety of roles on the expeditions. He was a blacksmith, carpenter, cook, and hunter, becoming an invaluable member of the group. He even learned to speak Inuit so that he could communicate with local guides and assistants.

Peary made several unsuccessful attempts to reach the North Pole starting in 1898. Their final attempt began in July 1908, starting out with a team of twenty-four men, including several Inuit guides, and 133 dogs to haul supplies. Only Peary, Henson, and four Inuit would make the full journey; the support staff gradually dropped off on the journey to avoid the problem of feeding so many people in the harsh Arctic conditions. Peary had trouble determining exactly where the North Pole was as the two men alternated breaking the trail. Henson, Peary, and their Inuit guides arrived at what Peary judged to be the North Pole on April 6, 1909. When Peary calculated the location, he discovered that Henson had actually been the first person to reach it. Henson noted in his memoirs that Peary's attitude toward him changed almost immediately upon the successful conclusion of their expedition. Peary may have felt disappointment that, at the end of his many years of attempts, he was not the first person to set foot upon the North Pole.

However, there may be another reason. Many explorers and other experts have expressed doubts about Peary's claim of reaching the Pole. The explorer may have been harsh toward Henson because he was the only other English-speaking person who could provide an account of the journey, and could therefore reveal that the team's location was considerably farther south than the actual Pole. To complicate matters, another explorer—Frederick Cook (1865–1940)—had also just returned from the Arctic, and claimed to have reached the North Pole a full year before Peary's expedition. Peary's own poor documentation and position measurements further clouded the issue.

Falls into Obscurity after Expedition

Despite the controversy, Peary was welcomed back to the United States as a hero. Henson was largely ignored, viewed only as a manservant who followed Peary's commands. This reflected the prevailing belief that African Americans were not equals with whites. Henson, in need of money and perhaps wanting some recognition for himself, arranged for a series of lectures in which he talked about the expedition, and also published his autobiography and account of the trip, *A Negro Explorer at the North Pole* (1912). Peary reacted poorly to these actions, believing Henson had betrayed him by trying to steal credit for his accomplishments. Peary may have also been upset by Henson's version of events on the expedition. Henson's account depicted Peary as an exhausted, injured man who had to be pulled on a sled to complete the final part of the journey.

Henson was eventually given a low-level job with the United States Customs House in New York, where he remained for twenty years. As the dust settled around the North Pole controversy, Peary was remembered as the daring explorer and Henson was hardly remembered at all. Only in his final years were his accomplishments recognized, when he received an invitation to the White House from President Harry Truman (1884–1972) in 1950 and a citation from President Dwight Eisenhower (1890–1969) in 1954. Henson passed away the following year at the age of eighty-eight. The U.S. government rebuffed suggestions that he be recognized for his accomplishments by being buried in Arlington National Cemetery; they argued that it was not appropriate because he had not served in the military. Thirty-three years later Henson received a hero's burial in the famous cemetery.

★ SAMUEL ELMER IMES
(1883–1941)

Samuel Elmer Imes became the second African American to earn a doctorate in physics in 1918. His work at the University of Michigan played an important role in the recognition of quantum mechanics as a valuable way of viewing the physical world. He also developed the undergraduate physics program for Fisk University, a historically black college where the study of pure science had previously been neglected.

Imes was born in Memphis, Tennessee, to Benjamin and Elizabeth Wallace Imes. His parents were a college-educated African American couple, a rarity for the time period. They were based in Oberlin, Ohio, but worked as missionaries for the American Missionary Association (AMA), educating former slaves throughout the South. Imes went to grammar school in Oberlin, but attended high school in Normal, Alabama, where his parents were working.

Imes began attending Fisk University in Nashville, Tennessee, in 1899. He graduated with a degree in science in 1903, and spent some time teaching science and math for the AMA in Georgia and Alabama. Imes returned to Nashville around 1909 and became a teacher at Fisk. He worked towards his master's degree at the same time, successfully completing his master's program in 1910. He continued to teach at the school until 1914.

Samuel Elmer Imes. *Fisk University Library. Reproduced by permission.*

Imes realized that colleges for African Americans simply were not capable of providing the kind of in-depth study he wanted. Most were intended purely for vocational training so that students could obtain jobs as skilled tradespeople. Imes, on the other hand, wanted to study advanced physics. He enrolled in the doctorate program at the University of Michigan in 1915 and earned his doctorate in physics in 1918. He was only the second African American to earn a doctorate in physics in the United States; the first, Edward Bouchet, had earned his doctorate more than forty years earlier.

Imes performed important work at the University of Michigan, measuring the behavior of molecules. He published his findings in *Astrophysical Journal* and *Physical Review*, and soon other physicists recognized the importance of his work. His studies supported the validity of quantum mechanics, a fairly new set of ideas aimed at describing the behavior of atoms and even smaller particles. These findings were important because the usefulness of quantum mechanics was still being debated among physicists.

No black colleges in the South offered facilities that could accommodate his research, and Imes was not allowed to teach at white institutions. Imes therefore remained in the North, settling in New York City in 1918. There, he met the writer Nella Larsen, a significant literary figure in the Harlem Renaissance. The Harlem Renaissance was a flourishing of the arts that occurred in the Harlem neighborhood of New York City during the 1920s and into the 1930s. Imes and Larsen married on May 3, 1919, and moved to Harlem. Imes's own literary and scholarly pursuits made him a notable figure of the Renaissance in his own right. The marriage eventually dissolved after Imes began an affair with a white woman named Ethel Gilbert. Their divorce in 1933 received significant coverage in the African American press because of Larsen's celebrity.

Imes relied on consulting work until 1922, when he secured a position with the Federal Engineers Development Corporation. He worked for a total of three different companies throughout the 1920s, primarily studying magnetism. He earned four patents for processes and devices that arose from his work.

Financial problems led Imes to return to Fisk University in 1930 to head the physics program. He set about reworking the undergraduate physics curriculum to prepare physics students for graduate work at other colleges. This involved creating courses that would be recognized as valid by the most prestigious universities in the country. Imes also actively sought talented students for his program. His first three physics students graduated from the program in 1935.

Imes was not content to let his students specialize in science at the expense of a more classical education. He himself had started out with a much broader education in the arts, languages, and philosophy, and he felt that this well-rounded approach was an important part of any scientific education. For this reason, he developed his own course that showed students how science fit within the broader context of human society. He also wrote a book for the course, titled *Cultural Physics*.

Fisk lacked the kind of advanced equipment Imes required to perform his research, so he often traveled to the University of Michigan during the summer so that he could continue his work. He also spent time performing experiments at New York University. Imes passed away from throat cancer in 1941 at the age of fifty-seven.

★ ERNEST E. JUST
(1883–1941)

Ernest E. Just was a biologist who spent much of his professional life studying the structure of cells. His research led him to write numerous papers and books that changed prevailing conceptions about cells and reproduction. His most famous work was *The Biology of the Cell Surface.* He taught at Howard University for most of his career and performed research alongside the country's greatest scientific minds.

From a South Carolina Schoolhouse to Dartmouth

Just was born in Charleston, South Carolina, the son of Charles Fraser Just, a wharf builder, and Mary Matthews Cooper, a laborer and teacher. The family had two other young children, but both died of illnesses when Ernest was still an infant. The Justs had two more children after Ernest. His father died when Ernest was three. As Ernest got older, he contributed to the family income by working various jobs whenever he was not in school. He spent much of his youth living on James Island, off the coast of South Carolina, where his mother taught workers in the phosphate mining industry and worked gathering phosphate herself. The school

A U.S. postage stamp released in 1996 honors scientist Ernest E. Just. *AP Images*

he attended was a segregated school for African American children, as was common throughout the South. The schools were supposed to be of equal quality for both black and white students, but schools for blacks were always under-funded. Many black children were expected to end their education after elementary school and start earning a living.

Just's mother knew that he had a gift for intellectual pursuits, and knew that staying in Charleston would likely prevent him from reaching his true potential. He left home to attend South Carolina State College, a vocational school for African American students, in 1896. He finished his schooling there at the age of fifteen. He was certified to teach in African American schools, but his real desire was to continue his own education. Just left South Carolina aboard a ship bound for New York City at the age of seventeen, working as a member of the crew to pay his fare.

Just worked hard as a cook to earn enough money to attend a prestigious school, but his chosen institution was not in New York. He wanted to go to Kimball Academy in New Hampshire, one of the oldest private boarding schools in the nation. The school was known for its high standards and its relative accessibility for those of modest means; the school launched a program in 1880 whereby one hundred dollars covered a student's entire room and boarding costs for a year. The student was simply required to work one hour each day assisting in the kitchen or garden. Still, the expense was equal to about what a typical African American laborer earned working full-time for a year. Just showed up at Kimball without a confirmed acceptance letter and without enough money to cover tuition. He was fortunate enough to qualify for a special scholarship, and was admitted.

Just was the only African American student at the school when he arrived. It was his first time attending classes with white students, but Just found the faculty and students to be welcoming. He started out slightly older than his classmates, but managed to finish all his course work in three years instead of four. He was both popular and successful at Kimball, serving as editor of the school newspaper and graduating in 1903 with honors.

Just next attended Dartmouth College, a small but esteemed Ivy League school that was founded before the American Revolutionary War. He took classes in biology and discovered in himself a passion for the subject that would determine his career. He graduated, again with honors, in 1907. His academic excellence should have given him access to teaching positions at any number of institutions, but employment opportunities for African Americans were largely limited to black institutions due to segregation. Just took a position teaching at Howard University in Washington, D.C., which was quickly earning itself a reputation as one of the most prestigious black colleges in the country. He was the head of the department of zoology by 1912.

Woods Hole Fulfills a Desire to Do Research

Just continued pursuing his own research when he was not teaching. His greatest interest was in cells and their structure, as well as the process of egg cell fertilization that forms the basis of most animal reproduction. The research facilities at Howard were limited, so Just began to spend his summers at the Marine Biological Laboratory (MBL), a research center founded in Woods Hole, Massachusetts, in 1888. Professors and researchers of all types visited Woods Hole in order to study different aspects of marine life and to exchange ideas or collaborate with other scientists.

Just met many prominent scientists at the MBL who, like himself, were interested in the development of life from its earliest stages. Jacques Loeb (1859–1924) earned fame there by studying parthenogenesis, the process of producing offspring without male participation, in sea urchins. Frank Rattray Lillie (1870–1947) served as the director of the MBL during Just's time there, and was also the chairman of the department of zoology at the University of Chicago in Illinois. Just began his research at the MBL by assisting Lillie in his studies on sandworm reproduction.

Just continued to study the egg cells of sandworms and sea urchins over the course of several summers, following up and improving upon Loeb's research into parthenogenesis. His many academic papers earned him a reputation as one of the foremost cell biologists in the country. He also took some time away from Howard University so he could complete his doctorate in zoology under Lillie's guidance at the University of Chicago. Just was only thirty-one when he received an unparalleled honor in 1915. The National Association for the Advancement of Colored People (NAACP) chose him as the recipient of the very first Spingarn Medal, an award created to highlight outstanding achievements in any field by an African American.

Just also assisted as editor of several publications in the fields of zoology and biology in addition to writing numerous academic papers. He participated in research fellowships that took him to France, Italy, and the Soviet Union, and his work was honored by scientists worldwide. He was the first American to attend the Kaiser Wilhelm Institute in Berlin, Germany, one of the world's premier research institutes, which boasted the participation of world-renowned scientists like Albert Einstein (1879–1955) and Max Planck (1858–1947). His success did not make him immune to the effects of segregation in the United States, however. Just was not offered the kinds of teaching opportunities given to his white peers.

Work Interrupted, and a Legacy

Just spent time performing research in France in the late 1930s. He had grown increasingly unhappy with his job at Howard University. He was especially upset at the university's failure to pay him back pay that he believed he was owed. This problem was made worse by the fact that Just was not able to obtain research grants as easily as his white counterparts, despite the recognized significance of his studies. He decided to remain in France, and continued his research until the outbreak of World War II. Nazi Germany, led by Adolf Hitler (1889–1945), had seized control of several parts of Europe, and continued into France, occupying much of the country in 1940. Just, unable to get out of the country, was held in an internment camp for a time by Nazi forces. Fortunately, an influential contact secured his release, and Just was able to return to the United States. He unfortunately had to leave behind much of his valuable research documentation.

Just's most enduring legacy is a book he published in 1939, *The Biology of the Cell Surface.* The book combines all of Just's previous research on cell biology and reproduction into a compelling description of the parts of the cell and how they interact. Just emphasizes the importance of the ectoplasm, which is the outer surface of a cell where the cell interacts with the world around it. Previous biologists had concentrated only on the nucleus of the cell, believing that it contained all the important information needed for the cell to exist and reproduce. Just demonstrated that the ectoplasm acts as both a guardian and a filter for the rest of the cell, and plays a key role in reproduction.

Just was virtually penniless when he returned to the United States in 1940. He reluctantly returned to his position at Howard. He did not teach long; Just's life was brought to an early end by pancreatic cancer in 1941, at the age of fifty-eight. His contributions to science are still recognized as some of the most significant biological research ever performed by an African American, and they forever changed the way scientists view cell structure.

★ LEWIS H. LATIMER
(1848–1928)

Lewis H. Latimer was a draftsman and inventor who worked with two of the most famous American inventors of the nineteenth century. He taught himself the art of scientific drawing, and his experiences in a patent attorney's office inspired him to create his own inventions. Latimer devised the most successful filament used in the first electric lightbulbs, though he is seldom recognized for the achievement.

From Young Veteran to Veteran Draftsman

Latimer was the son of George and Rebecca Latimer, two escaped slaves who made their way from Virginia to Boston six years before Lewis was born. George was caught by his former owner, who had been told of his whereabouts. Rebecca was helped into hiding by Northern abolitionists, who believed that slavery was immoral and fought to end the practice. George's case went to trial, and he was ordered to return to his owner. Public sentiment in Boston for George was so strong that a local minister collected enough money to buy George his freedom. George's case was the first of several famous Boston fugitive slave cases. George left the family when Latimer was ten years old. Latimer had to leave school in order to help support his family. He got a job in Boston working in a local attorney's office at the age of thirteen.

The Civil War between the Union forces in the North and the Confederate forces in the South began in 1861. Latimer joined the fight on the side of the Union three years into the conflict, when he was just sixteen years old. He enlisted in the Union Navy and worked as a cabin boy aboard the USS *Massasoit,* which saw combat along the James River in Virginia. He returned to Boston at the end of the war in 1865.

Latimer once again got a job at a law office. This law office, called Crosby and Gould, specialized in helping inventors file patent applications with the United States Patent Office. Applicants must include detailed drawings or blueprints indicating the structure and composition of their inventions as part of the patent process. Latimer watched draftsmen create scientific drawings for the office's patent applications, and decided that he could earn more money by doing the same. The head draftsman at the firm agreed to let him try, and was pleasantly surprised at the quality of his drawings. He became a draftsman and worked for the firm for eleven years, eventually becoming the person in charge of checking all scientific drawings before any patent application was submitted.

In 1876, Latimer collaborated with scientist and engineer Alexander Graham Bell (1847–1922) on the patent application for a device Bell had invented. Latimer created drawings for Bell and guided him through the patent process. The invention was the telephone, which forever changed human culture and earned Bell a place in the history books. Latimer created his own invention during this time, receiving a patent for an improved version of a railroad car toilet in 1874. Latimer would go on to patent other devices of his design.

An Electrifying Career

Latimer left Boston in 1879 and moved to Bridgeport, Connecticut, where he took a job as a draftsman for a machine shop. There he met an inventor named Hiram Maxim (1840–1916), who learned of Latimer's experience at a patent office and hired him as a draftsman for his own company, the United States Electric Lighting Company. Maxim was working on designing efficient and practical electric lightbulbs. Thomas Edison (1847–1931) had already been granted patents for incandescent lightbulbs, and Maxim wanted to carve out his own piece

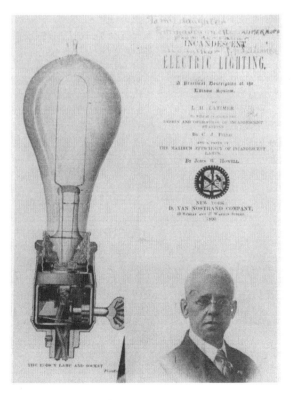

Title page of Lewis Howard Latimer's book on incandescent electric lighting with an image of Edison lamp and socket. *Photographs and Prints Division, Schomburg Center for Research in Black Culture, The New York Public Library, Astor, Lenox and Tilden Foundations*

of what he saw as a potentially huge business. There was still much work to be done, though. The main problem with lightbulbs was the filament, the thin carbon strand in the center that, when heated by electric current, gave off light. Filaments at the time wore out very quickly, making the prospect of electric lighting a very expensive one.

Latimer's experiences in a patent office left him with broad mechanical knowledge and a good mind for problem-solving. He tried out various materials and methods for creating new, longer-lasting filaments, and ultimately struck upon a winner in 1882. His filament design out-performed every other bulb made at the time, and paved the way for mass adoption of electric lighting. Maxim took credit for the invention. Latimer left the company for the Olmstead Light and Power Company of New York that year.

Latimer stayed at Olmstead two years before receiving a job offer that cemented his reputation. He joined a company owned by Thomas Edison that eventually became General Electric. Latimer did not normally work with Edison directly, but was a key figure in creating and enforcing the patents Edison received for his many inventions. Latimer was responsible for helping to defend the company against lawsuits from other inventors and businesses who claimed Edison's electrical patents unfairly kept them from competing in the industry. One of these companies was United States Electric Lighting Company, Latimer's former employer.

Latimer worked for General Electric for thirty years, and at the same time enjoyed some success as a writer. His 1890 book, *Incandescent Electric Lighting: A Practical Description of the Edison System,* was the first on the subject, and was widely read for years. Latimer also published poetry, which was later collected in *Poems of Love and Life* (1925). Latimer retired from General Electric in 1912, but continued working as a draftsman and as a teacher for the rest of his life. He passed away in 1928, at the age of eighty.

★ GARRETT MORGAN
(1877–1963)

Garrett Morgan was one of the most prolific and versatile inventors of the early twentieth century. His successful inventions range from African American beauty products to safety equipment for firefighters. He is also acknowledged as the inventor of the traffic signal, from which modern signals have evolved. Though he grew up in poverty and received no formal education, he became one of the most successful businessmen of his time through his own inventiveness.

Ingenuity Leads to Successful Businesses

Morgan was born into a large, poor farm family in Paris, Kentucky. He had ten siblings, and his parents, Sydney and Elizabeth Reed Morgan, were of mixed-race heritage. Like many African American children in the South, he was only able to attend school through the fifth grade. Higher education was not offered, and most African American children went straight into jobs as laborers or domestic workers. Morgan had a different plan. He decided to move north at the age of fourteen with the hope that he could find greater opportunities.

Morgan first ended up in Cincinnati, Ohio, where he worked briefly, performing odd jobs for a white landowner. He then continued north to Cleveland, Ohio, where he settled permanently. He obtained a position working on sewing machines at a company named Roots and McBride. He proved to be exceptional at building and repairing mechanical things, and was an instant success. He invented a belt fastener for sewing machines that earned him his first paycheck as an inventor in 1901.

Garrett Morgan.
Fotosearch/Hulton Archive/
Getty Images

Morgan eventually went into business for himself. He opened his own sewing machine shop in 1907, and soon after he married Mary Anne Hassek. He was so successful that he was able to buy a house and send for his now-widowed mother to join him in Cleveland. Morgan expanded into a tailoring business in 1909. His success as a businessman was impressive, but it was his success as an inventor for which he is best remembered. His first major invention was based on a discovery made while he tried to solve an entirely unrelated problem.

As the story goes, Morgan was having difficulty sewing wool fabrics on his machines because they generated friction against the sewing needle, causing the needle to get hot and scorch the fabric. He guessed that if he placed a lubricant on the needle, he could reduce the friction, thus eliminating the heat. He had tried out one particular batch of potential lubricant, when his wife called him to dinner. He wiped his hands off on a cloth made of wiry textured fur, only to return after dinner and find the fur on the cloth had become straight instead of wiry. Something in his lubricant recipe had the ability to straighten naturally crooked fibers. He tried the formula out on his neighbor's dog, which was a wiry-coated Airedale terrier. The test was such a success that the neighbor could not even recognize his own dog.

Morgan immediately saw the potential in his mystery solution as a beauty product for African Americans. Many African Americans of this time period attempted to win acceptance in mainstream society by imitating white concepts of beauty. Some attempted to accomplish this by straightening their naturally curly hair, but this was a difficult process. Heated combs had been invented to help relax and straighten black hair, but they were troublesome and potentially unsafe. Morgan made additional refinements to his lubricant and marketed his solution—now in cream form—as the first chemical hair relaxer, called G. A. Morgan Hair Refining Cream. It was an immediate hit, and prompted a whole series of hair-care items aimed at African American customers.

Inventions for the Common Good

The substantial income Morgan earned from his businesses allowed him to invent products that he considered important for human safety. The first of these was a special breathing hood designed for firefighters and engineers who are regularly exposed to dangerous fumes. At the time, there was no good system for allowing someone to survive in a smoke-filled space. Morgan's device worked on a very simple principle: during a fire, deadly smoke gathers at the highest levels of a room or area, because it is heated by the fire. At floor level, the air remains relatively clear and safe. Morgan's device covered the user's head and featured tubes that extended down to floor level. In this way, the wearer only breathed in the safe air taken from ground level. This air was further filtered by moist sponges to prevent soot and other particles from entering the hood.

This simple device proved highly effective, especially for people dealing with fires. Morgan patented the device and formed a new company, the National Safety Device Company, to create and sell the hoods. Stocks issued for the company shot up to twenty-five times their initial value after just two years. The invention earned Morgan a gold medal at a safety exhibition in New York City in 1914. Still, he faced prejudice as an African American when trying to sell the device to buyers in the South. For this reason, he hired a white man to assume the role of the company owner.

Morgan himself had an opportunity to prove the effectiveness of his safety hood in his own hometown in 1916. On July 24, more than thirty workers who were digging a tunnel under Lake Erie became trapped after an explosion in the tunnel. The tunnel was filled with poisonous gas and smoke, preventing the rescue of the trapped men. Someone quickly informed Morgan about the crisis, and he and his brother hurried to the tunnel with safety hoods. Both of them descended into the smoky passage wearing safety hoods, and both returned carrying survivors. They made numerous trips back and forth through the tunnel, ultimately saving more than twenty of the men. Morgan was hailed as a hero by the city's residents.

Morgan's next major invention was, yet again, completely unrelated to the fields in which he had achieved his previous successes. As automobiles began to dominate the streets of Cleveland, so too did accidents between the vehicles and horse-drawn carriages. Some signals to regulate traffic flow had already been invented, but none of them worked very well. Morgan came up with a design that allowed an operator—or automated system—to direct traffic coming from any direction to stop, go, or proceed with caution. These basic signals still exist to this day in the form of red, green, and yellow traffic signals. Morgan patented his signal in 1923, and General Electric paid him forty thousand dollars for the rights to the device.

Morgan never rested on his previous accomplishments, and he thrived on finding new avenues to explore. He launched an African American newspaper in 1920, the *Cleveland Call.* The newspaper merged with another paper in 1928 to form the *Call and Post,* a long-running and popular publication. Morgan also ran for Cleveland city council in 1931. Though he was unsuccessful, it is significant that he ran for political office at a time when the majority of African Americans in the South were still being denied the right to vote.

Morgan developed glaucoma in his later years, a condition that results in damage to the optic nerve and eventual blindness. He continued to work on new inventions for as long as his vision allowed. He passed away in 1963 at the age of eighty-six, just months after the United States government honored him as the inventor of the traffic signal.

★ HAROLD DADFORD WEST
(1904–1974)

Harold Dadford West was a biochemist who gained fame for his work studying the basic building blocks of life. West served as the first African American president of Meharry Medical College, the premier black medical college in the nation, from 1952 to 1965. He also was the first black member of the State Board of Education in Tennessee.

West was born in Flemington, New Jersey, to George and Mary Ann West. West suffered from acute asthma attacks throughout his life, in which his lungs would become inflamed and his breathing constricted.

This condition, usually brought on by an allergen (a substance that can trigger an allergic reaction) or other environmental trigger, may have spurred his interest in biochemistry. He finished high school in 1921. His quest for knowledge took him to the University of Illinois, where he earned his bachelor's degree four years later.

West took a teaching position at Morris Brown College, an African American school in Atlanta, Georgia. The primary purpose of Morris Brown, as was true at many African American colleges in the South, was simply to provide black students with enough education so they could work as teachers in segregated schools; the school did not have advanced science courses or resources. West became the head of the science program when he started at the school. He had no opportunities there to continue his own education or perform research. He stayed just two years.

West accepted a position as an associate professor of biochemistry at Meharry Medical College in Nashville, Tennessee, in 1927. Meharry was the first medical college for training African American doctors and nurses in the South. Its facilities were among the best available to many African Americans at the time. West continued his education by earning his master's degree and doctorate in biochemistry, both from the University of Illinois in 1930 and 1937, respectively. Prestigious fellowships from both the Julius Rosenwald Fund and the Rockefeller Foundation made his continuing education possible. He became a full professor at Meharry in 1938 and, as at Morris Brown, became the head of his own department.

West was able to use the facilities at Meharry for his own continuing research. West was especially interested in amino acids, special chains of molecules that are sometimes referred to as the building blocks of life. Amino acids are used to make proteins, which among other things play a key role in the functioning of cells. West became the first person to successfully synthesize, or create from other components, an amino acid called threonine. His studies, widely published in medical journals, often centered on the role nutrition—or lack of nutrition—plays in the development of various diseases.

West became the first African American president of Meharry Medical College in 1952. He remained in this position until 1965, when he gave up his administrative responsibilities so that he could concentrate on teaching and research. He also devoted his time to the State Board of Education; he was the first African American to serve on the board. He retired as professor in 1973, and died just one year later at the age of sixty-nine.

❖ AFRICAN AMERICAN INVENTORS ADVANCE RAILROADS

The American railroad system began just before 1830, and became a major industry in the country. African Americans were largely excluded from contributing to the industry's development until slavery was abolished following the Civil War (1861–65). Their newfound freedom allowed several African Americans to make significant contributions to railroad technology and safety throughout the last half of the nineteenth century.

The first major contribution made by an African American was the invention of an improved smokestack for steam train engines, patented by Landrow Bell in 1871. The new design solved a problem common in smokestacks: As the train moved forward, sparks and embers were expelled from the stack along with smoke. These embers posed a risk to passengers and engineers, partly because they were a fire hazard. Landrow's cone-shaped design trapped the sparks and embers and returned them safely to the ash pan.

Other African Americans received patents for similar improvements to existing designs. Dozens of patents were issued for new kinds of railway switches, train car couplings, and fenders to prevent running over people or animals. Elijah McCoy (1843–1929) invented a lubricating cup in 1872 that automatically oiled locomotive engines. Inventor Elbert R. Robinson (d. 1925) devised both a new way to cast metal wheels and an improved connector system for electric trolleys. As passenger travel increased, some African American inventors found ways to improve comfort aboard long rail trips. Lewis Latimer (1848–1928), who later earned fame for his association with Thomas Edison (1847–1931) and the invention of a better lightbulb, shared credit for the invention of an improved toilet for railcars.

The most significant African American inventor in the field of railroad technology was Granville T. Woods (1856–1910), sometimes referred to as "the black Edison." He began as a fireman aboard the Danville and Southern railroad in 1872, and soon moved up to engineer. His inventions covered a broad spectrum of

Granville T. Woods invented a number of devices that improved railroad technology in the late nineteenth century. *AP Images*

devices and systems related to rail travel. He patented a more efficient type of steam boiler furnace in 1884. The following year, he patented a device that combined voice and telegraph signals on a single wire for transmission. He also invented a mechanical brake powered by electricity.

One of Woods's greatest achievements was a method for transferring electricity from a track to a moving train. This was accomplished through iron blocks on the track that connected briefly with the train as it passed, providing a charge. The device improved communications between trains and stations, and helped to prevent accidental collisions between trains.

❖ THE END OF SLAVERY BRINGS PATENTS AND RECOGNITION FOR AFRICAN AMERICAN INVENTORS

The end of slavery in the 1860s allowed African Americans to participate in many parts of society from which they previously had been excluded. A few African Americans came up with significant inventions before and during the Civil War (1861–65), but their status as slaves prevented them from patenting their creations. Once that restriction was lifted from millions of African Americans, many of them created or improved devices that continued to benefit Americans in modern times.

Improving the Trades and Domestic Life

The types of inventions patented by African Americans during the last half of the nineteenth century follow a general trend. The first patents were sought by African Americans who worked in specialized trades and came up with new or better ways to perform their jobs. Joseph Dickinson built and repaired reed organs in the 1870s, and patented several improvements in design to these musical instruments. Elijah McCoy (1843–1929) worked as an oilman for the Michigan Central Railroad, and invented a lubricating cup in 1872 that kept important steam engine parts well oiled without the need for constant human monitoring. His basic design was ultimately used in several different industries since its application was useful for any machine with parts that needed lubrication. He eventually held dozens of patents for lubrication devices.

David Fisher was involved in the furniture-making trade, and his inventions addressed specific obstacles in that field. The first, a joiner's clamp patented in 1875, held two parts of a piece of furniture together as they were being glued, allowing the worker to continue assembling the piece instead of having to hold the parts together until the glue dried. His second invention was the furniture caster, a wheel mounted on the bottom of a heavy piece of furniture to allow workers to move pieces around the shop. The caster proved so popular that most large pieces of furniture are still made with casters so they can be moved easily. Jan Ernst Matzeliger (1852–89), originally from Dutch Guiana, moved to the United States and began to work for a shoemaker in Massachusetts. After noting that the final assembly of a handmade shoe was a long and tedious process, Matzeliger invented a machine in 1883 that allowed a shoemaker to assemble more than ten times as many shoes in a single day as he could by hand.

After these early, specialized inventions, more and more African Americans sought patents on items that improved domestic life. Since many were employed as cooks, laundry workers, and cleaners, their goal was usually to make their own jobs and home duties easier. In 1879, Thomas Elkins came up with an early design for a refrigerator that kept perishable items cool for longer periods of time—important for a poor family who cannot afford to have food spoil. Willis Johnson invented a machine in 1884 that beat eggs; in fact, it mixed any ingredients placed inside it and was the early ancestor of modern kitchen mixers. Sarah Goode became the first African American woman to earn a patent in 1885. Her invention was a folding bed that stored away in a piece of cabinet furniture, which could then be used as a desk. Albert Richardson invented a variety of domestic conveniences, but his most famous came in 1891. Richardson designed the definitive butter churn, which allowed anyone to create butter easily.

Sarah Boone patented an early version of the ironing board in 1892. Thomas Stewart revolutionized cleaning in 1893 with his invention of the modern mop. Joseph Lee, a veteran of the food industry, created the first bread machine in 1894. Lloyd Ray's 1897 invention was an improvement on the dustpan, allowing the pan to be handle-mounted and fold flat—a design still used by many professional sweeper pans today.

Making Significant Improvements to the Modern World

As African Americans became increasingly accepted into mainstream American society, many inventors focused on making improvements to the world beyond the kitchen and broom closet. Henry Brown invented the first personal-use strongbox for storing valuables and important documents in 1886. Miriam Benjamin invented a system for calling for service from a waiter or attendant in 1888. A customer simply pressed a button located on his or her chair, which sounded a signal for the employee, and then activated a light on the chair so that the employee could easily locate the person in need of assistance. A system very similar to Benjamin's is still used on airplanes.

Several other devices created by African Americans during the last decade of the nineteenth century proved both popular and enduring. William Purvis noted the inconvenience and mess involved in using ink pens. A person was required to keep a supply of fresh ink on hand, which was bulky and could leak and stain clothing. Purvis solved this problem in 1890 by inventing the first fountain pen, which contained ink in its barrel that automatically flowed from the tip as it was used. Philip Downing saw the inconvenience in having to make constant trips to the post office to mail letters, and invented the postal drop mailbox in 1891.

Charles Brooks saw a way to improve the labor-intensive task of cleaning city streets, which was done by workers pushing brooms and picking up trash by hand. He invented the street sweeper in 1896, a vehicle that automatically brushed the streets free of dirt and debris. Street sweepers very similar to his original design are still used regularly in urban areas. John Love, noting the aggravation of having to use a knife to whittle down the point of a pencil whenever the tip became dull, invented the first pencil sharpener in 1897. And in 1899, George Grant, an avid golfer, became frustrated by golf balls that would not remain stable and still while he swung. He solved his problem with a simple device that is now an essential part of the sport: the golf tee. Grant's invention provides a fitting example of how far African Americans had come since the Civil War—from working as slaves on plantations in the South, to inventing better ways to hit a ball on the golf course.

❖ BOUCHET BECOMES FIRST AFRICAN AMERICAN PH.D. IN SCIENCE

Education for African Americans, especially in the South, improved dramatically after the Civil War with the creation of many schools and training institutes. The primary goal of most of these institutions was to provide basic literacy and to prepare students for trades and jobs involving physical labor. Very few focused on higher academic learning, which meant there were limited opportunities for African Americans who achieved advanced degrees and education. Such was the case for Edward Bouchet (1852–1918), who studied advanced physics yet was denied the chance to share his knowledge with students by teaching at a university.

Bouchet is often referred to as the first African American to receive a Ph.D., which is not accurate. He was actually the first African American to earn a doctorate at an American university. The first African American to receive a Ph.D. anywhere was Patrick Francis Healy (1834–1910), a Jesuit priest who studied religion and philosophy at the University of Leuven in Belgium. He earned his doctorate there in 1865. Healy was born in Georgia to a wealthy white plantation owner and his slave common-law wife. Healy and his nine siblings were technically slaves because their mother was a slave. Southern law mandated that a black person's status as a slave or free person depended on the mother's status, and it was illegal to free slaves in the South. Healy's father did not treat them as slaves, however. He sent Healy and his brothers north so they could receive a quality education, and Healy eventually continued his education in Europe.

Edward Bouchet was the first African American to earn a Ph.D. in a science, but racism prevented him from advancing in his career. *Fisk University Library. Reproduced by permission.*

Healy openly admitted his racial heritage although he was light enough to "pass" for white. His light complexion, family wealth, and European education provided him with unique opportunities not available to most African Americans. He was one of only a handful of people in the entire United States to hold a Ph.D., since the only university offering that advanced degree at that time was Yale University. He received a teaching position at Georgetown University, and later became the school's president.

Bouchet's experiences were somewhat different. He was born in New Haven, Connecticut, in the shadow of Yale University. He was forced to attend a segregated school as a child, but he was eventually able to enter the prestigious Hopkins Grammar School. He graduated at the top of his class and entered Yale, where he was the first African American to earn a bachelor's degree in 1874. He finished in the top 5 percent of his graduating class, and was the first African American nominated—though not elected—to Phi Beta Kappa, an honor society known for the academic excellence of its members. Yale's chapter of Phi Beta Kappa was inactive during Bouchet's college years, so he did not actually become a member until ten years after he graduated, in 1884.

Bouchet continued at Yale after receiving his undergraduate degree, studying physics. He completed his doctoral dissertation in just two years on ray optics, a field concerning the properties of light. The dissertation earned him a doctorate in 1876. This made him the first African American to earn a Ph.D. in the United States, the first African American anywhere to earn a Ph.D. in science, and one of only six people in the United States to earn a Ph.D. in physics.

Bouchet did not receive the opportunities given to Healy. The most notable difference between the two men was that Bouchet was visibly African American. Even though he was one of the two most educated African Americans in the country, Bouchet could not obtain a teaching position at any university. African American schools had not yet begun to offer advanced subjects such as physics, and white colleges refused to hire him. He ended up working for the Institute for Colored Youth (ICY, now Cheyney University) in Philadelphia, Pennsylvania, a school that did not even offer degrees until 1913. He taught physics and chemistry at the school for twenty-six years. The school gradually shifted away from academics in favor of vocational, skills-based training, and dissolved the academic department altogether in 1902. Bouchet was out of a job.

Bouchet moved from job to job, working as a high school teacher, a hospital manager, a customs inspector, and finally as a high school principal in Gallipolis, Ohio. He worked for five years there, but quit when his health began to fail. He died in 1918 at the age of sixty-six. African Americans like Booker T. Washington (1856–1915) and George Washington Carver (1864–1943) would eventually make significant contributions to science and education. Yet it would be forty-two years before another African American, Elmer Samuel Imes (1883–1941), would earn a doctorate in physics.

❖ TUSKEGEE ESTABLISHES AN AGRICULTURAL EXPERIMENT STATION

In 1897, Booker T. Washington, founder of the Tuskegee Institute in Alabama, received a grant from the Alabama state legislature for one thousand five hundred dollars for the purpose of establishing an agricultural experiment station. This was the first of its kind for an African American school. The trend for creating agricultural experiment stations began with the passage of the Hatch-George Act of 1887, which called for experiment stations in each state to study the particular problems and challenges facing those in the field of agriculture. The economy of the South was predominantly based on agriculture, so problems with growing crops could—and did—lead to devastating economic conditions. The experiment stations were overseen by the United States Department of Agriculture.

George Washington Carver (1864–1943) had just arrived at the Tuskegee Institute to head its Department of Agricultural Research, but he had already learned a great deal about agriculture from his own firsthand experience. He immediately set to work studying the various crops and plants grown in the area, and devised experiments to evaluate the best varieties to grow under specific soil and weather conditions. The station was also in charge of an educational outreach program, sharing knowledge of its agricultural findings with local farmers by visiting them with a "portable school" on a wagon.

The Tuskegee Institute received very little funding from the government, and the various departments were expected to contribute to the school's operating budget in whatever way they could. The school emphasized practical skills, so students contributed their labor and skills to earn a modest profit. Washington expected the Agricultural Experiment Station to earn a profit as well. Carver and his students were already

Tuskegee Institute students plant sweet potatoes at the historically black college's agricultural experiment station, c. 1913. © *Corbis*

growing a surplus of crops, so it made sense to sell the unused portion at market value. Other experiment stations—at schools that received greater amounts of funding—sold their crops for a profit, so the idea was not far-fetched or unreasonable. Carver was so dedicated to his research, however, that he did not have the time or patience to deal with arranging for the sales of crops. This caused occasional tension between Washington and Carver, though Washington generally left Carver to pursue his own research.

The product of that research was forty-four pamphlets published over the course of forty-five years. Each pamphlet was dedicated to a different area of research at the station and summarized the findings of Carver and his team. The most famous of these bulletins was *How to Grow the Peanut and 105 Ways of Preparing It for Human Consumption,* published in 1915. Carver also published bulletins covering the many ways of utilizing sweet potatoes, tomatoes, and cowpeas. The bulletins covered other aspects of farming as well, including ways to recharge soil that has been depleted of nutrients and methods to increase yield in a corn crop. Though it was just one of many such stations, the knowledge gained and shared by Carver at the Tuskegee Agricultural Experiment Station helped to change the way that Southern farmers viewed both their land and their livelihood.

❖ HISTORICALLY BLACK COLLEGES INTRODUCE SCIENCE PROGRAMS

A large number of schools were built across the South to educate African Americans after the Civil War. These schools were not intended primarily for academic study. Many were "normal schools," the mission of which was to train African Americans as teachers. Those teachers could then provide basic education to other African Americans in lower-level schools across the region. Some schools provided education in trades or farming. Because these colleges were concerned mainly with spreading basic education and teaching vocational skills, few of them offered studies in the sciences.

At the beginning of the twentieth century, African American college students began to make their way into traditionally white universities to complete advanced science degrees that they could not earn at black colleges. After they earned these degrees, however, they found that the only schools willing to hire them in teaching positions were the African American colleges. By returning to these underdeveloped institutions, these well-educated scientists brought with them sufficient knowledge to expand the schools' science programs.

Howard Offers Broad Science Curriculum

Like many historically black colleges, Howard University in Washing-ton, D.C., was founded just after the Civil War, in 1867. Unlike some other

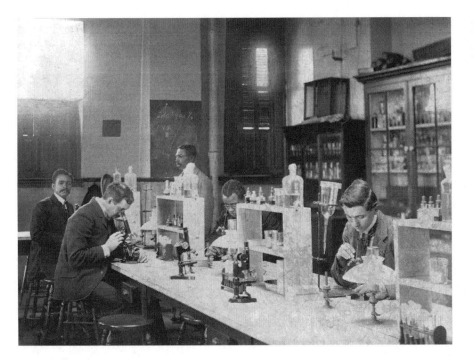

Students work in the bacteriology laboratory at Howard University at the turn of the twentieth century. © *Corbis*

colleges, it was meant to provide a broad education in the arts and sciences rather than a focus on teaching or trade skills (though it was a teacher's college as well). The curriculum included classes in chemistry and the life sciences.

Biologist Edward E. Just is responsible for developing the successful zoology program at Howard. After earning his biology degree at Dartmouth, he helped launch the zoology department at Howard when he was hired there in 1907. At first, Just found the university's lab and research facilities to be inadequate for his work. Slowly, as the program grew and the school's funding increased, the department rivaled similar departments at traditionally white schools.

Howard soon branched out into other sciences as well. Between 1907 and 1910, the university added programs in civil, electrical, and mechanical engineering as part of its School of Manual Arts and Sciences. The following year, the school developed a four-year curriculum and moved into its own building on campus. Professors such as Perry Blaine Perkins, who received his Ph.D. in physics from Yale University, provided instruction in subjects like physics, including electricity and magnetism, beginning in 1909. Howard was the first African American learning institution to offer degrees in engineering, with the first civil engineering degree awarded in 1914.

Tuskegee University president Frederick Patterson (left) with George Washington Carver in 1940. Patterson established the school's veterinary program.
© *Bettmann/Corbis*

The Tuskegee Institute Branches Out

The Tuskegee Institute in Alabama was established as a normal school in 1881. Tuskegee's first leader, Booker T. Washington (1856–1915), believed strongly that African Americans needed to learn practical work skills in order to be able to support themselves and become productive members of society. For this reason, Tuskegee Institute also focused on providing farming and trade skills education.

Tuskegee Institute gradually expanded beyond its initial mission, achieving particular success with the School of Veterinary Medicine, which opened its doors in 1945. The driving force behind the Tuskegee Veterinary School was Frederick D. Patterson (1901–88), president of Tuskegee Institute from 1935 until 1953. Patterson had earned his degree in veterinary medicine in 1923, and worked at several universities before accepting a teaching position at the Tuskegee Institute. He was selected as the head of the agriculture department in 1933, and two years later he was chosen as the new president of the Tuskegee Institute.

Patterson made it one of his goals as president to open a school of veterinary medicine at the college. There were only a handful of veterinary schools in the country in the 1930s, and even fewer where an African American could receive a veterinary degree. The degree could be used in many ways; a veterinarian could work in private practice, or as an animal inspector for the government, or even as an animal researcher. Patterson saw that such a degree could offer the perfect opportunity for African Americans who could not break through in other, more established professions.

The first class at the Tuskegee veterinary school consisted of thirteen students who were taught by seven different instructors. Five students graduated with degrees in veterinary medicine in 1949. Maintaining small class sizes was important to school officials, and after fifteen years the student-to-teacher ratio was still just three-to-one. The school had turned out 142 graduates by 1961, most of whom opened their own private veterinary offices. The school remained one of fewer than thirty accredited veterinary schools operating in the United States as of 2010.

❖ AFRICAN AMERICAN PILOTS OPEN OPPORTUNITIES IN THE SKIES

The aviation industry had its origins in the early 1900s when daring inventors risked their lives by climbing into machines of their own creation in an attempt to attain the power of flight. It only took about a dozen years for those first successful attempts to result in a brand-new way of traveling, conducting war, and even just looking at the world. Some African Americans saw in aviation an opportunity, a new chance to break out of the traditions of segregation and discrimination they had lived with for so long. Indeed, African American pilots did not lag far behind their white counterparts in accomplishments, but they still had to struggle for every step of progress they made.

Coleman, Powell, and Banning Open Doors for African American Flyers

The first prominent African American aviator in the United States was a woman named Bessie Coleman (1892–1926). She had no special background in engineering, nor was she connected in any way with other early aviation pioneers. She simply heard stories from her brother, who had fought in France in World War I (1914–18), of women and African Americans flying planes. This inspired in her a dream of becoming a pilot. She could not find a school in the United States willing to train an African American woman, so she went to France and earned her international pilot's license in 1921.

Coleman was ahead of her time, and there were no practical careers for a pilot in the United States. Training other pilots was a possibility, but existing schools were for whites only. She seized upon the only option she had, as a stunt pilot performing for crowds at festivals, fairs, and other events. She dreamed of opening her own flight school where African Americans could train as pilots. Her tragic death in 1926 after being thrown out of a plane prevented her from accomplishing her goal, but a man named William J. Powell (1897–1942) would help bring her dream to reality.

Powell was a native Kentuckian who had experienced many of the same obstacles and challenges that Coleman had faced. He was denied admission to the U.S. Army Air Corps (later known as the U.S. Air Force) because he was African American. Powell tried to find a civilian flight school willing to train him to be a pilot, and was finally accepted to a school in Los Angeles in 1928. He became not only a pilot but also an aeronautical engineer. Powell launched the Bessie Coleman Aero Club in 1929, and also opened a flying school named after Coleman. His goal, like hers, was to train African Americans interested in flying and encourage them to seize the opportunities presented by this new industry.

One famous member of the Bessie Coleman Aero Club was James Herman Banning (1899–1933). Banning grew up in the Midwest, and

C. Alfred Anderson, with his arm around the shoulders of his wife, and Albert Forsythe (right) pose in front of their plane before attempting to become the first African Americans to complete a round-trip transcontinental flight in 1934. © *Bettmann/Corbis*

learned to fly at an airfield in Des Moines, Iowa. He moved to Los Angeles and joined the Bessie Coleman Aero Club in 1929, becoming its chief pilot. He partnered with another African American pilot, Thomas C. Allen, to build a working plane from scrap parts. The pair flew it from Los Angeles to Long Island, New York, in 1932. Banning and Allen were the first African Americans to make such a trip, averaging about eighty miles per hour while in the air. The journey took three weeks to finish since they needed to raise money for fuel at every stop. Just as his career was beginning, Banning died in a tragic plane crash in 1933 in San Diego, California. The following year, C. Alfred Anderson and Albert Forsythe (1898–1986) became the first African Americans to complete a round-trip transcontinental flight.

Brown, Young, and Green Fight for Acceptance

Like William Powell, Willa Brown (1906–92) was inspired by Bessie Coleman's determination and spirit. She became the first African American woman to earn a pilot's license in the United States in 1937. Brown was chosen to run the Civil Air Patrol (CAP) training program in Chicago, Illinois, in 1941. The CAP was the civilian arm of the U.S. Army Air Corps. Brown was enlisted as a military officer, and therefore became the first

African American officer in the CAP. Brown was responsible for training hundreds of soldiers to fly for the U.S. Army Air Corps, including some of the African American pilots who earned a reputation as the Tuskegee Airmen during World War II (1939–45). Brown's efforts were an important step toward ending segregation in the United States military.

Perry Young (1919–98) was also connected to the Tuskegee Airmen. He first took flying lessons in 1937 while attending college, and earned his pilot's license in 1939 at the age of nineteen. During World War II, Young became an instructor at Tuskegee Army Air Field, training over 150 of the Tuskegee Airmen for battle. Young was unable to find work as a commercial pilot for more than ten years after the war, despite the prestigious reputation of the Tuskegee pilots. He spent time as a private instructor, and was also the first African American to earn a helicopter pilot's license in the United States. Young finally broke through the color barrier on December 17, 1956, by becoming the first African American commercial pilot in the United States, flying for New York Airways. He remained a pilot for the company for twenty-two years.

African American pilot Marlon Green (1929–2009) followed the path cleared by Young. He left the U.S. Air Force in 1957 after nine years of service flying a variety of aircraft, from cargo planes to bombers. He attempted to find work in the rapidly expanding commercial airline industry, but was turned down by every major airline. He believed that his race was the only issue with his application, so he applied to Continental Airlines without identifying himself as an African American. The ruse worked; the company was impressed enough by his credentials to bring him to Denver for flight tests. He had more experience than all of the other candidates, yet he was one of only two who were not hired.

Continental had signed an agreement, along with other airlines, that they would not discriminate against African Americans in hiring. Green sued Continental Airlines on the basis that they had violated this agreement. He resorted to working at a dairy, cleaning milk cans, while awaiting the outcome of his lawsuit. The case reached the United States Supreme Court in 1963. The justices ruled unanimously that Continental had acted in violation of antidiscrimination laws. The airline offered Green a job, and in March of 1965, he became the first African American pilot for a major airline.

❖ AFRICAN AMERICANS HELP LAUNCH THE APOLLO MISSIONS

The U.S. space program in the early 1960s was trailing behind the accomplishments of the Soviet Union. Soviet cosmonaut Yuri Gagarin

Robert H. Lawrence, First African American Selected to Be an Astronaut

While Ed Dwight was the first African American to be selected for astronaut training, Robert H. Lawrence (1935–67) was the first African American to be selected as an actual astronaut. Lawrence was raised by a single mother in a poor Chicago neighborhood. He overcame the difficult circumstances of his childhood to earn a Ph.D. in physical chemistry while also reaching the rank of major in the United States Air Force. Lawrence applied twice to NASA's astronaut training program, but he was rejected. He was accepted into another program instead, the Aerospace Research Pilot School. He completed the program in June 1967. Lawrence was one of seventeen men selected to serve as astronauts for the Manned Orbital Laboratory (MOL),

Pilot Robert H. Lawrence died in a crash six months after being picked to be NASA's first black astronaut. *Time & Life Pictures/Getty Images*

a planned space station. Just six months later, Lawrence was killed in a plane crash while he was training another pilot in advanced flying techniques. The MOL project was cancelled two years later, before any of its astronauts had a chance to travel into space. NASA refused to acknowledge Lawrence's historic place among American astronauts for thirty years. In 1997, on the thirtieth anniversary of his tragic death, his name was added to the Space Mirror Memorial at Kennedy Space Center, a tribute to those who died during missions or training for the American space program.

(1934–68) became the first human in space in 1961. This accomplishment was a major blow to the image of the United States, since the United States and the Soviet Union were locked in the Cold War at the time. The Cold War was an intense political and economic rivalry between the United States and the Soviet Union falling just short of military conflict that lasted until the Soviet Union dissolved in 1991. President John F. Kennedy (1917–1963) was committed to landing Americans on the moon before the Soviets could get there. The National Aeronautics and Space Administration (NASA) moved ahead full-force with its Apollo program to accomplish this goal. The program recruited the finest minds from different scientific and military fields, a number of whom were African American.

Vance Marchbanks (1905–1988) was a key participant in the American space program even before the Apollo project. He was born into a military family and earned his medical degree from Howard University. He later became a surgeon in the United States Air Force during World War II. He also flew during the Korean War (1950–53), and conducted research on pilot fatigue that earned him a commendation medal. Marchbanks was selected as a medical specialist for the Mercury space program in 1960. NASA developed the Mercury program from 1959 through 1963 with the goal of putting a human into orbit around the Earth. It was as part of the Mercury program that John Glenn (1921–) became the first American to orbit the Earth. Marchbanks was responsible for developing systems to monitor the vital signs and general health of all astronauts during their missions. His work set a standard for medical monitoring on all future space missions.

O. S. "Ozzie" Williams (1921–) was an aeronautical engineer for the Apollo program who designed one of its most critical rocket systems. He attempted to enroll in an engineering program at New York University after completing high school in Brooklyn, New York. The dean discouraged him due to his race. Williams ignored the dean and completed his aeronautical engineering degree in 1943. He continued studying for his master's degree while working as a designer for Republic Aviation, where he helped create the P47 Thunderbird plane for use in World War II. Williams worked as a designer for various types of aerospace systems throughout the 1940s and 1950s, and became a leading expert on liquid-fueled rockets. He began working with NASA as a propulsion engineer in 1961.

Williams and his team were responsible for designing the landing propulsion system for the Apollo lunar module. Williams's propulsion system allowed astronauts to guide the spacecraft gently and safely to the moon's surface. This propulsion system, consisting of sixteen small rockets, was responsible for saving the lives of the astronauts aboard the Apollo 13 module in 1970 when their main propulsion system failed partway through their mission.

George R. Carruthers (1939–) contributed to the Apollo program as an astrophysicist. Carruthers was the son of a civil engineer who worked for the U.S. Army Air Corps. His interest in space was obvious from a young age; he built his own working telescope when he was only ten years old. He attended the University of Illinois at Urbana-Champaign, where he studied both engineering and astronomy. He earned his Ph.D. in aeronautical and astronomical engineering in 1964, and began work at the United States

Ed Dwight in 1983. Dwight was the first African American to train as an astronaut but was ultimately not selected by NASA. *AP Images*

Naval Research Laboratory that same year. He made a major contribution to the Apollo program with his creation of a moon-based observatory. The device could detect molecular hydrogen in space, and offered ultraviolet images of Earth and other celestial bodies. It was launched and put into operation during Apollo 16 in 1972. Carruthers received the Exceptional Scientific Achievement Medal from NASA for his accomplishments.

One notable role in which African Americans did not participate during the Apollo program was as astronauts. One African American, Ed Dwight, was selected for training as an astronaut in 1962, after proving himself as a U. S. Air Force pilot and as an aeronautical engineer. He completed his space-flight training, only to be told that NASA chose not to select him as an astronaut for the program. Dwight wrote a report documenting the racism and harassment that he endured while training, but it did not help. He ultimately resigned in 1966 and went on to become a successful sculptor. Robert H. Lawrence was later selected as an astronaut for another American space program (see sidebar), but died in a crash before getting an opportunity to fulfill his duties. It was not until 1983 that the first African American, Guion Bluford (1942–), made history by traveling into space.

GEORGE WASHINGTON CARVER'S CONGRESSIONAL TESTIMONY ON THE PEANUT (1921)

African Americans had to confront stereotypes about their lack of intelligence for most of the twentieth century. African Americans had been denied an education by law during slavery, and made slow progress towards equal education after slavery was abolished in 1865. Many white Americans thought that African Americans were not capable of higher learning, particularly in the sciences.

African Americans made a significant step forward in challenging this stereotype through the work of prominent African American scientists like George Washington Carver. Carver was associated with the Tuskegee Institute from 1896 until he died in 1943. He headed the Agricultural Experiment Station there, and conducted many experiments related to farming and crops. His most famous research concerned the peanut, for which he discovered dozens of uses. George Washington Carver appeared before the House Ways and Means Committee of the United States Congress in 1921 in order to share his knowledge of the many uses of the peanut. His obvious intelligence and charm won over the committee, and he was allowed to speak longer than the ten minutes he had originally been given. This simple visit proved to be a defining moment in public perceptions about African Americans in the sciences. The following is an excerpt from his appearance before the Ways and Means Committee.

·······················

The Chairman: [Joseph W. Fordney, R-Michigan] All right, Mr. Carver. We will give you 10 minutes.

Mr. Carver: Mr. Chairman, I have been asked by the United Peanut Growers' Association to tell you something about the possibility of the peanut and its possible extension. I come from Tuskegee, Ala[bama]. I am engaged in agricultural research work, and I have given some attention to the peanut, but not as much as I expect to give. I have given a great deal of time to the sweet potato and allied southern crops. I am especially interested in southern crops and their possibilities, and the peanut comes in, I think, for one of the most remarkable crops that we are all acquainted with. It will tell us a number of things that we do not already know, and you will also observe that it has possibilities that we are just now beginning to find out.

If I may have a little space here to put these things down, I should like to exhibit them to you. I am going to just touch a few high places here and there because in 10 minutes you will tell me to stop.

This is the crushed cake, which has a great many possibilities. I simply call attention to that. The crushed cake may be used in all sorts of combinations—for flours and meals and breakfast foods and a great many things that I have not time to touch upon just now.

Then we have the hulls, which are ground and made into a meal for burnishing tin plate. It has a very important value in that direction, and more of it is going to be used as the tin-plate manufacturers understand its value.

The Chairman: If you have anything to drink, don't put it under the table.

Mr. Carver: I am not ready to use them just now. They will come later if my 10 minutes are extended. [Laughter.]

Now there is a rather interesting confection.

Mr. [John N.] Garner [D-Texas]: Let us have order. This man knows a great deal about this business.

The Chairman: Yes, let us have order in the room.

Mr. Carver: This is another confection. It is peanuts covered with chocolate. As I passed through Greensboro, S.C., I noticed in one of the stores that this was displayed on the market, and, as it is understood better, more of it is going to be made up into this form.

Here is a breakfast food. I am very sorry that you can not taste this, so I will taste it for you. [Laughter.]

Now this is a combination and, by the way, one of the finest breakfast foods that you or anyone else has ever seen. It is a combination of the sweet potato and the peanut, and if you will pardon a little digression here I will state that the peanut and the sweet potato are twin brothers and can not and should not be separated. They are two of the greatest products that God has ever given us. They can be made into a perfectly balanced ration. If all of the other foodstuffs were destroyed—this is, vegetable foodstuffs were destroyed—a perfectly balanced ration with all of the nutriment in it could be made with the sweet potato and the peanut. From the sweet potato we get starches and carbohydrates, and from the peanut we get all the muscle-building properties.

Mr. [John Q.] Tilson [R-Connecticut]: Do you want a watermelon to go along with that?

Mr. Carver: Well, of course, you do not have to have it. Of course, if you want a dessert, that comes in very well, but you know we can get along pretty well without dessert. The recent war has taught us that. . . .

Mr. Garner: Let me ask you one question now.

Mr. Carver: Yes, sir.

Mr. Garner: I understood you to say that the properties of the peanut combined with the properties of the sweet potato was a balanced ration, and that you could destroy all other vegetable life and continue to sustain the human race?

Mr. Carver: Yes, sir. Because you can make up the necessary food elements there. Then, as I said before, in addition to that you have your vitamins. You know the war taught us many, many things we did not know before. We did not know anything about these vitamins, and we did not know anything about these various peculiar compounds which are brought out by the complex handling of these various products, and science has touched these things in a way that is bringing to life or bringing to light what was intended should be brought to light, and there is scarcely a vegetable product that we have not learned something about.

Then again, if we think of how the peanut is used, it is the only thing that is universally used among civilized and uncivilized people, and all sorts of animals like it, and I do not know of a single case—that is, I mean normal—that complains because peanuts hurt them. I remember a little boy that we have in our town. Well, he is one of our professor's boys. He made up his Christmas budget, his Santa Claus budget. He started out with peanuts first, and then he would mention a horse, and then peanuts, and then a dog, and then peanuts, and peanuts were the beginning and the ending. He eats peanuts all the time. So that it is a natural diet that was intended that everybody should use. Then again, if you go to the first chapter of Genesis, we can interpret very clearly, I think, what God intended when he said, "Behold, I have given you every herb that bears seed upon the face of the earth, and every tree bearing a seed. To you it shall be meat." That is what he means about it. It shall be meat. There is everything there to strengthen and nourish and keep the body alive and healthy.

The Chairman: Mr. Carver, what school did you attend?

Mr. Carver: The last school I attended was the Agricultural College of Iowa—the Iowa Agricultural College. You doubtless remember Mr. Wilson, who served in the cabinet here so long, Secretary James Wilson. He was my instructor for six years.

Mr. [William R.] Green [R-Iowa]: What research laboratory do you work in now?

Mr. Carver: At the Tuskegee Institute, Tuskegee, Ala[bama].

Mr. Carew: You have rendered the Committee a great service.

Mr. Garner: I think he is entitled to the thanks of the committee. [Applause.]

The Chairman: Mr. Carver, if you wish to make any statement in any brief, just file it with the clerk or the reporter and it will be made a part of your remarks. We will be very glad to have you do so.

Mr. Garner: File it any time within the next week.

The Chairman: Yes. File it any time within the next week.

Mr. Garner: Any brief along the same line you have been speaking of here we would be glad to have you file.

Mr. [Allen T.] Treadway [R-Massachusetts]: Did the institute send you here or did you come of your own volition?

Mr. Carver: The United Peanut Association of America, sir, asked me to come.

Mr. Treadway: In order to explain to us all this variety of uses of the peanut?

Mr. Carver: Yes, sir. You have seen, gentlemen, just about half of them. There is just about twice this many more.

Mr. Treadway: Well, come again and bring the rest.

The Chairman: We want to compliment you, sir, on the way you have handled your subject.

ERNEST JUST DESCRIBES THE ESSENCE OF LIFE (1939)

Ernest E. Just was an African American scientist who conducted research on the structure of cells during the first half of the twentieth century. He captured his conclusions about the parts of cells and how they interact in his landmark book *The Biology of the Cell Surface*, published in 1939. The quality and depth of his research proved that African American scientists could perform at the same level as their white counterparts. The following excerpt from Just's book offers an eloquent description of how living things are similar to—and yet different from—non-living matter.

• •

Contiguous
In parallel to or alongside; very near or in contact with

The realm of living things being a part of nature is **contiguous** to the non-living world. Living things have material composition, are made up finally of units, molecules, atoms, and electrons, as surely as any non-living matter. Like all forms in nature they have chemical structure and physical properties, are physico-chemical systems. As such they obey the laws of physics and chemistry. Would one deny this fact, one would thereby deny the possibility of any scientific investigation of living things. No matter what beliefs we entertain, the noblest and purest, concerning life as something apart from physical and chemical phenomena, we can not with the mental equipment which we now possess reach any estimate of living things as apart from the remainder of the physico-chemical world.

Constitutes
Makes up or defines the substance of

But although any living thing, being matter, is a physico-chemical system, it differs from matter which **constitutes** the non-living. This difference exists and would continue to exist were some chemist at this moment to succeed to **synthesize** out of non-living matter a living thing. The analysis of living things reveals that they are

Synthesize
Create from component parts or elements

composed of no peculiar chemical elements—instead, they are made up of those most commonly occurring. The difference can not then be attributed to the elements. To be sure, certain complex compounds, as proteins, carbohydrates and lipids (fats and fat-like substances)—themselves compounded mainly of the commonly occurring elements, carbon, hydrogen and oxygen, and never of rare elements—are peculiar to living matter; but the synthesis of protein-like bodies, of sugar and of fat as well as the synthesis of thyroxin (a compound in the internal secretion of the thyroid gland), of products of other internal secretions and of vitamins must **dissipate** whatever belief may have lingered on since Wohler's classic synthesis of urea (more than a hundred years ago) that some unknown vital principle sets apart the chemistry of living things from that of non-living.

And yet there is a difference which expresses itself in the chemical make-up of the living thing. It is its organization. The difference with respect to chemistry thus lies in the **peculiar** combination of compounds which together make a **heterogeneous** system. This acts as a unit-structure, whose behavior or **manifestations** are those of a single thing and not the sum-total of the **multitudinous** chemical components in an **agglomerate** mass.

Living matter has an organization peculiar to itself. Nowhere except in the living world does matter exhibit this organization. Life, even in the simplest animal or plant, so far as we know, never exists apart from it. Resting above and conditioned by non-living matter, life perhaps arose through the chance combination of the compounds which compose it. But who knows? A living thing is not only structure but structure in motion. As static, it reveals the **superlative** combination of compounds of matter; as a moving event, it presents the most intricate time-pattern in nature. Life is exquisitely a time-thing, like music. And beyond the plane of life, out of infinite time may have come that harmony of motion which **endowed** the combination of compounds with life.

Dissipate
Eliminate or get rid of

Peculiar
Unique

Heterogenous
Containing a mixture of different elements or parts

Manifestations
Physical forms

Multitudinous
Large in number; many

Agglomerate
Clustered or lumped together

Superlative
Of the highest kind or quality

Endowed
Furnished or provided with

Research and Activity Ideas

1. African American inventors are responsible for creating many products that improved the quality of life of users even into modern times. Using the Internet, look up one of the inventions mentioned in this chapter by accessing the United States Patent and Trademark Office Web site at http://patft.uspto.gov or by using Google Patents http://www.google.com/patents. Read the original patent application and examine the drawings of the invention. Create a short presentation discussing why this invention was important. Did it make improvements on an existing design? How is this invention still important today?

2. George Washington Carver was famous for his humanitarian outreach to poor farmers in the South. He established a movable school, called the Jesup Wagon, that traveled through the rural South giving demonstrations on agricultural techniques, testing soil, and distributing simple, clear farming bulletins. Using your library and the Internet, research the kinds of agricultural advice Carver shared with Southern farmers. Develop a five-minute oral presentation in which you explain one of Carver's techniques, why it is helpful and effective, and how it is employed. Your presentation must include a visual aid. Potential topics include composting, crop rotation, and pest management.

3. Why do you think so many African American inventors dedicated themselves to working to improve safety and technology in the railroad industry? Research the role of African Americans in the railroad industry, and write a short paper in which you offer an answer to this question.

4. Inspired by Bessie Coleman, Willa Brown (1906–92) decided to become a pilot. Like Coleman, Brown broke down many barriers facing African Americans and women who wanted to be aviators. Use your library and the Internet to research Brown's life. Create an illustrated timeline of her life, either on paper or for presentation on a computer, and share it with your class. Make sure your timeline highlights at least ten key events in Brown's life.

5. Most historically black colleges began as institutes for training African Americans in basic trades like farming or blacksmithing. This was because there were few opportunities in the advanced sciences for blacks at the time. Choose a historically black college or university and trace the development of the school's science programs through the years. Write a short report detailing your findings. Be sure to include any notable students, teachers, or research projects performed at the school.

For More Information
··

BOOKS

Abdul-Jabbar, Kareem, and Alan Steinberg. *Black Profiles in Courage: A Legacy of African American Achievement.* New York: Perennial, 2000.

Fouché, Rayvon. *Black Inventors in the Age of Segregation: Granville T. Woods, Lewis H. Latimer, and Shelby J. Davidson.* Baltimore, MD: Johns Hopkins University Press, 2003.

Gubert, Betty Kaplan, Miriam Sawyer, and Caroline M. Fannin. *Distinguished African Americans in Aviation and Space Science.* Westport, CT: Oryx Press, 2002.

Haber, Louis. *Black Pioneers of Science and Invention.* Orlando, FL: Odyssey Classics, 1992.

Henson, Matthew A. *A Negro Explorer at the North Pole.* Montpelier, VT: Invisible Cities Press, 2001.

Kessler, James H., J. S. Kidd, Renée A. Kidd, and Katherine A. Morin. *Distinguished African American Scientists of the 20th Century.* Phoenix, AZ: Oryx Press, 1996.

Logan, Rayford W. *Howard University: The First Hundred Years 1867–1967.* New York: New York University Press, 2005.

Manning, Kenneth R. *Black Apollo of Science: The Life of Ernest Everett Just.* New York: Oxford University Press, 1983.

McMurry, Linda O. *George Washington Carver, Scientist and Symbol.* New York: Oxford University Press, 1982.

Mickens, Ronald E., ed. *Edward Bouchet: The First African American Doctorate.* River Edge, NJ: World Scientific Publishing, 2002.

Potter, Joan. *African American Firsts: Famous, Little-Known and Unsung Triumphs of Blacks in America.* New York: Dafina Books, 2002.

Russell, Dick. *Black Genius: Inspirational Portraits of America's Black Leaders.* New York: Skyhorse Publishing, 2009.

Wilson, Donald, and Jane Wilson. *The Pride of African American History.* Birmingham, MI: DCW Publishing, 2003.

PERIODICALS

DeGroot, Morris H. "A Conversation with David Blackwell." *Statistical Science,* vol. 1, no. 1 (February 1986): 40–53.

Sanders, Charles L. "The Troubles of 'Astronaut' Edward Dwight." *Ebony,* vol. 20, no. 8 (June 1965): 29–36.

"Tuskegee Veterinary School." *Ebony,* vol. 16, no. 3 (January 1961): 25–32.

WEB SITES

"Garrett Morgan." Black Inventor Online Museum. http://www.blackinventor
.com/pages/garrettmorgan.html (accessed on January 26, 2010).

"Universal Legacy." BessieColeman.com. http://www.bessiecoleman.com/Other%
20Pages/universal.html (accessed on January 26, 2010).

Where Do I Learn More?

BOOKS

Barbeau, Arthur E., Florette Henri, and Bernard C. Nalty. *The Unknown Soldiers: African American Troops in World War I*. Cambridge, MA: Da Capo Press, 1996.

Bartleman, Frank. *Azusa Street*. New Kensington, PA: Whitaker House, 1982.

Bogle, Donald. *Bright Boulevards, Bold Dreams: The Story of Black Hollywood*. New York: One World/Ballantine, 2005.

Brophy, Alfred, and Randall Kennedy. *Reconstructing the Dreamland: The Tulsa Race Riot of 1921, Race Reparations, and Reconciliation*. London: Oxford University Press, 2002.

Cooper, Anna Julia. *A Voice from the South*. Xenia, OH: Aldine Printing House, 1892.

Du Bois, W. E. B. *The Souls of Black Folk*. Ed. Henry Louis Gates Jr. New York: W. W. Norton, 1999.

Hill, Laban Carrick. *Harlem Stomp! A Cultural History of the Harlem Renaissance*. New York: Little Brown, 2003.

Katz, William. *The Black West: A Documentary and Pictorial History of the African American Role in the Westward Expansion of the United States*. New York: Harlem Moon, 1971.

Large, David Clay. *The Nazi Games: The Olympics of 1936*. New York: W. W. Norton, 2007.

Lemann, Nicholas. *The Promised Land: The Great Black Migration and How It Changed America*. New York: Vintage, 1992.

Love, Spencie. *One Blood: The Death and Resurrection of Charles R. Drew*. Chapel Hill, NC: University of North Carolina Press, 1996.

Malcolm X, with Alex Haley. *The Autobiography of Malcolm X.* New York: Grove Press, 1965.

Robeson, Paul. *Here I Stand.* Boston: Beacon Press, 1958.

Robinson, Jackie, and Alfred Duckett. *I Never Had it Made: An Autobiography of Jackie Robinson.* New York: Putnam, 1972.

Thomas, Vivien T. *Partners of the Heart: Vivien Thomas and His Work with Alfred Blalock: An Autobiography.* Philadelphia: University of Pennsylvania Press, 1998.

Till-Mobley, Mamie. *Death of Innocence: The Story of the Hate Crime that Changed America.* New York: One World/Ballantine, 2003.

Ward, Geoffrey C. *Unforgivable Blackness: The Rise and Fall of Jack Johnson.* New York: Vintage, 2006.

Wells, Ida B. *Southern Horrors and Other Writings: The Anti-Lynching Campaign of Ida B. Wells, 1892–1900.* Ed. Jacqueline Jones Royster. New York: Bedford/St. Martin's, 1996.

Wood, Sylvia. *Sylvia's Family Soul Food Cookbook: From Hemingway, South Carolina, To Harlem.* New York: William Morrow Cookbooks, 1999.

Woodward, C. Vann. *The Strange Career of Jim Crow.* New York: Oxford University Press, 1955.

WEB SITES

African American Odyssey: A Quest for Full Citizenship. Available at the Library of Congress Web site. http://memory.loc.gov/ammem/aaohtml/exhibit/aointro.html (accessed on March 1, 2010).

Chicago Defender. http://www.chicagodefender.com (accessed on March 1, 2010).

Documenting the American South. http://docsouth.unc.edu/index.html (accessed on March 1, 2010).

Duke Ellington: Celebrating 100 Years of the Man and His Music. http://www.dellington.org/ (accessed on March 1, 2010).

Jazz. Available on the PBS Web site at http://www.pbs.org/jazz/ (accessed on March 1, 2010).

Madame C. J. Walker Official Web site. http://www.madamcjwalker.com (accessed on March 1, 2010).

Mintz, S. "America's Reconstruction: People and Politics after the Civil War." *Digital History.* http://www.digitalhistory.uh.edu/reconstruction/index.html (accessed on March 1, 2010).

The Nation of Islam Official Web site. http://www.noi.org/ (accessed on March 1, 2010).

Rosa and Raymond Parks Institute for Self Development. http://www.rosaparks.org/about.html (accessed on March 1, 2010).

Tuskegee University. http://www.tuskegee.edu/ (accessed on March 1, 2010).

Index

Boldface type indicates entries; *Italic* type indicates volume; (ill.) indicates illustrations.

missionary work, *2:* 307; *4:* 761,
792–93, 793 (ill.), 794

bacteriologists, *4:* 824–25, 832,
833–34, 861 (ill.)

Baer, Max, *4:* 701

Baker, George. *See* Divine, M. J.

Baker, Josephine, *1:* 80, **85–88,**
86 (ill.), 139, 140

Baldwin, James, *1:* **88–89,** 88 (ill.),
133, 134–35

ballet, *1:* 81, 91–93

Ballet Russe de Monte Carlo, *1:* 92

Baltimore Afro-American (newspaper),
1: 184; *2:* 224, 258

Baltimore, Charles, *4:* 625, 662

bandleaders, *1:* 84, 120–21, 124;
2: 243, 244 (ill.); *4:* 732 (ill.)

The Banjo Lesson (Tanner), *1:* 107

banking, *1:* 154, 181–83, 182 (ill.)

Banning, James Herman, *4:* 863–64

Baraka, Amiri, *4:* 718

Barnett, Ross R., *2:* 402

Barrymore, Lionel, *2:* 268–69

Baseball Hall of Fame, inductees,
2: 224; *4:* 709, 712

baseball managers, *2:* 224; *4:* 707, 709,
711–12, 736–37

baseball players, *4:* 738 (ill.)
    media portrayals, *2:* 219; *4:* 712
    player biographies, *4:* 683,
        707–13, 707 (ill.), 710 (ill.)
    segregation and integration,
        2: 222–23, 224; *4:* 709–13,
        736–37

Baseball Writers' Association of
America, *2:* 224

Basie, Count, *1:* 121

basketball players, *4:* 684, 685, 729–31,
730 (ill.)

Baskett, James, *2:* 264

Bassett, Ebenezer, *3:* 418, **420–23,**
420 (ill.)

Battle of Pearl Harbor (1941), *4:* 646,
647–48

Battle of San Juan Hill (1898),
4: 655–56, 656 (ill.)

The Bean Eaters (Brooks), *1:* 91

Beat, E. A., *3:* 522

Beattie, John, *3:* 492

Beatty, Talley, *1:* 92

beauty contests, *1:* 158–59

beauty products. *See* cosmetics; hair
styles and products

beauty standards, white-centric, *4:* 727,
729, 850

bebop, *1:* 121–22. *See also* jazz

Bechet, Sidney, *1:* 124

Beckwith, Byron de la, *1:* 15–16,
15 (ill.), 47

Belafonte, Harry, *1:* 121; *2:* 215

Bell, Alexander Graham, *4:* 847

Bell, Landrow, *4:* 853

Benjamin, Miriam, *4:* 856

Bennett College, *2:* 345, 365, 367–69

Bennion, Mervyn, *4:* 648

Benson, Stephen, *2:* 298

Bentley, Charles, *3:* 518

Bentley, Gladys, *1:* 140, 141, 142

Benton, Thomas Hart, *4:* 654

Bergmann, Gretel, *4:* 734

Berlin Olympic Games, 1936, *4:*
684, 705 (ill.), 706, 733–35,
735 (ill.)

Bessie Coleman Aero Club, *4:* 822, 837,
863–64

Bethune, Mary McLeod, *2:* 396; *3:* 419,
423–27, 424 (ill.), 466; *4:* 628

Bethune-Cookman College, *2:* 396;
3: 423, 425–26

The Betrayal (film; Micheaux), *2:* 243

Bevel, James, *1:* 20

Bibb, Henry, *2:* 288–89

big band music, *1:* 84, 121.
    See also jazz

The Big Sea (Hughes), *1:* 139–42

Biggers, John, *1:* 132

Billings, Frank, *3:* 518

biochemists, *4:* 823, 831–33,
851–52

biologists, *4:* 821–22, 824–25, 833–35,
843–46, 861, 872–73

The Biology of the Cell Surface (Just),
4: 843, 846, 872–73

Birth from the Sea (Biggers), *1:* 132

The Birth of a Nation (Griffith), *2:* 242,
254; *3:* 594, 594 (ill.)

Index